The Complete Idiot's Refer

## Who Are These People?

**Suspects:** Potential customers you have yet to meet.

**Prospects:** Contacts with realistic potential.

**Customers:** Folks who have decided to buy.

**Business Partners:** Customers that depend on your company to grow and prosper, and with whom you develop a mutually rewarding relationship in the long term.

**Your job never stops:** You want to turn suspects into prospects, prospects into customers, and customers into business partners.

## Ways Salespeople Sell

**The Complex Sales Model:** Associated with the sale of products, services, and solutions to organizations; may require group decisions and long time-frames.

**The Simple Sales Model:** One-on-one sales notable for speed in reaching an "up-or-down" decision and directness of approach.

**Commodity Sales:** Typically bulk items and long-term sales.

**End User Selling:** Selling directly to the person or organization using the product.

**Wholesale Selling:** Selling to the distributor.

**Retail Selling:** Everyday "across-the-counter" sales—from high-end to bargain-basement.

**Consultant Selling:** "Total solution" selling.

## Six Ways to Reduce Defections Among Current Customers

✔ Develop a relationship with more than one contact in an organization.

✔ Ask appropriate contacts for referrals (doing so builds loyalty).

✔ Keep adding value—become the person your customers call on for help.

✔ Keep the lines of communication open.

✔ Ask your customers for their opinions (and listen to what they say).

✔ Create special packages and prices for special customers.

## The Template of Ideal Prospects

The Template of Ideal Prospects (TIP) discussed in Chapter 6 is a list of characteristics shared by your most important customers. Use it to...

➤ Isolate (if you haven't already) what your very best customers have in common.

➤ Evaluate current prospects.

➤ Pursue the best matches first.

alpha
books

# The Parinello Principle

75 percent of your sales activities will yield a 125 percent quota performance. If 75 percent of your work time is managed properly and allocated directly to supporting the sales process. This means three-quarters of your time should be devoted to the following activities, in the following order, every day:

➤ **Priority One:** Take the steps that are necessary to bring closure and commitment to each and every one of your "on-the-edge" prospects (those about to emerge from the bottom third of your "sales funnel").

➤ **Priority Two:** Take the steps that are necessary to convert as many suspects into prospects as you can in the time available, typically by arranging and attending meetings. (That is, bring people into the top of your funnel.)

➤ **Priority Three:** Take the steps that are necessary—typically by providing information and consultation to people you've already met—to move prospects from the middle to the bottom of your sales funnel—or out of the process altogether.

# FFAB Stands For...

**Functions:** How does someone use your product?

**Features:** What are the individual characteristics of your product?

**Advantages:** How will your product solve the individual's or organization's needs?

**Benefits:** What good things will happen when someone uses your product?

# Five Different Buyer Scenarios

Or, how your prospect operates (and what to do about it).

➤ **Stonewall:** Talk to someone else in the organization, try to secure a referral.

➤ **The Analytical Approach:** This buyer is factual, serious, and exacting. Keep the conversation focused on specifics, make sure you can back up every statement.

➤ **The Expressive Approach:** This buyer likes long-winded discourses, let him/her talk, focus on his/her feelings about the product.

➤ **The Amiable Approach:** This buyer works by consensus, let him/her talk to the rest of the team.

➤ **The Driver Approach:** This buyer cuts to the chase. Stick to the big picture, be direct.

# What People in Your Target Organization Want to See

*Leaders* want to see benefits.     *Influencers* want to see features.

*Directors* want to see advantages.     *Consumers* want to see functions.

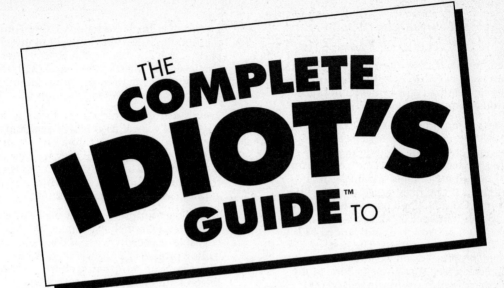

# THE COMPLETE IDIOT'S GUIDE™ TO

# Dynamic Selling

*by Anthony Parinello*

## alpha books

A Division of Macmillan General Reference
A Simon and Schuster Macmillan Company
1633 Broadway, New York, NY 10019-6785

## Tony's Advice Works!

The following comments were supplied by team members at Moore Corporation LTD, (San Ramon, California), the leading global partner helping companies communicate through print and digital technology.

Tony's commitment to our success, his knowledge of the sales process, and his passion for winning are absolutely unparalleled. By becoming our sales "Yoda," Tony has helped me to build a team of "Jedi Knights." We've quadrupled the activity in our sales funnel, lifted our typical point of entry within target organizations by a minimum of two levels, and landed $12 million in new contracts. The first telementoring session we had with Tony sparked an idea that propelled one of my sales representatives to win a $200,000 account that had been stalled for over three months. Tony has demonstrated an uncanny ability to become thoroughly immersed in the sales process with each and every team member. His compassion for my team and his extraordinary generosity is world class.
—*Mike Adani, Vice President*

With Tony's tactics and strategies, you'll have fun as your pursue new mastery in sales. You'll feel the blood flowing through your veins in a new and exciting way, because Tony's approach to sales will immediately enhance your position within your accounts. You'll gain tremendous confidence and determination, but more importantly, you'll have a blast. The ideas in this book have tremendous upside potential for your career growth. Take advantage of them.
—*Steve S. Hirano, Sales Representative*

Salespeople need confidence to succeed. Tony's techniques have helped boost my confidence both personally and professionally. I've learned to look in the right places, instead of in the usual places, for my sales opportunities. When Tony's kind of sales preparation becomes second nature, every sales call is taken to the next level—and productivity soars. That's unshakable confidence!—*Kathy Pierce, Sales Representative*

Listening is crucial to selling. Using Tony's methodology, I'm able to position myself as a partner and consultant. I'm able to listen "between the lines"—and that's a skill that differentiates me from the competition!
—*Linda Murphy, Sales Representative*

Tony's selling techniques are different than anything I've ever used before. It would be impossible to ever get "into a rut" by implementing these ideas. And they work! If you don't have fun selling using Tony's methods, then you will probably never enjoy selling.
—*Doug Gelatti, Sales Representative*

Tony takes our profession to the "No Fear" level. He's extremely passionate and knowledgeable, especially when it comes to cold-calling prospects. For several years I'd focused my telephone prospecting efforts on people in lower- and middle-management levels. Then Tony took me to the top! Now I'm meeting with presidents, CEOs, and senior management people, and I'm expediting the sales process. The results we've experienced have been phenomenal, because Tony was on our side. Now he's on your side, too!
—*Dave Irish, Sales Manager*

There is nothing Tony suggests in this book—or in any of his seminars, workshops, tapes, or telementoring sessions—that he doesn't do himself every day. That's the reason he earns the respect of so many salespeople. To me, he's more than a top-level author, more than a compelling professional speaker, more than a mentor. He's a friend and colleague who does the same thing I do for a living. He's shown me how to get customers to view me as a resource, someone who's part of the team—rather than a salesperson trying to meet quota.—*Chad Robertson, Sales Representative*

Tony has shown me how to take action and make things happen—rather than wait for things to happen. As a result of implementing his ideas, I won my company's Rookie of the Year award, became the third-ranked salesperson in a company of 1,000 salespeople, and emerged as the #1 sales rep in the West. Now it's time for you to take action—and read this book!—*Peter T. D'Errico, Sales Representative*

*In loving memory of my mother, Josephine Rose, and my brother Al. You are the reason I soar.*

*"Be yourself."—Bro.*

## ©1998 by Anthony Parinello

Macmillan Publishing books may be purchased for business or sales promotional use. For information please write: Special Markets Department, Macmillan Publishing USA, 1633 Broadway, New York, NY 10019.

THE COMPLETE IDIOT'S GUIDE name and design are trademarks of Macmillan, Inc.

International Standard Book Number: 0-02-861952-8
Library of Congress Catalog Card Number: 97-073171

00  99  98    4  3  2  1

Interpretation of the printing code: the rightmost number of the first series of numbers is the year of the book's printing; the rightmost number of the second series of numbers is the number of the book's printing. For example, a printing code of 98-1 shows that the first printing occurred in 1998.

*Printed in the United States of America*

**Brand Manager**
*Kathy Nebenhaus*

**Director of Editorial Services**
*Brian Phair*

**Executive Editor**
*Gary M. Krebs*

**Managing Editor**
*Bob Shuman*

**Senior Editor**
*Nancy Mikhail*

**Development Editor**
*Lisa A. Bucki*

**Production Editors**
*Brian Robinson*
*Mark Enochs*

**Editorial Assistant**
*Maureen Horn*

**Cartoonist**
*Judd Winick*

**Book Designer**
*Glenn Larsen*

**Cover Designer**
*Michael Freeland*

**Indexer**
*Chris Barrick*

**Production Team**
*Angela Calvert*
*Mary Hunt*
*Pamela Woolf*

# Contents at a Glance

# Contents

# Foreword

Most successful salespeople recognize that it is impossible to win solely via one's own sales skills. While "independence" and "autonomy" may characterize the sales profession, sustained success comes from a continuing desire for self-improvement. From raw rookies to seasoned professionals, salespeople who rise to the top know that they need help, input, moral support, and an occasional kick in the pants. In short, they need a coach.

Tony Parinello is one of the country's outstanding sales coaches. We included Tony's training in our Data General University program, and the improved productivity of the participants was remarkable: a 45 percent increase in additions to the pipeline, and a 54 percent increase in deal size. Overall, people who learned from Tony had double the pipeline and double the deal size of those who did not have the benefit of his program.

While this book is no replacement for a one-on-one session with Tony, I believe it is the best coach-in-a-book you will find. All the passion, experience, efficiency, and enthusiasm of a Parinello seminar are present. Even if you are not a salesperson, this book will give you the strategies you need to transform your career.

Succeeding in sales means knowing your territory (however that territory is defined) and making the most of your opportunities within it. Those are challenges for which Tony Parinello can help salespeople summon extraordinary reservoirs of energy. Tony is a motivator par excellence who knows what it takes to get people to turn selling into something more than a job. He knows how to make it an all-consuming passion.

Tony practices exactly what he teaches. He will not advocate any technique that he has not field-tested and used himself extensively. If an idea does not have the legitimate potential to deliver dramatic results, Tony does not include it in the program. As a result, salespeople have a tendency to think of his advice as coming, not from a "trainer" or "consultant," but from a trusted senior colleague who regularly puts up big numbers, knows the ropes, and is willing to share his best moves with everybody in the profession.

If this is the kind of "coach" you are looking for—and it may be the best kind—you will want to read what Tony has written in *The Complete Idiot's Guide to Dynamic Selling*.

The strategies you are about to encounter have inspired remarkable achievements among salespeople of virtually every description and industry specialty. They have also won Tony Parinello a reputation as one of the country's most creative and dynamic sales trainers. He has turned around numerous companies and careers—helping subpar performers emerge as key contributors, helping superstars move their performance to the next level, and helping organizations go from the red into the black. It is not surprising that Tony's many advocates—salespeople, sales managers, and top executives from around the country—revere him.

When you show a team of stars how to hit even higher goals, or you turn a troubled department into a pack of goal-oriented overachievers, people tend to notice. Tony's pulled off both tricks plenty of times. If you want to know how, all you have to do is start reading his book.

This volume will show you the best ways to put Tony's unique approach to the world of sales into practice. If you are a salesperson looking for practical, powerful strategies that will help you increase your income in a hurry, look no further. This is the book for you. I advise you to read it now—before your competition does!

*Ron Skates, President and CEO, Data General Corporation (Westborough, Massachusetts), one of the world's leading and most respected computer firms.*

# Introduction

I'm guessing that, if you're reading this book, you're a professional salesperson—or, if you're not, that you're either considering entering the world of sales, or you've got some important reason for learning more about it (for instance, you've been given the job of supervising and motivating salespeople). So my first word to you is a simple one: Congratulations!

Congratulations, because you're now involved in the most dynamic profession I know of. What's so dynamic about selling? Take your pick! It's a constant swirl of energy and movement: People, products, cultures, needs, desires, personalities, egos, goals, dreams, competition, pressure, stress, rewards, and, yes, money. Sales is all of this and more. It's a challenging but extraordinarily rewarding way to make a living, and I'm proud to say that it's been MY way of making a living for more than a quarter century. My aim is to pass along, in this book, what I've learned over that period of time, and to help you become more of a success.

## What You'll Learn in This Book

*The Complete Idiot's Guide to Dynamic Selling* is divided into six main parts. In it, you'll learn that sales work has certain steps that cannot be ignored. At the same time, it will become clear to you that sales involves dealing with the human mind, and that there are emotional and desire-related aspects of the work that require a certain instinctive approach. I've tried to balance the hard-and-fast rules outlook with the "follow your own instincts" approach, because I think any sales training system that relies exclusively on one or the other is incomplete.

The rest of this section describes the six volumes of your sales "encyclopedia."

## Part 1: The Greatest Job in the World—Honest

Here's where you'll explore the different kinds of jobs that are available in sales. You'll take a good look at what's best for you and how your existing skill set can be applied to your career in sales. You'll also learn about the different types of selling situations in which you're most likely to find yourself involved.

## Part 2: Day by Day

Here, you'll learn the real meaning of the old saying "It comes with the territory"—and a whole lot more. In this part of the book, you'll find out about territories, suspects, prospects, customers, and business partners. You'll also learn how to set meaningful goals and manage your own time. Finally, you'll find out what the competition's up to.

## Part 3: Great Beginnings

Have you ever stopped to ask yourself why people buy things—what any individual's needs and wants have to do with the act of buying and selling? In this part of the book, you'll learn how to approach people with different styles, and you'll learn how to use opening statements to break preoccupations and open the doors of opportunity for your first in-person appointment.

## Part 4: In Depth

Here's where you take a close look at the mechanics of selling. In this part of the book, you learn that the fastest way to sell something is to let the other person talk himself or herself into buying it—and the fastest way for that to happen is to ask the right questions. Of course, the flip-side of asking questions is being able to answer questions that you're asked—questions that may take the form of objections. Part 4 will show you how to deal with skittishness along the way...and get you ready to create and deliver a strong presentation.

## Part 5: Building (and Maintaining) Alliances

"Closing"? Well, let's just say this is where you learn to open up new business relationships. In this portion of the book, you'll learn how to negotiate and how to follow up on all your work thus far and get your contacts into the "yes" column. Once you earn that commitment, you'll learn how to maintain it. You'll also learn how to win powerful referrals from the contact base you've developed.

## Part 6: The Long Term

Selling is about relationships, and the most important relationships endure. This chapter shows you how to make sure your customers get the results you promised—and how you can benefit handsomely from that process. What's the alternative? Jumping from company to company, and city to city, and dashing behind the Diet Coke display at the local supermarket because you just spotted someone who looks a lot like an old customer of yours?

## End Matter

In addition, you'll find a helpful series of appendices that give you step-by-step information on dealing with some potentially challenging elements you may encounter at various points in the sales process. There's also a glossary of important terms, and, at the end of the book, information about my career-long telementoring program, which will allow you to take advantage of working with a personal success coach.

# And That's Not All!

This book also provides you with bite-sized chunks of information that will help you understand the world of sales, and how you can succeed in it, even better. These boxes give you extra information:

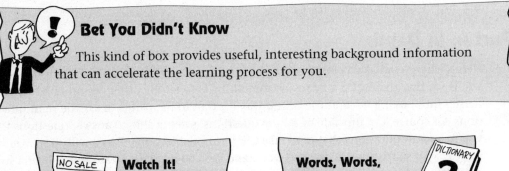

**Bet You Didn't Know**

This kind of box provides useful, interesting background information that can accelerate the learning process for you.

**Watch It!**
This kind of box will help you avoid potentially catastrophic mistakes in your sales work.

**Words, Words, Words**
This kind of box will help you understand unfamiliar words and phrases.

**Sales Accelerator**
This kind of box offers easy-to-understand tips and strategies that will help you increase your income and improve your relationships with customers and prospective customers.

# Acknowledgments

There are many, many people involved in the development of a book such as this one. My thanks go out to the all the good people at Macmillan who helped to put this volume in your hands, and especially to: Kathy Nebenhaus, Dick Staron, Lisa Bucki, Mark Enochs, and Brian Robinson. I'd also like to thank my friend Brandon Toropov for all his help on this project. My gratitude also goes out to the team members at Parinello Incorporated: Diane Durbin and Catherine Jones, who were a part of this project from the first moment to the last. Thanks are also due to my sister PhyllisAnn Casisa, who never stopped encouraging me, and my sister-in-law Sharon Parinello, for prodding me when I needed it most. A word of gratitude also goes out to my father, Anthony Parinello Senior, the Chairman of the Board, who, for some reason, liked the idea of my writing an *Idiot's Guide* from the get-go! I'd like to thank the many customers and alumni over the years who have helped me to make my programs the best they can be. Finally, here's to you—for making me a part of your journey to greater success.

## Special Thanks to the Technical Reviewer

It's one thing to write a book and *hope* it all makes sense; it's another to see to it that the work is hanging together in the way it should. I was lucky to have a technical editor, Ron Karr, who helped me to present this material in a logical and accessible way. Ron spent many long hours reading and making suggestions for clarification, and I'm very grateful for his insights. He is no armchair salesperson.

Ron specializes in helping organizations dominate their marketplace and get closer to the people they serve. Ron brings to his audiences real-life knowledge gained during a highly successful 15-year career in sales and managment. He has conducted seminars and keynote addresses before organizations including The NFL, Met Life, Mutual of Omaha, Hertz, Southwestern Bell Yellow Pages, and Marriott Hotels. He has authored numerous video and audio programs, as well as dozens of articles that regularly appear in trade journals. Currently, Ron is a faculty member of the American Management Association (AMA) and an active member of the National Speakers Association (and is past president of its NY Tri-State Chapter). Ron Karr's new book is *The Complete Idiot's Guide to Great Customer Service*, from Alpha Books.

## Trademarks

All terms mentioned in this book that are known to be or are suspected of being trademarks or service marks have been appropriately capitalized. Alpha Books and Macmillan General Reference cannot attest to the accuracy of this information. Use of a term in this book should not be regarded as affecting the validity of any trademark or service mark. The following trademarks and service marks have been mentioned in this book: Infoseek, Yahoo!, Hewlett Packard, Moore Business Solutions, Data General Corporation, AT&T, General Electric, GTE, LDDS WorldCom, Procter & Gamble, Sprint, Merck, Fujitsu, Octel, Output Technologies, MCI, Vantive, Dunn & Bradstreet, Xerox, IBM, Century 21, Transamerica, SkyTel, and Mobil Oil.

# Part 1
# The Greatest Job in the World—Honest

*If you're reading this book, it's probably because you want to learn more about selling successfully. Whether you're a veteran salesperson, a newcomer to the game, or a managerial professional looking for new ideas, you want the lowdown on a very simple question: How can sales work be made more effective? To answer that, you should begin by looking at the world of sales in depth in this part of the book.*

*Most businesses—and, for that matter, huge chunks of the national and international economy—would simply self-destruct if there were no such thing as salespeople. Salespeople are the means by which Organization A spotlights, and implements solutions for, the problems within Organization B. It's a noble profession, one I'm very proud to call my own. In this first part of the book, you'll get an overview of the sales world: How it operates, who does best within it, what kinds of jobs it offers, the advantages of work in this area, and, yes, some of the potential disadvantages. One you've gotten familiar with these fundamentals, you'll be in a good position to take advantage of the advice and strategies that appear later in this book.*

# Getting Started

The day I decided to become a salesperson, I was out of a job, out of money, and (I thought) out of luck.

I remember sitting at the kitchen table with my parents, my sister, and her family. "Mom," I said, "I've figured out what I'm going to do, what career I'm going to pursue." My dad said, "What's that?" (That's the way it worked. I talked to my mom and my dad answered for her.) I said, "I'm going into sales." All around the table, eyebrows started to rise. For a long time nobody said anything. My sister glared at me, then asked, "Why don't you get a real job?"

*A real job.* Well, I thought it was a real job. And, as it turned out, I was right...even though my mom begged me to sleep on the decision, and my dad never did make any official comment on my career choice. (My brother, who showed up later, didn't much care what I did for a living, as long as I paid him back the 600 bucks I owed him.)

That was almost 30 years ago, and today I couldn't think of any career other than sales. Over the years that followed my dinner-table discussion with my folks, I've had the honor of being named to 16 President's Clubs for above-quota performance. I've won just about every sales award you can win—from rookie of the year to most valuable player of the year, and nearly everything in between. I tell you this not to brag on myself (although that's fun, too), but to let you know that the preconceptions of others shouldn't alter the way you look at what you do for a living. I love to sell, and I want you to love to sell, too.

In this chapter, I want to show you why this is the best job in the world, despite what anyone else may have to say about it. I also want to clue you in on the kinds of sales jobs that you may encounter in your travels, and give you some advice on landing the right position for you.

## Why Take a Job in Sales?

Because sales is—or, at any rate, should be—a real gas. My personal definition of sales—which may or may not match up with the "official" dictionary definition—looks something like this:

> *Sales* (noun): The act of 1) proactively understanding the needs and problems of others, then 2) using the art of honest persuasion to highlight possible solutions to those problems, and finally 3) encouraging others to believe in what you say and invest their money and time in what you propose.

Note that this definition does not accept any conception of "sales" that's rooted in manipulation, short-sighted opportunism, or dishonesty. In my experience, that type of "selling" always backfires. Just as a brain surgeon would never start in on invasive surgery without first making a diagnosis, a salesperson who is worthy of his or her title would never try to impose a solution without attempting to develop a complete understanding of the needs and problems of the person to whom he or she is trying to sell. A salesperson must always diagnose first—and prescribe (or operate!) later.

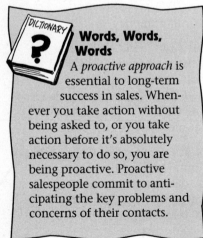

**Words, Words, Words**

A *proactive approach* is essential to long-term success in sales. Whenever you take action without being asked to, or you take action before it's absolutely necessary to do so, you are being proactive. Proactive salespeople commit to anticipating the key problems and concerns of their contacts.

Whether you're fresh out of college, tired of your desk job, re-entering the job market after raising your children, or beginning a second career after retiring from the first, you are wise to set your sights on the world of sales. There is no other career that combines extraordinary income and career potential in quite the same way. What's more, sales is among the most equal-opportunity professions imaginable: If you can achieve, there's a place for you in sales, regardless of your gender, nationality, age, or level of education.

I firmly believe that the more you enjoy doing what you do as a salesperson, the greater your emotional and financial rewards will be.

No matter what has led you to the decision to join the world of sales, I would argue that you should stay in sales because you like doing what you're doing. If you don't like it, you need to find a way to make selling your passion, despite the demands and occasional challenges of the job. I think this book will help you to do just that.

> ### Bet You Didn't Know
>
> Although sales is among the most accessible of all professional fields, offering opportunity to achievers of virtually all social and work backgrounds, you should know that there are some people who probably aren't cut out for the job, including people who are traumatized over (temporary!) rejection or setback, can't stand being the center of attention, feel uncomfortable establishing alliances with others, and/or don't work well under pressure. If one or all of these traits describes a permanent or long-standing feature of your own work life, and you are not willing to work to overcome these barriers, you should think long and hard about entering the world of sales.
>
> The most common barrier to success in sales is probably the fear of rejection, a topic I'll be addressing in detail at various points in this book. For now, you should understand that rejection is not "failure," but rather part of the job description. Day-to-day work in the sales field requires constant rejection—even for superstar performers. Salespeople who never get rejected aren't running enough plays in the first place, and they won't be successful!

## Solving Problems

Some people tell me that I'm a born salesperson. I don't buy that. Although lots of people are likely to find sales a satisfying way to make a living, I don't think anyone is a "born" salesperson. People who are enthusiastic; who are willing to commit to solving problems because that's what they love to do; who realize that, without problems, there would be no need for salespeople in the first place; who accept that state of mind is a key factor in determining outcomes—people who share these qualities can, I believe, become successful salespeople.

How do you know if you're likely to succeed in a sales career? The best answer to this common question comes in the form of another question: How good are you at listening to problems? If you love listening to the problems of other people (that is, if you enjoy the process of identifying, without prejudice or preconception, exactly what obstacles somebody else is facing), or if you have a way of letting your conversational partners know, almost without effort, that you hold their opinions and feelings in high regard, then you will, in all likelihood, make a good (or great!) salesperson.

## Autonomy

Speaking from personal experience, I have to say that the most frightening aspect of my sales jobs wasn't staring a high quota in the eye at the beginning of each year, making cold calls, or conducting presentations. It was the prospect of losing my autonomy, my independence. That's why I always gulped hard and mumbled when people offered me "promotions" that would have left me sitting behind a desk like everyone else who wasn't a salesperson. Eventually, I had to go out and start my own company so people would stop trying to turn me into a manager!

**Sales Accelerator**

True sales success requires commitment in the form of persistent effort and, from time to time, some long hours.

There's an old joke about a sales manager who's approached by a new team member. The fresh-faced young recruit asks, "Boss, I'm looking for a way to work part-time—you know, half days—and still sell more widgets than anyone else in the department. How do you think I should do it?" The sales manager smiles and says, "That's easy. Pick any 12 hours of every day and work like crazy."

Short of actually running your own business, working as a salesperson is the closest thing to entrepreneurial freedom you're going to find. If you still want to pull a paycheck signed by someone else, but you want the thrill of independence, self-sufficiency, and achievement, sales is the job for you.

All the same, you should know that this freedom comes with some very real risks: The risk of being distracted, for instance, and managing your own time poorly; and the risk of getting so carried away with the notion of "freedom" that your day lacks any structure whatsoever. I know I'm not the only salesperson to have fallen prey to this "born free" syndrome, and I'm certainly not the only one to have gotten into hot water as a result. This book will give you the tools you need to manage your most important resource—your own time—for optimum efficiency. After all, a successful salesperson has to work not only hard, but smart. That is to say, simply following a predetermined routine is not enough. You have to focus your efforts on reviewing your routine regularly—to make sure you're doing the *right* things.

## "Wait a Minute..."

Perhaps you're thinking to yourself, "All this problem-solving and autonomy stuff sounds fine, but how accurate is it in defining what sales really is? What about the brochures and flyers I get in the mail? What about e-mail I receive and Web sites I visit? What about television and radio advertising? No one ever takes the time to try to understand my needs in those situations. And if those attempts to win me as a customer don't count as selling, what is?"

Actually, those efforts to convince you to buy don't come under the "selling" category, although it's common enough to remark that a car company, a computer maker, or a local lawn doctor are all trying to "sell" when they engage in the activities just described. Common as the "selling" label may be, however, it's not completely accurate.

## The How and the What

There's a big difference between sales (which is a tactical, proactive approach, focused on the way one individual achieves the goal of resolving problems for a customer or customers(s)) and marketing (which is the strategic component, focused on the what, the overall goal).

Effective marketing will define the market, and perhaps even soften it up in such a way (by providing name recognition or brand name information, for example) that effective salespeople can approach customers within it proactively.

## People People

Some marketing efforts don't require salespeople; however, all salespeople act in the pursuit of marketing goals. And to do that, they interact with people, some of whom are more interested than others in what is being offered for discussion.

The names salespeople use to refer to the folks they deal with every day are many. To get the most out of this book, you should take a few minutes now to familiarize yourself with the simple definitions in the "What's in a Name?" list that follows. You'll be coming back to them again and again.

---

**What's in a Name?, or The Hierarchy of Contacts**

✓ **Suspects.** This word describes individuals or companies who are potential customers, but who have not yet had any contact with you or your organization.

✓ **Prospects.** These are people whom you have contacted, or who have contacted you, and who represent a realistic potential for future business.

✓ **Customers.** As you might expect, these are the folks who have made a decision to purchase what you have to offer.

✓ **Business partners.** The people and organizations in this category not only have bought from you, they've come to depend on you. Business partners depend on your company's resources to grow and prosper.

---

One way to look at the salesperson's job is as the continuous (and never-ending!) job of defining and upgrading, people and institutions based on the four-part model above. We want to turn as many suspects as possible into prospects; we want to turn as many prospects as possible into customers; and we want to turn as many customers as possible into loyal business partners. How do we do it? Listen attentively to problems and make recommendations, for starters!

# Different Sales Jobs

Let's assume you want to enter a sales job for the first time, or explore options beyond your current situation. What kinds of jobs are available within the broad category of "sales"? They include inside sales, outside sales, direct sales, and indirect sales. I describe each of these next.

# Inside Sales: Telephone

Just as the name implies, if you have this job, you never go outside to meet suspects (or, for that matter, prospects, customers, or business partners) face-to-face. You call them on the phone.

Inside "outbound" salespeople typically spend hour after hour on the telephone, typically talking to more than 100 people in the course of a single day. They generally work from within a cubicle, dialing for dollars.

Inside "inbound" salespeople handle only calls placed via an 800 line as a direct result of advertising or some other media blitz. This work means you handle the calls of interested individuals, not suspects, and is not to be confused with inside outbound sales work. In outbound telephone sales, there are no calls coming in. The outbound salesperson's job has three important phases: dial, dial, dial! The inside inbound salesperson's job can be summed up just as simply: Answer, answer, answer!

# Other Inside Sales Jobs

If you prefer inside sales and you want to encounter your suspects, prospects, customers, and business partners face to face, you can choose sales work that allows your department or showroom floor to become your sales territory. (Retail and automotive settings come to mind.) You'll be expected to interact on a person-to-person basis—and, in many cases, you'll also be expected to use the telephone to perform your sales work.

# Outside Sales

The outside salesperson is the road warrior (or worrier!). He or she traverses a territory in search of suspects, prospects, customers, and business partners. This salesperson works face to face, eyeball to eyeball. There's lots of one-on-one interaction. Wardrobe, physical stamina, and personal grooming are usually much more important factors for the outside salesperson than for the inside salesperson (although inside salespeople who work in retail and automotive showrooms must, of course, look businesslike at all times).

Spending lots of time out of the office gives one a feeling of greater independence, of being your own boss. This factor may sound appealing, but it also means that personal discipline is an essential requirement of the job.

Another essential element will probably be travel. We all know the stereotypes associated with the classic "traveling salesperson" story: wrinkled suits, scuffed shoes, baggy eyes. How accurate are such stereotypes? Not very. Today's successful outside salesperson is typically a thoroughly professional-looking emissary from the central office (and, thanks to today's telephone and wireless computer technology, a very well-connected one).

## Direct Sales

This salesperson works directly for the actual "label" manufacturer of specific products. He or she enjoys product support, pre-sales resources, and plenty of personnel backup from the "factory." Name recognition of the product will probably be high. Direct sales contrasts strikingly with…

## Indirect Sales

Here, you work for the reseller of a major label manufacturer. You represent a product manufactured by a company other than the company for which you work (although your organization will likely add value in some way to the product you sell). If you decide to work for resellers, you may get less factory support, and you may find yourself competing, at some level, with the original supplier's sales force.

"Inside/direct, outside/indirect—I'm confused!" I don't blame you one bit. Like everything else in sales, the type of work you choose leaves you with plenty of choices and configurations. For example: Imagine you're selling a full line of products for the dental industry. Your product line includes compounds, chemicals, instruments, diamond drills (ouch!), the works. You're selling face-to-face to dentists (outside selling), and you represent several different suppliers, each of which has its own outside direct sales force that competes with you! That would be outside indirect selling.

**Words, Words, Words**

*Hunter* salespeople and *Farmer* salespeople have different overall goals in their sales work. All sales organizations need a healthy mix of new market share (obtained by "hunting" for new customers) and revenue from loyal existing customers (obtained by cultivating and supporting, or "farming," current accounts). Successful Hunters usually have different strategies and may require different skills and tactics than successful Farmers. Many salespeople are expected to both hunt and farm within their territories.

**Sales Accelerator**

The healthiest mix of company revenue will probably look something like this: 75 percent of revenues from new business (hunting) and 25 percent of revenues from existing customers (farming). Not surprisingly, Hunters are often compensated more aggressively than Farmers.

# Ways Salespeople Sell

Choosing a sales career is a little like selecting a new car. You have a wide range of options to choose from, some of which affect other options you will be considering on the same car.

Whichever sales role you decide to assume, you will need to choose from among many different sales environments. Take a look at some of the most important of these now. Some of these selling environments overlap; all are important to understand as you survey the "lay of the land" and make choices about what is—and isn't—right for you. (By the way, you'll be learning more about types of selling in Chapter 4.)

## The Complex Sales Model

In a complex sales model or environment, the process (rather than the product or service!) is what's "complex." Selling in this environment requires several sales calls because many different buying influences, such as committees, are involved. In this environment, a salesperson will almost certainly make more than one product presentation, demonstration, factory tour, and/or site visit in order to win a commitment to buy. In other words, you'll be expected to jump through all the hoops. And yes, all of this work requires time, effort, and plenty of patience.

This environment—often referred to as "long sales cycle" selling—is generally associated with the sale of products, services, and solutions to organizations.

## The Simple Sales Model

A simple sales model or environment is notable for the speed and uncomplicated progress of the overall sales cycle. Everything's done quickly—typically, as the result of a single visit or phone call. That's all the person you're dealing with needs to decide one way or the other about what you have to offer.

Let's take a look at how different sales jobs align with the complex and simple sales models. Consider that one product, service, or solution could fit into both the complex or simple sales models. For example:

### Sales Jobs and Their Alignment with Differing Sales Models

| Product | Complex Model | Simple Model |
|---|---|---|
| Long-distance service (inside telephone selling) | Sold to the business marketplace | Sold to the residential marketplace |

It's unlikely that you'd sell long-distance service into totally different markets, since the service options for consumers would vary greatly from those offered to businesses. (So, for that matter, would your product training.) Take a look at another example.

## More Sales Jobs and Their Alignment with Differing Sales Models

| Product | Complex Model | Simple Model |
|---|---|---|
| Financial services (outside/indirect selling) | Retirement packages sold to the business marketplace as employee benefits | Personal financial plans sold to individuals or families |

## End-User Selling

If the individuals or companies that will actually be using the products, services, or solutions you are selling buy from you, then you are engaged in end-user selling. This type of sale may involve a long-term relationship in which the customer receives ongoing support and (in some cases) product training from you, the salesperson.

## Wholesale Selling

Here, the individuals or companies you're selling to are the distributors of your products, not the end users. Typically, this type of selling is conducted under long-term contracts; "quotas" are set for the customer to meet. Such targets incorporate impressive price reductions. In this role, the salesperson may end up providing ongoing product support as part of the overall sales activity.

**Words, Words, Words**

If you're in *commodity sales*, you're selling something that is typically bought in bulk and consumed continuously. Products, such as industrial solvents, oil and gas, and certain paper goods are generally considered commodities. You'll find stiff competition here, close price points and delivery issues being daily challenges. (Later in this book, you'll learn how to make your "commodity" look better than anyone else's.)

## Retail Selling

This is probably the easiest of all the models to observe and understand, because it's the one in which all of us participate directly, usually on an everyday basis. The higher end of this environment would be the "prestige" department stores, that often assign personal salespeople to their (high-income) customers. On the low end are the vested salespeople at low-price-driven retail chains who stock shelves, straighten out inventory, and clean up their departments—pausing occasionally to answer questions from shoppers.

## Consultative Selling

This selling environment is also known as "total solution selling." These are travel agents, event planners, interior decorators, and other professionals who take the services of several suppliers and consult with the end user, who selects the correct array of products and/or services. Each element sold through this consultation with the end user results in a commission, credit, or bonus from the supplier with which the "consultant" works.

# A Love Thing

What could be more important to your successful career choices than a general knowledge of the various sales roles and selling environments?

An indefinable thing called passion.

Passionate salespeople, by and large, are successful salespeople. People tend to get passionate about the things they love. So it stands to reason that you'll be most likely to experience success if you're selling something you already love.

Take a few minutes, right now, to answer the questions in the "Your Passions Quiz" with total honesty. Pull out a pencil and paper and write responses to the quiz questions.

---

**Your Passions Quiz**

1. What do I love to help others do?

2. What do I love seeing people accomplish?

3. What do I love learning about?

---

If you wrote that you love to sit on a beach and drink foamy, ice-cold drinks with tiny umbrellas perched atop small slices of fruit, you should either take a break for a reality check or find a job selling vacations to burnt-out salespeople.

If you said that you love to help others to plan their weddings, or pick out the best attire for a formal affair, perhaps you should consider a sales career as a wedding consultant/salesperson—one of the people who handles everything from catering to gowns to honeymoon reservations. If, on the other hand, you said, "I love to help people select the very best look for their day-to-day wardrobes," perhaps a career as a personal shopper in an upscale department store is right for you.

Sell what you love...and love what you sell! When you love something, you believe in it. When you talk about the thing you love to people, they'll listen, they'll sense your enthusiasm, and they'll believe in you. And when people believe in you, they'll do business with you.

# One Really Crucial Sales Job: Getting the Job Offer

Don't just apply for a job at any company. Design the right company to work for.

What do I mean by "design"? Try finding the perfect company and then approach that company about a sales job, whether or not you know of an opening (or even the existence of the job in question)! It's been my personal experience that good salespeople have a way of creating jobs for themselves.

The "right" company may not be hiring. The company may be launching a corporate austerity program with the aim to sell more with fewer salespeople. The company may not have a local office in your area, a problem if you don't want to relocate. Do any of these obstacles mean you can't get a job with the company in question? No, no, and a thousand times no!

## How to Make Openings Appear

Remember, your first decision has already been made. You know what to do. You're not looking for any sales job; rather, you're looking for a particular type of sales job. Let's assume you know that you love to help others plan weddings, and you're certain that you want a sales job in that area.

Your next step is to look for the very best company in the country in the wedding planning business. Ask your local librarian, friends, and appeal to your own experience or the experience of family members. Call the makers of the finest wedding accessories you can find; ask them where you can find the nation's leading wedding planning organization. There may be a couple of nominees—select the one that's right for you, the one that's most likely to make you feel great about your day, every day.

**Watch It!**
Don't take (or stay in) any old sales job. Find the right sales job for you. You'll spend something like 96,000 working hours on the job over the course of your lifetime. If you're going to invest that much time, be sure you invest it with a company that represents a truly perfect fit with what you want to do. Don't settle for anything less!

## Just the Facts, Ma'am

Your research indicates that ABC Bridal Consultants is the outfit that most excites you. Find out all you can about that company—including the name of the owner or president, and his or her executive assistant's name. (How? There are lots of different ways to track down this information, but for now, you can simply call the reception desk and ask for names and spellings.)

Before you write a letter to the owner or president of the operation, however, you're going to call a few good salespeople. A few really good salespeople. Count on it; the best salespeople will return your call! The great ones always do. If no one calls you back, you should ask yourself whether or not you really want to work for this outfit.

**Sales Accelerator**

Looking for a sales job? At least initially, you should forget about contacting the human resources department or the local sales manager. Target the head person in the organization.

When one of the sales reps calls you back, ask one simple question, the question that will tell you everything you need to know about the company this person works for: "Can you take a minute to talk to me about what separates you from your biggest competitor?"

Keep a pen and a pad of paper handy; you're going to write down what you hear. The information you receive during these calls will give you everything you need to know when it comes time to pitch your cause to the top banana.

You may hear answers like these when you ask the magic question, "What separates you from the competition?"

➤ "Quality is critically important to us."

➤ "We are the industry's leading innovators."

➤ "We stand behind our products and our service."

➤ "We use the latest computer technology."

➤ "We keep up with what our customers need."

➤ "We offer free so-and-so."

Take a good long look at your list of answers from each salesperson, and perform the following exercise:

1. Get a big piece of paper and draw a line vertically, right down the middle.

2. On the left side of the line, write down the information you got from the sales reps with whom you spoke, summarizing and combining identical or similar answers.

3. On the right side of the line, list all your personal gifts. That is, write down all you feel you personally have to offer to the company you want to sell for. Write nonstop for as long as you can (at least, say, five minutes). The object here is to list things that will get an employer excited about you; your reliability, your sound judgment, your good humor, your adaptability, and so on.

4. Review the lists, and look for direct "hits" between what you have to offer and what the company sees as its main advantages over the competition. If you want, you can draw a line between each match to get a clear picture of how you can help the company continue being better than the competition.

## Take a Letter

In Appendix B, "Letters, In-Depth," you'll find a model of a letter targeted toward CEOs. It deals specifically with your job search campaign. The point of the letter is to show your prospective employer—initially, the very top person in the organization—what gives you the edge—and the right—to work for the target company. You're going to demonstrate what you've got in common with the organization, and how your strengths can help the company overachieve when it comes to important goals.

## The Offer

Letters, calls, faxes—you're going to keep after the top people in the organization (the CEO and his or her assistant, who may well be the most important person of all!). Later on in the book, you'll learn more about the kind of campaign that works best with these folks. For now, just bear in mind that you'll be applying tactful, persistent, unfailingly polite pressure day in and day out until something interesting happens.

Eventually, you're going to win a face-to-face meeting with somebody, probably the CEO or someone in his or her circle. (Trust me. Salespeople who show that kind of persistence tend to make CEOs very interested indeed.) Once you do, you're going to make this company an offer it cannot refuse: You'll work for 30 days for free. That's right—if, after 30 days, you're not what you said you'd be, the company owes you nothing. If, on the other hand, the company likes what you have to offer, they pay you retroactively, from day one.

And, speaking of money…

## Money

What compensation plan is right for you? There are three basic combinations:

➤ Base salary.

➤ Base salary with commission.

➤ 100 percent commission (no base salary).

**Sales Accelerator**
Treat the job interview like a sales call. That is to say, study the organization's products, marketplace, and competition. Be prepared to explain how you would develop new prospects, nurture existing customers, and plan for the long term. Read this book from cover to cover and be ready to discuss key points in detail!

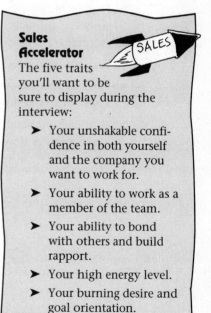

**Sales Accelerator**
The five traits you'll want to be sure to display during the interview:

➤ Your unshakable confidence in both yourself and the company you want to work for.

➤ Your ability to work as a member of the team.

➤ Your ability to bond with others and build rapport.

➤ Your high energy level.

➤ Your burning desire and goal orientation.

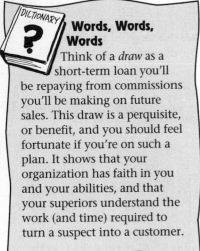

**Words, Words, Words**

Think of a *draw* as a short-term loan you'll be repaying from commissions you'll be making on future sales. This draw is a perquisite, or benefit, and you should feel fortunate if you're on such a plan. It shows that your organization has faith in you and your abilities, and that your superiors understand the work (and time) required to turn a suspect into a customer.

Base salary jobs in sales are rare. If you take one, the rest of this book will still be invaluable to you, but, as a practical matter, your title and responsibilities will probably be closer to that of a staff or support person than that of a salesperson, whose income is based on (you guessed it) selling. When you take a sales job that's a base plus commission—or structured, perhaps, by means of a draw against future commission earnings—you're usually trading some consistency (a smaller guaranteed base salary) for a lower upside potential. And if you opt for 100% commission with no guaranteed salary, your income potential is, quite literally, unlimited…but you're assuming more risk.

Most salespeople, seduced by the prospect of three dependable square meals a day, opt for some form of base salary plus commission.

## The Least You Need to Know

➤ Sales means solving problems.

➤ If you sell what you love, and love what you sell, you'll probably be successful.

➤ Four labels are helpful in categorizing the world of people who might buy from you: suspects, contacts, customers, and business partners.

➤ There are a wide variety of selling roles and environments, so pick the combination that makes the most sense for you.

➤ Target a specific company, one you'll feel great about working at—whether you know of an opening there or not.

➤ While in job search mode, do your homework and appeal straight to the top—then make an offer they can't refuse.

# What Is Your Organization Doing Already?

Knowledge really is power!

Salespeople often tell me that they feel as though they're "in the dark" about their company's current position or future direction.

Sometimes it sounds to me as though these salespeople believe there ought to be a *Department of Clarification for the Befuddled*, whose duty it is to supply earnest-looking members of the sales department with the latest critical information about corporate objectives.

The truth of the matter is that it's our own responsibility to become familiar with our company's plans, goals, and objectives. In this chapter, you'll learn how to find out who's doing what in your outfit, and what you should to with that information once you dig it up.

# Assuming Responsibility

As sales professionals, our awareness of what our company does must cross all departmental lines. We must commit to finding out everything that relates to our customers, and that's just about everything in our organization. Why do we have to do this? Because, to our prospects and customers, we are the company, and should be able to communicate about it!

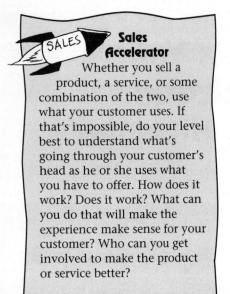

**Sales Accelerator**

Whether you sell a product, a service, or some combination of the two, use what your customer uses. If that's impossible, do your level best to understand what's going through your customer's head as he or she uses what you have to offer. How does it work? Does it work? What can you do that will make the experience make sense for your customer? Who can you get involved to make the product or service better?

You are the first (and sometimes the only) contact your prospects and customers will have with your organization. It is your responsibility to talk to and, if necessary, meet with all the various departments within your organization. It is your responsibility to understand what it is that your company does that no competitor could possibly do.

If you sell widgets, get out and visit your manufacturing facility, repair facility, and shipping and customer care centers. If you resell parts manufactured elsewhere, consider finding some way to go to that facility and take a look at the processes that are critical to making your product what it is. If your company offers a service, take a trip out to the front lines and take a look at what your customer is receiving.

## Why Bother? You Learn!

During the years that I sold computers for Hewlett-Packard, I took many a prospect and many a customer on HP factory tours. Showing off our facilities was a pleasant experience because they were pretty impressive operations. This was (and, I'm sure, still is) top-notch, high-tech stuff, complete with all the accouterments: passage through "clean rooms" that required white smocks, hats, and gloves; acres of blinking lights and beeping machines; and guys with clipboards.

On one such tour, my customer expressed amazement at the amount of sophisticated test equipment that was used to measure and control the Hewlett-Packard manufacturing process. I have to admit that, once this equipment was pointed out to me, I was amazed, too. I did a little digging after the tour and found out that every single piece of equipment being used on the Hewlett-Packard line was manufactured by (guess who?) Hewlett-Packard.

I knew that HP had gotten its start in the test and measurement world, but I had no idea that we made all the stuff necessary to control an entire manufacturing plant, from start to finish. In the weeks that followed, I decided to act on a hunch: I began to get the test equipment salesperson in my office involved in my most important new sales opportunities. He added value to my sale, and he was able to look into different areas of the prospect's company, areas I was not aware of and would probably never have asked about.

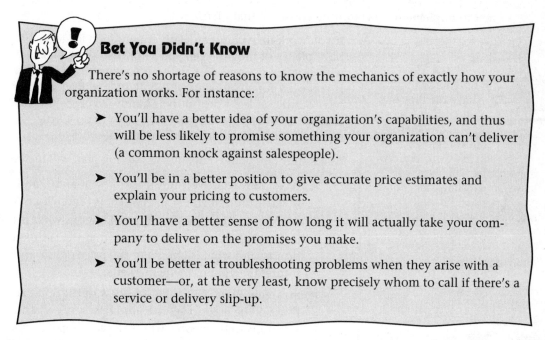

**Bet You Didn't Know**

There's no shortage of reasons to know the mechanics of exactly how your organization works. For instance:

➤ You'll have a better idea of your organization's capabilities, and thus will be less likely to promise something your organization can't deliver (a common knock against salespeople).

➤ You'll be in a better position to give accurate price estimates and explain your pricing to customers.

➤ You'll have a better sense of how long it will actually take your company to deliver on the promises you make.

➤ You'll be better at troubleshooting problems when they arise with a customer—or, at the very least, know precisely whom to call if there's a service or delivery slip-up.

## Money Talks

So, could I have simply kept on selling computer systems, and let the measuring guys keep to themselves? Sure. But I didn't. I found out a little more about a new (to me!) area of my company, and I figured out how it might relate the new information to my customers. What happened? My sales started to get bigger. Each and every sale I made where I introduced my test equipment counterpart resulted in above-average initial orders.

By knowing exactly—not approximately—what my company did, I was able to increase the size of my entry-point orders. From that point on in my sales career, I made sure to keep my eyes open for any new advantage my company could offer my prospects and customers, and for any initiative, in any area, that affected my daily sales routine.

## The Battle Plan

Each and every successful company that has something to sell to individuals or organizations has an overall plan—a strategy—that sets out how the organization is going to move products, services, and solutions to the marketplace as quickly as possible. Your organization is no exception. The key questions are: How much do you know about that plan?

And how can you use what you know to assemble your own personalized marketing plan overview?

Knowing what your company's marketing plan is will save you tons of time when it comes to implementing your little corner of that plan.

**Watch It!**
If you don't take the time to identify the most important objectives guiding your company's efforts, you may miss out on opportunity. The more you know about what your company offers, and how it's promoting what it offers, the better off you'll be when it comes to keeping prospects and customers happy.

**Sales Accelerator**
You owe it to yourself to track down some version of your organization's (or unit's) marketing plan. No matter what field you're in (retail, automobile, other), you can always sit down with a supervisor and ask, "What are we trying to get accomplished—and how are we planning to pull it off?" No matter what type of selling you do, you need a plan, and that plan should mirror your company's. Get the straight scoop!

If you work for a company with enlightened leaders who have plenty of time to keep you informed, the "Big Plan" will show up on your desk without your having to ask for it. If you work for a company with enlightened leaders who have a little bit less time on their hands (or perhaps even a little bit less enlightenment), you'll have to do a little digging. That's okay. Track the information down.

At a minimum, your company's marketing plan will include:

➤ **Basic Research.** This means studies, analysis, and investigation of where the market is (and who is and isn't in it); what the size of the market is; what the buying habits of the market are; what the competition is; and what is known of the price points and future direction of niche market(s).

➤ **Strategic Plan.** This is an overview of the approach that will be used to get the products, services, and solutions to the people who will (you hope) decide to buy. You should know: Will direct mail be used? Will advertising support your efforts? Will telemarketing campaigns play a role in identifying potential customers? Will your company invest in trade shows and conventions? If so, who will attend? Will resellers or consulting firms serve as partners? Who will support the direct sales force? How?

➤ **Tactical Plan.** This is the step-by-step process you and your colleagues will follow. This plan sets out what needs to happen in each of the areas identified by the strategic plan if success is to be achieved. This is the plan that helps ensure the overachievement of revenue goals, dominance in the marketplace, compression of the production or deployment process, and containment of costs.

So—you're a responsible salesperson, one who's headed for the top. As such, you must be completely familiar with your company's plans. You know that you need your own roadmap for overachievement…and you know that your own roadmap to overachievement must be based on that of the company for which you work. (If the two plans are headed in opposite directions, there's a problem somewhere!) If you're working for a company that doesn't *have* the marketing resources to create a full-fledged plan, then you'll need to create a simple, easy-to-follow plan of your own. This can be modeled after what's been done by other successful salespeople in your organization. If you're the first and only salesperson in the company, you'll want to put on the "marketer's hat" and create a grassroots plan for territory development that follows the guidelines set out in Chapter 4.

The rest of this section provides some pointers on making the most of some key individual elements of your company's overall plan and a few ideas on making the most of a few elements that may not show up in company documents.

## Advertising

What does your company pay for in this area? What is it planning to pay for? Do you use trade journal, magazine, newspaper, television, or radio advertising? Do they skip advertising altogether? Whatever your company is planning, find a way to track down a copy of each advertising piece in question.

Get hold of a video if the advertising runs on television; find an audiotape if your outfit buys radio spots; get reprints if the advertising runs in printed formats. Read and review all of it, so you're familiar with how your company promotes itself. Keep everything on file.

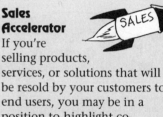

**Sales Accelerator**
If you're selling products, services, or solutions that will be resold by your customers to end users, you may be in a position to highlight co-operative advertising credits to your advantage when the competition starts lowering prices. (Perhaps your company already spends co-op dollars to encourage fans of Stephen King novels, or purchasers of high-end cosmetics, to purchase at the retail level.)

## Direct Mail (and Its Variations)

This is the "sale by mail" approach that has exploded in recent years, and has radically changed both how consumers buy and what they know about what they buy (or even think about buying!). In the past, direct mail was used primarily for selling commodity items, magazines, and a few other categories. Nowadays, all manner of items are sold through the mail, up to and including fresh fruit!

Variations on the "sell-by-mail" approach include such direct response vehicles as Internet home-page marketing, fax broadcasting, and e-mail blitzing. (Another classic direct-response medium, of course, is good old-fashioned display advertising.) Once again, whatever your company is doing, track down copies or printouts, review them, and keep them on file.

## Word of Mouth

This means goodwill and name recognition. Unless you're working for a start-up operation, this will already be established (for better or worse) before you join the sales team. Your aim here is to determine the best untapped avenues of opportunity. If you sell for a company that has a board of directors, get the list of names of the people who are currently on the board. If any of your executives serve on some other company's board of directors, get the names of those companies.

## The Main Event(s)

And speaking of your company's top executives…what colleges did they attend? What clubs and associations do they belong to? What charitable events do they help to coordinate? What events do these groups have scheduled? Write it all down and keep it on file, remembering as you do so that networking is an endless—and endlessly lucrative—process of building partnerships. That process is fueled, in large part, by planning—or taking part in—"big events."

Partners! Did I mention partners? Don't forget to write down business partners (formal and informal) that interact with your business and any other organization that is likely to have a positive opinion of your outfit, including suppliers. Who knows what events they're planning or where such contacts can take you?

And remember: If your company is sponsoring any community event—charitable or commercial—you should get involved! Whether it's a fund-raiser, a food drive, a golf tournament, or a 10K run, you owe it to yourself to participate…and meet and greet 'til you stop and drop.

Other events you should consider taking advantage of include (but are not limited to):

> **Sales Accelerator**
> Word of mouth has far greater potential positive (or negative) impact than advertising or other promotional tools. If a close friend of yours swears by Widgetmaster widgets, you're probably far more likely to consider purchasing them for your own widget needs. If he spends most of his time swearing at Widgetmaster products, odds are you won't be placing an order with that company.

➤ Customer conferences and seminars

➤ Trade shows

➤ Special customer appreciation outings (such as ballgames)

➤ Contests and so on

## Meet the Press

Media relations is another important area of marketing. It sure makes it easier to sell if you can walk into a meeting with a potential customer and pull out a positive article from a major newspaper or the most important trade magazine in your industry!

Consider developing a punchy, straight-to-the point press release that highlights some genuinely newsworthy aspect of your product, service, or solution. Mail it out, and follow up by phone as your schedule permits. The closer your release matches up with the actual "house style" of the journal or broadcast outlet you send it to, the more likely it is to appear verbatim.

# The Customer Counts!

One final point to consider as part of your "outreach" strategy can be summed up in a simple (but too frequently overlooked) question: What are you doing to keep your current customers happy and up to date?

These days, good customer service is often (and rightly!) considered to be part of any smart marketing campaign. This makes perfect sense, because how you treat the customer *after* the sale can mean repeat business, and marketing to current customers can often pay hefty dividends. So ask yourself: How can you keep customers better informed? How can you make it easier for them to contact you about questions and problems? What kind of service are they actually receiving? Who in your organization is in charge of making sure customers you're responsible for are getting the very best treatment, whether it be over the phone, on paper, or in person? How can you improve the level of service your customers receive?

You might decide to help launch a newsletter for current customers—one that regularly features stories about new services, and provides updates on the best ways of getting in touch with you or your organization. Such a newsletter is a great way to "prime the pump" for a later in-person visit to a current customer's site, a visit that allows you to review current projects and future needs.

## Bet You Didn't Know

Before you commit to any set of strategies for your sales plan, you should strongly consider doing some role-playing with a colleague or your sales manager. The object? Find out whether what you're planning will actually appeal to your (probably distracted) potential audience.

Research indicates that today's decision makers are bombarded with up to 178 messages each and every day. These may take the form of pieces of paper delivered via the U.S. Postal Service, telephone calls, voice mail, faxes, internal memos, while-you-were-out slips, e-mail, sticky little yellow notes, and (my favorite) people who "just swung by to ask a quick question." That's the reality of the world your suspects, prospects, customers, and business partners live in. Before you add to the traffic, test your message. Listen to it yourself and ask whether it's something you'd put the world on hold to attend to.

# Your Plan

Most good sales managers will require each and every salesperson in the department to develop a written plan. Whether your sales manager asks you to do this or not, I firmly believe you should develop a detailed plan that will outline precisely how you plan to find and cultivate customers. Your existing customers and business partners can help you cultivate new customers, too. Their stories of success will be of great interest to others who face similar problems. Make sure your sales plan includes strategies for broadcasting these stories. (By the way, you'll find plenty of advice on gathering and circulating testimonials later on in this book.)

Your basic written plan should, at the very least, incorporate each of the following elements. Do the work on computer—as you progress through this book, you'll definitely want to go back to revise parts of your plan.

The following elements are basic components of a first-draft sales plan. To do full justice to your own industry and selling environment, you'll want to add specific features that address your own special challenges and opportunities.

Your sales plan should begin by identifying the following:

➤ The specifics of your territory (if applicable).

➤ The demographics of likely customers you will encounter. (Use your "best-guess" profile for now if your company marketing plan doesn't provide enough information.)

➤ A list of your current customers. Outline both the current products and services each customer purchases, and add ideas for future business with each customer.

> **DICTIONARY**
>
> **? Words, Words, Words**
>
> Your *sales plan* is a written document incorporating key goals and strategies that you review on a regular basis with your sales manager. Set it up! If you don't have a clear idea of how you're going to get where you want to go, you'll find success elusive. (And by the way, that principle holds true for companies as well as individual salespeople!)

➤ A detailed first draft approach of the "how" of your plan. How much time do you anticipate spending developing letters to prospects? Calling prospects cold? Calling current customers? In every case, you should find ways to augment and expand on your company's current selling and marketing efforts—with which you're now quite familiar, right? Use a personalized letter to key prospects, for instance, to add a "local" twist to the theme of a national direct marketing campaign.

➤ A summary of required activity levels. This should be based on your closing ratios (or the closing average in your company, if you're new). How many prospects must you typically present your products, services, and solutions to before one becomes a customer? Closing ratios change from time to time, based on all sorts of factors, including pricing, competition, new product releases, and, of course, your effectiveness as a salesperson.

➤ A sales forecast. Make your own realistic estimates of your performance, based on all of the previous points you've developed. Sales managers love this part of the plan. Even if your estimate is a little lower than your target or quota, you've taken responsibility for making things happen. (And you'll look like a hero when you do hit the company target!)

➤ A short narrative outlining the current state of your territory.

Take some time to work up your plan. Do it right and don't cut corners. Then present it to your sales manager. Review it every quarter, and update it whenever it seems appropriate to do so.

## Look at What's Been Done Already

Your company has already spent a lot of money putting together various promotional pieces, and if you've followed the advice in this chapter, you've assembled it and reviewed it carefully. Pull it out one more time—all of it—and ask yourself the following questions:

➤ What ideas here support my company's mission in a generic way?

➤ What is specific to the products, services, and solutions I offer?

➤ What different individuals/companies/niches does each piece of material appeal to?

➤ Are there groups of prospects that these materials target that I should be targeting, too?

➤ What can I adapt and incorporate within a powerful letter, fax broadcast, e-mail blitz, audiotape, personalized direct mail piece, flyer, or newsletter article?

If you make the best possible use of it, the material you've reserved can save you untold hours of work—and leave at your disposal thousands of dollars' worth of high-powered marketing ideas!

Try developing your own plan and see what happens. And remember—the more you know about what your company does, the more power you're putting behind your sales career.

## The Least You Need to Know

➤ Assume responsibility for gathering all the information likely to help you keep your customers' overall satisfaction level high.

➤ Take the time to review—and understand—your company's marketing/sales plan.

➤ Understand, on a fundamental level, exactly how your customers will use and benefit from what you have to offer.

➤ Take the time to track down every bit of marketing material your organization has developed that relates, even remotely, to what you sell for a living.

➤ Review all of this material carefully, adapting what you can to your own needs.

➤ Develop a detailed, written, personalized selling plan. Review it regularly and revise it when it's appropriate to do so.

# What You Bring to the Table

In the last chapter, you took a look at your company's marketing plan, which (typically) reflects a significant investment of time, talent, and energy on the part of the organization that hired you. That chapter was about the resources your employer offers to your sales work. This chapter is about the internal personal resources you can bring to bear in your sales career.

## No Two Identical Salespeople

I've worked with a lot of salespeople over the years, and I can tell you that I've noticed a wide variation of skills, attitudes, and aptitudes among the people I've trained. Although product knowledge is an exact science, one that depends very little on such factors as imagination and creativity, the same cannot be said for that intangible known variously as "charismatic personal style," "magnetism," or "interpersonal chemistry." This last factor, which may be described as an integral part of a given sales rep's personal selling style, seems to me to play the more important role in the establishment of a successful sales career. I don't believe there's any way a sales trainer can teach personal charisma, as such. It expresses itself differently in every case, and it arises in unexpected ways.

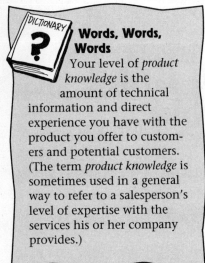

**Words, Words, Words**
Your level of *product knowledge* is the amount of technical information and direct experience you have with the product you offer to customers and potential customers. (The term *product knowledge* is sometimes used in a general way to refer to a salesperson's level of expertise with the services his or her company provides.)

I believe, however, that there are three basic elements within the successful sales rep's interpersonal arsenal that contribute to success. As luck would have it, continuous development of these three areas has, in many instances, helped sales people to bring about that elusive quality, known as "charisma," on their own. In other words, once you focus on the three areas I'll be discussing in depth in this section and the rest of the chapter, you may find your own inimitable brand of personal magnetism or appeal coming to the surface. My personal belief is that you can, over time and with a little bit of persistence, develop all three of the basic skill sets you'll be learning about in this chapter to a superior level. Once you do, you'll be in a perfect position to get the very most out of your (unique) personal selling style.

*Skill sets* are the talents you can bring to your sales efforts in any particular area. To improve your interpersonal chemistry, you can concentrate on developing three specific skill sets:

➤ Congruency.

➤ Intellect.

➤ Interpersonal bonding.

Your ability to make constant improvements in these three areas will have an immense impact on your overall sales performance and on the eventual development of that quality known as "personality" or "magnetism." You may run into people who tell you that this quality is the product of a set of pre-existing characteristics: "You've either got it or you haven't." Baloney! If you're committed to developing your skills in the three areas just outlined, your unique brand of confidence and personal charisma will emerge. I've seen it happen too many times to believe otherwise!

The short message is this: Don't get sidetracked by efforts to "increase your charisma." (That almost always backfires.) Instead, focus on improving the three individual selling skills you'll be learning about in this section, and the charisma will take care of itself!

# Congruency

Congruency means "unity, continuity, or compatibility." The type of congruency I'm talking about is congruency with positive values, as they are reflected in other aspects of your life. I'm talking about letting your own best instincts guide the sales process. I'm talking about making sure your moral values have a constant, pervasive, and tangible effect on your sales career.

I believe that all of us know, deep down, whether or not our actions are in continuity with our deepest, most constructive values. But it doesn't hurt to specify those values and reinforce them. The "My Inner Values Worksheet" offers a list of values you'll need to cultivate on a daily (hourly! minute-by-minute!) basis if you are sincere about improving your congruency skills. After each value in the worksheet, you'll find some questions you should be asking about your life in this area; take the time to write out some answers, and refer back to them regularly.

---

### My Inner Values Worksheet

➤ **Honesty.** Am I scrupulously honest in all my dealings with superiors, colleagues, customers, and potential customers? Do I stand by what I say? If what I promise doesn't appear likely to work out, do I take personal responsibility for setting the record straight ahead of time?

➤ **Integrity.** Am I a straight shooter with regard to what is spoken—and unspoken? Do I think in the long term for myself and my associates? Do I commit myself to act ethically in all situations?

➤ **Concern for others.** Am I genuinely empathetic? Do I listen well? Am I willing to repeat and rephrase what another person has said before I respond with my own concerns?

➤ **Respect for others.** Is my demeanor open, rather than challenging? Am I approachable? Do I keep things in perspective during my exchanges with other people?

---

What congruency really boils down to is this: Act from the heart, do what you know is right, and don't take shortcuts or strong-arm people—ever. Deep down, you probably already know that pressure tactics don't work in the long run. (All they ever really accomplish is to get you stressed out!)

What does all this talk of integrity, respect, and empathy boil down to? Something very simple: Your positive *inner values* are basically those convictions that instill trust in you from others. When your suspects, prospects, customers, and business partners trust you, they will share their problems and challenges with you. When that happens, you'll be able to put your values to work by solving problems and making sales.

Sometimes, during my seminars, when I start talking about establishing congruency with these positive values, the salespeople I train get a panicked look in their eyes. "Tony," they say, "this all sounds great in theory, but I've got to sell something this month. I'm not interested in smoke-and-mirrors selling any more than you are, but don't I need to be a little bit pushy to get the results I want?"

The answer is no, and I can back that up. Every high-achieving salesperson I've every worked with—every salesperson who's developed a pattern of long-term career success—has learned that there's a difference between being persistently confident about your product or service, and doing an impression of an ethically challenged bulldozer. Whenever you demonstrate your inner values, the ones you count on at a core level to keep your life in balance, you reinforce them for yourself, and for your prospects and customers.

Don't cut corners. Turn your ethical values into everyday action. Build congruency between what you believe and what you do.

# Intellect

No, nobody's saying you have to get an advanced degree to be a good salesperson. (There are some selling environments where an advanced degree in, say, psychology or social work wouldn't exactly hurt, of course, but I digress.) The issue here is to be able to understand, retain, and recite accurately the various features and benefits of your product, service, and solution. When you develop your intellectual skill set, what you're basically doing is committing to the proposition that you won't attempt to run a snow job on suspects, prospects, customers, and business partners.

I've already spoken about the importance of actually getting out and using what you sell. Just doing that, however, is not the same as cultivating this critical skill set. You must know your product, service, or solution backwards and forwards. That means, as a general rule, that you can easily—and without significant brain damage—show someone else how to use your product or service, or get the most out of it.

If you find you're coming up short in this category, it is incumbent upon you to track down some customers and ask them a few important questions. Use the "Build Your Intellectual Skill Set! Worksheet" to help get you started.

> **Sales Accelerator**
>
> If you've fully developed your intellectual skill set, you understand not only what your product is, but also what it does. If you are in any doubt about your status on this score, get out and talk to some customers! Customers virtually always understand the front-line problems and opportunities associated with your product, service, or solution better than the bigwigs in marketing.

---

**Build Your Intellectual Skill Set! Worksheet**

Ask your customers:

1.  What are you doing today that you were not able to do before you started using our products/services?

2.  How have our products/services affected your job?

3.  How have our products/services affected your department?

4.  How have our products/services affected your work group?

5.  How have our products/services affected your company as a whole?

6.  If we gave you a little creative license, what would you add, delete, or change about our products/services?

The answers to the "Build Your Intellectual Skill Set! Worksheet" questions will tell you a lot about the solutions you provide to other people.

Remember, if you don't know how to show another person how to use your product or service, you probably don't know as much about it as you should!

# Interpersonal Bonding

*Interpersonal bonding* refers to your ability to communicate effectively during one-on-one discussions and one-on-many presentations. Sometimes, a salesperson's existing communication patterns (which are typically established by exposure to an important adult role model who wasn't a salesperson) need to be changed. Ask yourself: "What specific areas do I need to develop more fully in my current communication style?" Here are some of the areas that the salespeople I train decide need to be improved:

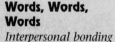 

**Words, Words, Words**
*Interpersonal bonding* is the way you communicate—both spoken and unspoken—with a customer through your body posture, body language, vocal delivery, and vocal pitch.

➤ **Body posture.** When walking or sitting, do you hold your head upright? Are your shoulders straight? Do you avoid slouching? Do you place both feet on the floor? Do you keep your back straight?

➤ **Body language.** Use appropriate—not invasive—eye contact. One person's successful body language is another's forced discomfort. Find a colleague whose physical style you admire and consider incorporating effective hand and arm movements from that style that could work for you, as well.

➤ **Vocal delivery.** Make sure there are appropriate rises and falls in your vocal style, and that you are not speaking too fast or too slow. Listen to your own vocal delivery on tape; if you speak in a monotone, consider practicing with the recorder until your style is varied and easy to understand!

➤ **Vocal pitch.** Many of us have years of experience in altering our vocal style to an unnatural tone. Unnatural is not what you want to be! Your "true" voice is the voice you would use to sing, for instance, "Happy Birthday to You." The closer your everyday speaking pitch is to this natural tone, the more confident and persuasive you will sound.

➤ **Listening skills.** During conversations, silently ask yourself, "Why is this person telling me this?" Keep a notepad with you at all times. If you feel tempted to interrupt, make a written note. You should also jot down intermediate questions that will help the other person clarify his or her points.

**Watch It!**
Don't make the mistake of believing that only the words that come out of your mouth affect how suspects, prospects, customers, and business partners will perceive you. Research indicates that 55% of all face-to-face communication is rooted in body language. A full 35% of your message is determined by the tone of your voice and your general vocal delivery, while only 7% is directly attributable to the words you select.

# Your Personal Value Inventory

Congruency, as we've seen, means continuity with your own positive values. Take the opportunity now to get specific about congruency. Take an in-depth look at the values that drive you.

Yes, it's time to do another "line-down-the-middle-of-a-big-piece-of-paper" exercise. This one will help you get a better idea of what you're moving toward in your life, as well as what may be standing in your way. (This exercise will serve as a kind of preliminary to the full-scale goal-setting work you'll be doing in Chapter 7—don't skip it!)

At the top of the left-hand side of your sheet of paper, put a big plus sign. At the top of the right-hand side of your sheet, put a big minus sign. On the left side, set aside five minutes and write continuously, without letting your pen stop moving for an instant.

I want you to write down everything you are aiming for and moving towards in your life. These are just a few of the entries that might fall on the left side of the line...

➤ "I want to own a nicer car."

➤ "A better place to live would be great."

➤ "Weight loss and increased health would seriously improve the way I view myself."

➤ "I want to find a person to share my life with."

➤ "Spending more time on my hobbies would really help me release stress."

➤ And so on.

Put this sheet of paper away for an hour and a half. Then come back to it and complete the exercise by writing nonstop for another five minutes, and specifying every doubt, fear, or concern you can think of in your professional life on the minus side of the paper. Here are some entries that might appear on your minus list:

➤ "I'll never be able to afford that."

➤ "There's too much risk."

➤ "I never finish what I start."

➤ "I could get rejected."

➤ "I never seem to beat quota."

➤ And so on.

# Analyze Your Inventory!

Now, take a color marker and connect each fear with the goal it cancels out. This process will highlight limiting self-talk and preconceptions that are standing in the way of your achieving what you're really capable of achieving.

Every time you make an attempt to try something new—to reach out to potential customers in a dramatic new way, to ask for that promotion, to get the very most out of your day—conflicts in your inventory can hold you back. These conflicts exert a powerful hold on your subconscious mind, and you have to find a way to overcome them.

Here are three techniques that have worked wonders for me:

1. **Visualize your goals and dreams.** Put strong images in your mind of exactly what it is that you want to perform, become, or achieve. See yourself shaking hands with an important new customer. Visualize the new house in its every detail. Put yourself in the quota club—participate, mentally, in the celebration honoring your achievement. I keep photos of my goals on my bathroom mirror, inside my top desk drawer, and on the sun-visor of my car. One of my goals this year is to invest in a 355 Ferrari Spider. I've got pictures of that machine everywhere!

2. **Eliminate negative influences in your life.** I know, I know, easier said than done. But there is a simple step you can take right now. If you're listening to the morning and evening news during your daily commute, you're not doing all you can to keep your mindset positive. Who needs all that gloom, doom, mayhem, victimization, and titillation? News is designed to take you off center. If a story doesn't seem likely to make a big chunk of the populace stop everything they're doing and respond emotionally, producers don't like to run it. Well, those are your emotions, not the news establishment's. Decide what you're going to do with them. Don't let the media manipulate you. Turn off the radio (and television!) news and read the daily newspaper instead. That way, you get to choose what you want to expose your psyche to—and what you don't.

3. **Compliment others.** At work, at play, at home—tell people how great they are and what they're doing right. Make sure you're the source of kind, encouraging, and completely sincere words. Not only will you get the same treatment in return, you'll be sending your brain a subconscious message: I am grateful for my surroundings, and by finding worth in other people, I myself become worthy.

# Your Rejection Response

Rejection comes with the salesperson's territory—right?

Well, yes and no. Responding gracefully and appropriately to situations most people would immediately label as "rejection" is a great way to demonstrate (and hone) your interpersonal bonding skills. Sure, getting a "no" answer is part and parcel of the salesperson's lot. Like everything else in life, however, what counts is not what happens, but what you do about it.

If you understand the circumstances, you can understand exactly what was "rejected"—and what wasn't. I'll go even further. If you truly are congruent with your own positive values, informed about the market and how your organization fits into it, and possessed of sound interpersonal skills, you'll never really feel "rejected." That's because you'll know, before the other person does, that what you have to offer is not right for the situation.

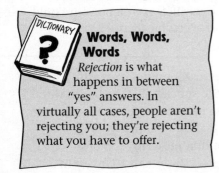

**Words, Words, Words**

*Rejection* is what happens in between "yes" answers. In virtually all cases, people aren't rejecting you; they're rejecting what you have to offer.

It's an old saying, but it's true: You really never are rejected until you give someone permission and power to reject you. My first direct experience with this principle came on the dance floor when I was a teenager. The first time I walked all the way across the floor to the ladies' side of the room to ask a pretty girl whether she wanted to dance the cha-cha, she said, "No." I had to walk all the way back to the guys' side, with all my buddies watching, knowing that I had failed.

That was a truly mortifying experience—enough to make me think about going food shopping at the A&P with my parents on a Friday night!

Afterwards, my brother Al took me aside and gave me a few pointers. He told me to bear in mind that, when something like that happens, it wasn't me being rejected, but the dance! He also told me that I had to learn to ask the right question, in the right way (certainly a lesson many a salesperson has picked up over the years). The next Friday evening, I followed my brother's advice to the letter. I walked up to the prettiest girl on the floor and asked, "Do you know how to dance?" "Of course," she replied. "Great," I said. "Do you want to show everyone on the floor how good you are?"

That approach might not have worked in every situation, but it certainly worked in this one. She took my hand and instantly led me out to the floor. My buddies couldn't figure out how I managed it. True to form, my brother Al cut in halfway through the song!

Suppose she'd said "No?" Hey, some people like the cha-cha, other people don't.

Although it's very easy to take rejection personally, the truth is that, in the world of sales, very little of the rejection you encounter is going to be directed specifically and pointedly at you—and you only have to accept as much of that as benefits you directly.

When was the last time someone told you, "You know, I really don't like you, so I'm not going to buy from you," or "I want to buy this product, but I don't want to have anything to do with you?" If you are consistently receiving messages like that, you owe it to yourself to figure out which of the signals you're sending is limiting your performance, and to make a positive change. But the truth is that these messages are actually quite rare, and they're usually passed along by people who have no idea what they're talking about.

**Sales Accelerator**

SALES

I've learned, over the years, to take revenge on rejection by learning from it when I can, and reminding myself that every rejection is just another form of saying "no." "No," of course, is part of the sales world. I listen to rejections, to find out whether there's some change in approach I should be making, but I don't accept them as assessments of my personal worth or the success of my overall plan. You shouldn't either.

**Watch It!**

NO SALE

Letting rejection affect your overall level of self-esteem can be hazardous to your career. If someone gets personal with you in saying "no," keep things in perspective. Ask yourself: Was what the person said correct? Was it stated by someone knowledgeable, someone in a position of authority? Does what this person said reflect similar comments from others who are knowledgeable and in positions of authority? Did the person who said this make (heh-heh) less money than you do?

# Mental Toughness: Beating Burnout

Mishandled day-to-day stress can make good interpersonal bonding difficult. If left unattended, stress problems can lead to full-fledged burnout that can make improvements in congruency, intellect, and interpersonal bonding—that is, all three skill sets—just about impossible. Obviously, it's in your best interest to beat burnout before it leads to a career crisis.

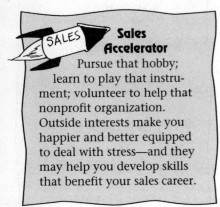

**Sales Accelerator**
Pursue that hobby; learn to play that instrument; volunteer to help that nonprofit organization. Outside interests make you happier and better equipped to deal with stress—and they may help you develop skills that benefit your sales career.

I've "hit the wall" four times in my career. All four times, I was at the top of my game at the time I stressed out and started careening into burnout.

Burnout can come when you're at the top or at the bottom. In my experience, it rarely occurs when you're somewhere in between, heading in either direction. If you're experiencing any of the Warning Signs of Sales Burnout (outlined below), you'll need to take some action to correct the situation.

---

**Warning Signs of Sales Burnout**

➤ You start to get sloppy; you forget about or ignore details.

➤ You don't meet the expectations you've set for yourself and it doesn't seem to bother you.

➤ You don't take action. You procrastinate. You may feel guilty about procrastinating, then procrastinate more, causing a snowball effect.

➤ You sleep a whole lot and still wake up tired.

➤ You aren't excited about much of anything.

---

In severe cases, burnout can lead you to increase your intake of alcohol or tobacco, or lead to serious substance abuse problems that can, of course, cause serious problems in your life as a whole.

How do you beat burnout? My list of Burnout Cures gives some steps you can take immediately.

---

**Burnout Cures**

To beat burnout take time out now and...

➤ Establish (or re-establish) balance in your life. Guard non-work time jealously. Make sure your priorities are acceptable to the people in your life who are most important to you. I know this is difficult, but it can be accomplished if you: a) schedule time each week on your calendar to do the things you enjoy, and take this commitment as seriously as you do appointments with prospects; and b) schedule "quiet" days or hours when you will not respond to calls. Let your office know of these times so backup staff can handle questions and calls. Another great long-term tactic, guaranteed to win you the time you need, is to make a non-refundable deposit for next year's vacation!

➤ Find a positive role model or mentor. Look to this person for guidance; model that person's balance and career commitment.

➤ Develop written short- and long-term personal goals; review them every day. Emphasize and celebrate choices you make; don't dwell on what you "have to" do. You don't "have to" do anything!

➤ Be the person your dog thinks you are.

---

Other strategies that may make sense for you include meditation, use of motivational or self-help tapes, and volunteering to help out those less fortunate than you are, any number of whom would trade places with you in a heartbeat. Exercise is also an important burnout-beater.

Life is short; we're here to make a difference and to learn to help one another, not to crash and burn. By keeping things in perspective, taking time out, and taking care of yourself, you can start to move back toward a passionate, fulfilling work life. I know, because I've done it!

# The Least You Need to Know

➤ You must develop your congruency skill set by putting your most constructive core values into action.

➤ You must develop your intellectual skill set by understanding not only what your product is, but also what it does.

➤ You must develop your interpersonal bonding skill set by learning to communicate effectively within one-on-one discussions and one-on-many presentations.

➤ Nobody can teach you to develop the elusive quality known as "charisma," but...

➤ Focusing on the three skill sets discussed in this chapter can help you make your own unique brand of charisma a reality.

➤ Rejection is what happens in between "yes" answers; it's a natural part of the sales process, not an assault on your value as a human being.

➤ Burnout can make improving your skill sets impossible—so keep an eye out for the warning signs (such as lack of motivation or energy), and take time out to take care of yourself.

# Types of Selling

> ## In This Chapter
>
> ➤ The beauty of the "willing win-win" approach
>
> ➤ What is direct selling?
>
> ➤ What is consultative selling?
>
> ➤ Keeping customers from jumping ship

A lot has changed over the past quarter-century in the world of selling: Buyers are better informed today than they have ever been. There's a lot more information out there, and it's left the consumer more confident, more skeptical about unrealistic claims, better prepared to make decisions, and less susceptible to pressure and persuasion. So, how do you appeal to today's customers?

In this chapter, you'll take a look at two very different sales models. No matter which method you decide makes the most sense for you, your preferred outcome must always be the same: A totally satisfied customer who makes a conscious decision to stick with you. The only way to pull that off, of course, is to listen carefully and make informed, intelligent recommendations, based on what you hear. The alternative? Make your prescription before you conduct a thoughtful diagnosis—and before you leave a trail of sales "malpractice" suits as you hop from job to job!

# Tech Talk

Is it my imagination, or can just about anyone now find out just about anything by executing a couple of well-targeted mouse clicks on a computer?

These days, buyers know exactly what types of technical wizardry are available to them, and they may even know how much it costs you to assemble your widget or put it on the showroom floor.

Given the technical tools and background information available to today's buyers, a salesperson is likely to wonder: Is it harder to sell today than it was, say, 25 years ago? I don't think so. I think it's just a different kind of sale, a sale that's likely to involve two informed parties, rather than just one. Today's selling also depends, increasingly, on your ability to offer support after the sale, based on what you learned during the sale.

# Toward Win-Win Selling...Again

There are two basic types of selling. But they both spring out of the same basic idea. Some years ago, a popular model for successful interpersonal transactions (including sales) appealed to a "win-win" philosophy, under which both participants in an exchange came out feeling they'd gotten a good deal. It sounds fine in theory, and for a while salespeople made good use of the model, but the many pressures of today's tight-margin, make-it-happen-this-quarter economy have, alas, made this type of selling less and less of a reality.

To put it frankly, too many buyers have gotten burned. When they check the fine print, they find unpleasant surprises they can't do anything about. When they open up the box, hook up the machine, or try on the outfit, they learn that what they got doesn't even remotely resemble what they were promised, and their only recourse is to wait for four or five hours on an 800-help line that doesn't really help very much at all. This over-promise, under-deliver syndrome has become common in virtually every product and service category. (Did you ever wonder why credit card companies started guaranteeing purchases made with their cards? They knew just how deep the currents of consumer resentment can run in our economy.)

It's your turn, your duty, to bring back true "win-win" selling. How? By using what I call a "willing win-win" approach. This means accepting an uncomfortable truth about the people to whom you're trying to sell.

# Why You Can't Make People Buy Anything

The "willing win-win" model is based on your accepting, at the outset, a single, simple idea: You can't really pressure anybody into buying anything. You can only let the customer buy what he or she wants to buy, when he or she wants to buy it.

You can try like the dickens to make sure the customer buys the product, service, or solution from you, but you can't transform him or her into a willing buyer by virtue of a convincing soft-shoe shuffle. Only the person you're selling to can decide when the time is right to buy. And you're not going to waste time trying to turn unwilling buyers into willing buyers because that approach doesn't make anybody happy.

## The Courage to Move On

Yes, you have a quota to meet. Yes, you have a family to feed. Yes, you've got to sell as much as you can in the shortest possible time. But you can't do any of that stuff if you're making promises neither you nor your organization can keep in order to rekindle interest that's ebbed in a prospect—or was never there in the first place in a suspect.

What we're really talking about here is dealing openly and honestly with potential customers, and making a commitment to spend the vast majority of your time with people who are clearly, and unmistakably, interested in moving the sales process forward with you.

When you get information that indicates you're looking at someone who's less than willing to talk to you about your products, services, and solutions, guess what? You need to find someone else to talk to. (*Note:* Later on in the book, beginning with Chapter 15, you'll be learning about the best ways to evaluate accurately, and respond to, the seemingly iron-clad "no interest" responses you're likely to get at various stages of your relationship with the prospect.)

## A Tale of Two Sales Models

Now it's time to look at two basic types of selling that will help you make the willing "win-win" approach a reality: direct and consultative.

The *direct selling* style is best suited to relatively simple sales environments, where one person is likely to give you a "thumbs-up" or "thumbs-down" decision in a relatively short period of time. The *consultative* style typically delivers good results for sales reps who must convince committees, review boards, and other imposing entities of the worthiness of their product, service, or solution—typically over a fairly extended period of time.

Don't get too hung up on questions of structure or hierarchy—or on permanent, hard-and-fast labels about selling to particular people. Different needs and different decision-making processes arise quickly and without warning among suspects, prospects, and customers.

Depending on the situation you face, you may decide to apply both the direct and the consultative approach to the same individual and/or organization over time. The next couple of sections look at each approach in more detail, so you can learn how and when to apply each approach.

# Direct Selling

Direct selling means solving a single pressing problem, typically in a short-term setting, and not digging too deeply beneath that problem.

There's nothing wrong with this approach; it doesn't imply a high-pressure philosophy or an uncaring attitude on the part of the salesperson. Direct selling is a quick, easy, and straightforward method of selling that gets right to the heart of the matter—and may even be less risky than a more in-depth set of discussions, in that there's less of an opportunity to indulge the temptation to over-promise. The time you spend discussing things with the prospect is limited. Either what you outline works...or it doesn't.

Think of the direct type of selling as analogous to a child carefully coloring in a picture in a coloring book. She colors inside the lines; she creates the picture that the book wants her to create. She has one problem to solve, one particular need to diagnose: completing a particular picture with a set of very clear borders.

That's a lot like the role of the salesperson who takes the direct approach to selling. The prospect outlines the problem, and the salesperson proposes some possible solutions, just as the child considers various colors of crayons before filling in an area on the page. The prospect makes a decision, and this sale is complete. It may lead to other sales situations, of course, and it probably should, but the structure is clear: The prospect outlines the problem, and you stay within the lines.

Here's how it might work out in real life. A law firm you happen to call is in a real jam and needs a solution to a problem, fast. The firm needs to open a remote office quickly, in order to provide a high level of service to a new (and huge) client in a faraway city. Somehow, the firm has to magic up an office, on the double. This prospect needs pretty much everything that constitutes an office: space, furniture, rugs, paintings, equipment for personnel, the works. You are an interior decorator/salesperson. You sell everything that has to do with opening a new office. You seize your opportunity.

Even though your primary job is to sell new furniture, rather than rent it, you accept the problem as the prospect has outlined it. This prospect is willing to rent for now—and pay you a modest premium—in order to resolve a pressing current problem, a problem they feel confident you can resolve.

In such a situation, I would argue, you must be willing to create a win-win solution in the direct-selling mindset. This solution must allow you to initiate an important new relationship, get the prospect exactly what he or she has outlined, make a little money now, and keep the door open for making a great deal more money later. You know time is tight. You tackle only the parts of the customer's problem that you know you can resolve quickly and conclusively, and you're completely up-front about what you can't accomplish. That way, you don't waste your time—or the prospect's—trying to get a deal that only makes sense for one side.

In six months or so, when the new law office has changed from a "who-knows-if-this-is-going-to-pan-out" facility to a "what-are-we-doing-renting-furniture-when-we-know-we're-here-for-the-long-term" facility, you can return and apply the consultative approach.

The best way to identify a direct selling opportunity? Ask yourself two questions:

➤ Have my products, services, or solutions successfully resolved this particular problem or situation before?

➤ Does this prospect have a good understanding of his or her problem or situation?

If the answer to *both* of these questions is "yes," then you can rest assured you'll be serving the prospect, and your organization, well by making a direct sale.

**Watch It!**
Direct selling is not a shortcut to a commission check. You still have to ask intelligent questions (as discussed in depth in Chapter 14). Direct selling does not mean you relinquish any of your responsibilities to undertake a complete "diagnosis" before you make an informed "prescription."

# Consultative Selling

Consultative selling means you take on the responsibility for a full, thorough, and all-encompassing professional diagnosis of the problem—for nothing, and with no preconception as to the outcome.

Look at it this way: Your work in the direct-selling model can be compared to that of a doctor who works in an emergency room and helps to identify and diagnose pressing problems that are pretty clear to all concerned (like a broken leg). Once you enter the consultative mode, however, you're running many more tests and conducting a full physical. You're looking at things in greater depth.

Why? Because there's more to see and understand about this prospect's situation. You're acting on more than an informed sense of how this problem usually gets resolved, so that you can deliver a solution that will work both now and for a significant period in the future. You're digging deeper in most cases because you're being encouraged to do so by the prospect.

Here are the important indicators that will let you know that you're looking at a prospect who's open to consultative selling. The presence of any one of these factors is a good signal that this is the situation you face.

➤ Your prospect is truly interested in exploring all the possible ways of resolving this problem or situation, and is willing to invest time to do so. Your prospect is on a search for "all the alternatives." His or her actions demonstrate to you that the decision in question is going to be based on choice, not necessity.

**Watch It!**
Don't use the word "consultative" in your discussions with suspects, prospects, customers, and business partners. They'll probably think you're getting ready to think up a way to charge them $275 per hour for your advice. Actually, that's about as far away from consultative selling as you can get.

➤ The topic of price is not at the top of the list; your prospect is more interested in total capability and overall cost of ownership than in initial price.

➤ Your prospect openly solicits your opinion and assistance in dealing with a wide range of challenges, some of which you may not be able to solve directly.

The fact that you're making a thorough review doesn't mean you are obliged to make an expensive recommendation. Quite the contrary! If you cannot prescribe a solution that will perform to, or exceed the expectations of, your prospect, you're going to say so. If it's in your prospect's best interest, you're going to recommend that your prospect seek help elsewhere. (In many cases, of course, your own recommendation is going to include a suggestion that your prospect work with you—and perhaps with someone else.)

## All the Angles

What does consultative selling look like in action? It might look like this.

You sell computer systems. The largest HMO in your territory, which has recently expanded, has just recruited a new CEO. His goals are outlined in a profile in the *Medical Business Daily News;* you clip the article and take it down to the local U-Frame-It shop—and turn it into a permanent memento. You send this to the CEO, along with a snazzy letter that highlights your organization's ability to help manage the heavy data load of organizations—just like the one the new CEO has just joined. You ask the new CEO to direct you to the individual(s) or department(s) that are responsible for the areas your ideas are designed to help.

At the same time, you gather information on the computer systems currently being used at the HMO's 25 facilities. As you'd hoped, they need upgrading. You brainstorm with your team and learn about two areas that your products can't address, so you take a preliminary look at an alliance with another vendor. Together, you are sure you can put together a proposal that will meet this company's needs.

By the way, the fastest way to get information on a prospect company is to call a salesperson who works for the organization in question. Call the main number and ask to be put through to the top sales rep in the office. (Trust me, you'll get through.) Most of the time, you'll have to leave a message, because this person will usually—surprise, surprise—be out selling when you call. Leave a message, and don't be surprised when that message is returned quickly. Once you have this person on the line, be honest. Tell the sales rep where you're from, what you want to know, and why you want to know it. You'll get the facts you need. Successful salespeople *love* to talk about their organizations.

## The Preliminary Work Pays Off

The CEO, impressed by your letter and your memento, refers you to a group of staffers. Because you've done your research on the company, you take part as an informed partici-pant, not an outsider trying to "sell something." Your probing and questioning turns up additional needs and additional opportunities. The people you're working with talk easily about these matters because they know you're interested in them, in their problems, and in their attempts to meet the objectives that the new CEO has laid out. You put together a killer proposal, and the likelihood of your getting the business skyrockets.

You colored outside the lines. You went out and found some problems to solve. You committed yourself to a full understanding of the prospect's needs. And it paid off.

Because you're selling in the consultative mode, you look beyond the immediate need. You work with a number of company insiders (including top-level executives) to develop creative approaches to all the situations to which you can provide solutions. Those solutions may come about either through your company's independent efforts, or as a result of work you do in league with others.

>
> **Sales Accelerator**
> When you sell in the consultative style, take time to understand all functional areas of interest that your suspects, prospects, customers, and business partners may have. If you don't sell solutions for all of their needs, hook them up with salespeople who do. For instance: You sell men's suits. You should know where to get the best shoes and accessories in town, as well as the best places for your customers to get their dry cleaning done.

# Winning with Customers You Already Have

Of course, the ultimate "win-win" situation is one in which the customer decides to keep winning by staying with your company. Fortunately, holding on to customers is easier than you may have been led to believe.

It's a good thing, too, because getting new customers is a whole lot more expensive than holding on to old ones—both for your company and for you. Marketing experts, surveys, and many sales managers estimate that it costs nine times as much to find a new customer as it does to add on business to an existing one. Add-on business is typically more profitable, too. No matter what type of selling you undertake, you're going to want to develop some strategies for keeping customer attrition to a minimum. You can use the six tips I outline next to retain market share and reduce customer defections:

> **Words, Words, Words**
> *Add-on business* is business you earn (by meeting and exceeding expectations) after your first sale to a customer.

1. Develop a relationship with more than one single contact in a customer's organization. If you're selling a solution used by the shipping and receiving department, get to know that department's manager and the manager of a related department (such as manufacturing or traffic), in addition to the purchasing department person who's your direct contact. There's strength in numbers! (And there's nothing wrong with developing a few "backup" contacts to point you toward key people if your primary acquaintance leaves the organization.)

2. Always ask for referrals. Doing so builds loyalty. Most customers will be happy, and a little bit flattered, when you ask for permission to contact the trade references they provided on their initial credit application (which most companies require from customers these days).

3. Keep adding value. Become known as the person your customers calls for help when something unusual comes up: a free consultant, if you will.

4. Keep the lines of communication open. Check in by phone. Send out a quarterly mailer that keeps your customer up-to-date on developments in your industry. That means you must become a trade magazine "junkie"! Read every journal, newsletter, and magazine that's related to the interests of your customer base.

5. Ask your customers for their opinions. Survey them periodically. Ask how your products and services are working out. Listen to the answers you get.

6. Create special packages and prices. Offer something special for your special customers. Lobby ceaselessly with the higher-ups until they allow you to (for instance) give prized customers advance notice of a sale or close-out.

Even when you take all of these steps, you may find that your customer is tempted to shop around elsewhere, either because the competition is offering a lower price or (even worse) because your own organization is planning to raise prices. Plan ahead! Continuously show your value by taking the following steps.

➤ Justify your prices. Do this periodically, not just when a price hike is in the offing. Make calculations; if necessary and appropriate, provide industry standards. Show what factors are affecting price shifts; help your customers put any price adjustments in the proper perspective.

➤ Read—and then reread—Chapter 23 of this book. It will tell you everything you need to know about measuring and demonstrating R.O.I. (Return On Investment) for your customers.

➤ Make sure you know how each of your customers defines "price." Once you move beyond the initial-sale phase of the relationship, your customer may change the working definition of the word "price." (This will almost always happen if your solution actually saves your customers time, money, or both.)

# The Least You Need to Know

> ➤ The "willing win-win" sales model is based on your accepting, at the outset, a single, simple idea: You can't really force anybody to do anything.

> ➤ Direct selling means doing what it takes to solve only the immediate, pressing problem the prospect or customer defines for you.

> ➤ Direct selling usually involves a single decision maker who gives you a rapid yes-or-no answer.

> ➤ Consultative selling means working with important constituencies within the target organization to identify all the possible solutions your organization can help bring about.

> ➤ Consultative selling usually involves a more protracted selling cycle than direct selling, and will usually expose you to a group, rather than a single decision maker.

> ➤ By developing relationships with multiple contacts and following up to monitor your results, you can increase the likelihood that your customers will keep doing business with you.

# Part 2
# Day by Day

*What groups of people will you be trying to turn into customers? How can you avoid wasting time in meetings and phone discussions with folks who represent a less-than-overwhelming statistical likelihood of turning into customers for you? Where can you find industry information? What should your average day look like? What should your goals be? Who's your competition—and what are they offering?*

*These are questions you'll be facing day in and day out as a professional salesperson. To get a head start on the right (ongoing) answers to them...turn the page!*

# Chapter 5

# Your Territory

## In This Chapter

➤ The nature of your sales territory

➤ Some advice on negotiating for new territory

➤ Finding out about everything and everyone within your territory

What is your sales territory, anyway? Is it really just a colored section of a map pinned to a wall in your office, your showroom floor, an existing customer base? Or is it something more, something akin to a diplomatic mission or a missionary outpost?

Salespeople have been known come up with some intriguing definitions of the word "territory" as it applies to their professional lives.

Such definitions might include "The area closely bordered by huge potential accounts I can't call," or "The region I can be sure will be split into two or more new territories and given to someone else after I've spent years developing it," or even "The group of possible customers that has the least likelihood of actually sitting down with me to talk about my organization's products and services."

You don't have to fall prey to all that frustration. In this chapter, you learn how to research, maintain, and, yes, get the most revenue possible from your sales territory. Even more important, you learn how to think about your sales territory. And once you start thinking in the right way about the people you're trying to reach, you'll be in a perfect position to manage your own sales territory at peak efficiency.

# More Than a Zip Code or Two

Most, but not all, sales territories are defined geographically. But in the final analysis, the territory you inherit is best viewed as opportunity, and not by any narrow labeling system. If there were a fixed, clearly identifiable set of potential customers in your sales territory, you may rest assured that your organization would not have hired you to develop it. If the higher-ups knew exactly where the customers were, they wouldn't have to pay salespeople to track those customers down!

Your job: Act as the company's diplomat to the vitally important "outpost" you've been assigned. Any diplomat who doesn't know the lay of the land is going to have a hard time fulfilling the assignment!

# What You'll Be Looking At

Here's a brief rundown of the different kinds of territory designations you're likely to run into over time:

➤ **Geographic area.** This, the most common method of designating sales territory, depends on tangible (roads or rivers) or hypothetical (zip codes or municipal lines) limits to define the boundaries of various sales areas. If you're in retail sales your geographic area could be your department or floor. Then again, in automotive sales your "geographic" area could be defined as your showroom—or your next walk-in customer.

➤ **Industry designation.** This approach to territory allotment divides up potential customers not by their physical location, but by the type of business they operate. One rep in your organization, for instance, might sell to automobile dealerships, while another might target health care providers. Another twist on this would be different "channels" within an industry or general business area. For example, if you're selling petrochemicals, you may have a territory that is comprised of end-users of your products, resellers of your products, and resellers that add value or ingredients and place their private label on your products and then resell them. In this last situation your reseller may in fact wind up being a competitor of yours!

➤ **"Installed" equipment community.** Under this arrangement, companies that already use a particular product or service (such as a network server) are designated to a particular salesperson. A variation: territory based on assigning salespeople application-specific users (anyone who can use a particular type of product, such as a certain piece of accounting software) as potential customers.

➤ **Named account lists.** Some organizations allocate specific target companies, or limit salespeople to current lists of ("installed") customers. In some cases you'll play the roles of both "farmer" and "hunter" with your account list; in others, you'll simply focus on maintaining existing relationships/purchasing patterns with specific customers.

➤ **None of the above, or a combination of one or more elements.** A company may simply decide that any prospect is fair game for any salesperson who manages to make the initial contact before someone else does. For example, in real estate sales, if get you get "the listing," it's in your territory. Alternatively, a company may combine methods, and assign a salesperson a group like this one: "All companies classified as process manufacturers, and having more than $4 million in gross annual sales, and in possession of a processor that will run our Zenith application."

In the end, your sales territory is defined not only by the lines on a map or the guidelines you receive from a sales manager, but also by your own persistence, initiative, and attitude. All the same, the outside world has a way of setting up mutually recognized "working borders" for the benefit of salespeople and prospects alike. This approach helps ensure that multiple sales-people don't contact the same prospect, and, perhaps more importantly, that groups of prospects aren't ignored altogether.

## What to Do with a Territory

When dealing with any sales territory, the question is not "What established accounts have I inherited?" but rather, "Where is the opportunity—and what do I have to do to come in contact with it?" Complaining about (or becoming sentimental about) your sales territory is a little like ascribing a certain performance level to a run of bad, or good, "luck."

Some territory arrangements can get pretty compli-cated, but even elaborate territory arrangements have been known to deliver commission checks that vary dramatically, depending on the salesperson who inherits the prospect group. Don't assume that an underperforming territory has to stay underperforming.

Is a particular territory ever really "cursed"? The answer seems to have more to do with the attitude of the salesperson in question than it does with otherworldly influences, or elaborate plots meant to ensure that "good" territory is allocated to a particular team member.

**Words, Words, Words**
Your *sales territory* comprises the potential customers you want to sign up as users of your organization's product or service. A particular sales territory may or may not be defined geographically.

**Watch It!**
Don't complain about "bad territory" or "bad luck" in dealing with a certain group of potential customers. In sales, you build up your own cus-tomer base, and you make your own luck. Take full responsibil-ity for developing and main-taining business within the territory you inherit.

Preconceptions and bad attitudes have "doomed" many a territory that got "undoomed" the minute someone else inherited it. If you take over a territory from another salesperson who tells you "not to bother calling such-and-such a company" because "they're hard to deal with" (or any other reason), then you should make that company the first company you visit!

# How to Negotiate with Your Sales Manager for a Better Territory

This one's simple. Don't.

That's right. Your best approach here is to forego the complaint cycle, politely decline the opportunity to give your sales manager the chance to label you as a chronic complainer (trust me, he or she meets more than a few in this line of work), and simply get down to work.

**Sales Accelerator**

Some "adopted" customers may have received less-than-exemplary treatment from a predecessor in your territory. How do you pick up the pieces?

Don't challenge the customer's perception of reality; listen nonjudgmentally to complaints. Take personal responsibility for doing whatever you can to make things better. Finally, do your level best not to disappoint the customer again.

**Sales Accelerator**

Keep an eye on the classifieds! Want ads in your local newspaper will show who the growth companies are. Then hit the road and get a look at them.

Research the territory, and carry out all the steps we'll be discussing in this chapter. Find out where the avenues of opportunity are. And then get down to the job of selling. If you demonstrate, through consistent action undertaken in good faith, the territory you've been assigned really is a waste of your time (and your organization's money), you won't need to do a lot of explaining to higher-ups.

Approach the task of developing and maintaining your territory with an open mind, and you'll keep everyone, including your sales manager, happy. That "bad" territory you inherit could turn into an acre sprinkled with diamonds, with each gem glistening, beckoning you to stride ahead confidently and pick up exactly what you need.

Sound farfetched? Ask any experienced sales manager whether he or she has ever seen a "lousy" territory turn into the launching pad for the next superstar of the department. I've seen just that transformation happen many, many times. All too often, a territory performs exactly as poorly as a salesperson has been convinced it should perform. When another sales rep inherits it, one who knows nothing about, or consciously rejects, the self-fulfilling prophecies promulgated by the last rep, guess what happens? Suddenly, everyone in the department is complaining about how such-and-such a rep has the "good" territory.

I've been selling for 26 years, and I've handled lots of different sales territories. Some of them had great reputations when I took them over; some didn't. I always had the ability to make each territory I worked great. The way I did it was pretty simple. I took full ownership of the territory rather than the other way around. You can develop the same skill.

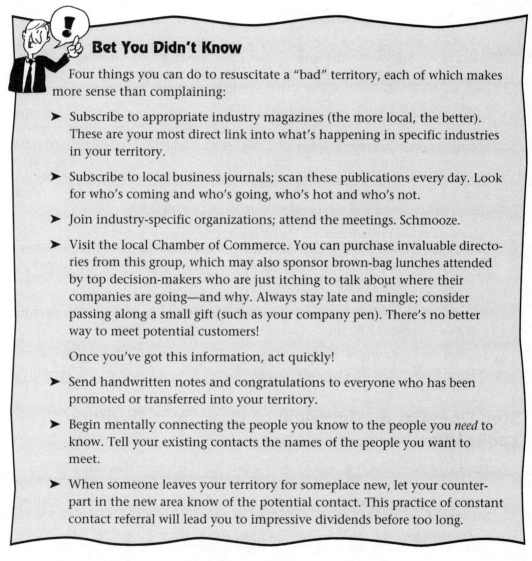

**Bet You Didn't Know**

Four things you can do to resuscitate a "bad" territory, each of which makes more sense than complaining:

➤ Subscribe to appropriate industry magazines (the more local, the better). These are your most direct link into what's happening in specific industries in your territory.

➤ Subscribe to local business journals; scan these publications every day. Look for who's coming and who's going, who's hot and who's not.

➤ Join industry-specific organizations; attend the meetings. Schmooze.

➤ Visit the local Chamber of Commerce. You can purchase invaluable directories from this group, which may also sponsor brown-bag lunches attended by top decision-makers who are just itching to talk about where their companies are going—and why. Always stay late and mingle; consider passing along a small gift (such as your company pen). There's no better way to meet potential customers!

Once you've got this information, act quickly!

➤ Send handwritten notes and congratulations to everyone who has been promoted or transferred into your territory.

➤ Begin mentally connecting the people you know to the people you *need* to know. Tell your existing contacts the names of the people you want to meet.

➤ When someone leaves your territory for someplace new, let your counterpart in the new area know of the potential contact. This practice of constant contact referral will lead you to impressive dividends before too long.

# Taking Ownership of Your Sales Territory

Life passes along some great lessons to each of us. I believe that one of those lessons is that when you work hard for something, you take better care of it. Haven't you found that to be the case in your own life? When you own something, you're more likely to take pride in it, to feel responsible for it, to make maintaining it as a part of your routine. That goes for your house, your car, your back yard, and your sales territory.

How do you go about developing this ownership, this sense of responsibility, when it comes to your own sales territory?

Ownership does not occur overnight. But if you're willing to put in some effort over time, you can eventually enjoy the many benefits of overseeing a sales territory that's truly yours. You can develop the same "territory mastery" one might associate with a senior diplomat, someone who is familiar with all the important power centers within a given state.

Remember, there are lots of different kinds of sales territories, and customizing your approach may be necessary. Retail sales, for instance, implies a territory that is limited to your department or showroom floor. In this case you must extend the boundaries and consider the demographic profiles of the people who enter into your department. The smartest and highest-paid retail salespeople I've seen take real pride in the ownership of their territories. And they never forget that "diplomat" function.

Regardless of the type of territory they work, they always seem to be doing something to take better care of it. They remove any and all boundaries and put "pride of ownership" first. In most cases, when you're dealing with a non-geographical and/or non-account territory assignment, you get to focus on the suspects and prospects that enter into your territory, and on how to make them feel comfortable with you and what you offer. Knowing the trends within your territory becomes critical to your effort to serve the potential customers who enter it, and to establish true ownership.

The five steps I outline in the rest of this section can help you achieve "territory mastery." Remember, if you apply these steps over time, you'll see a vast improvement in your sales performance.

# Step One: Get an Overview of What Your Territory Looks Like

Get a map that accurately represents your potential customer base. The map you use should typically be desk-blotter size, and backed with foam-core (you'll be sticking pins into it). This map should be framed and mounted in your office. Get an un-framed, un-mounted copy, too, one you can fold and keep in your briefcase. If your territory consists of only one or two accounts, plan on making a map of each building, floor by floor, and identifying all the businesses within it, department by department.

Your map provides visual confirmation of what's yours, where you've been, and where you need to go. And if you're interested in saving time, you'll appreciate that a single glance before you go out on a scheduled appointment will let you know what potential future customers are located near your destination. And let's face it, there's probably no greater joy for a salesperson than watching the customer base multiply.

# Step Two: Drive, Drive, Drive...

If at all possible, get in your car and drive around your territory. Get a look at every square mile, and record your comments and observations on a small hand-held tape recorder. You'll notice that territories tend to have centers of influence—key locations nearly everyone knows about—as well as a network of industries that complement each other. Develop a coloring system that will help you make sense of the economic activity within your territory, then make appropriate spots on you map with colored markers. Once you've done that, ask yourself, "Who are the major employers here? Which businesses take a lead role in this community? Which depend heavily on other businesses in this territory?" (By the way, if your territory isn't geographical but consists of a list of particular companies or an industry segment, you can gather research information in a binder or database system.)

The more first-hand facts you can gather about your territory, the better your commission check will look!

Early in my career, I had the responsibly of selling to one account. (Now, that's a simple territory!) For an entire year, I called on the same departments and people my predecessor had. No map, no research, no exploring into other areas; I was just collecting the low-hanging fruit. One day, I was running late for an appointment on the third floor. I normally take the stairs for the exercise, but that particular day I was in a rush, so I decided to jump into the elevator. I quickly pressed the "3" button...but the elevator went down, not up!

When the elevator doors opened, I couldn't believe my eyes. There was a huge laboratory filled with engineers and test equipment! I was a computer salesperson, so naturally, my mouth started watering. Within six months, I sold the engineers in that lab enough computers to net me a $30,000 bonus! After that experience, I always made sure I knew everything there was to know about my territory, no matter what it looked like. In the case of a single account in a single building, that means a map of the building!

**Sales Accelerator**

Let's say you've got the entire eastern seaboard as your territory, and you really don't want to spend your winter vacation skidding down the Garden State Parkway. Invest in an electronic "zoom" map, one that you can install on your computer. Some of these programs will allow you to input your customer locations and type of industry. You can also "surf" the Internet for important information about your territory.

**Sales Accelerator**

Never take the same route back to the office! Make a habit of driving in different areas; do some exploring. Make a commitment to constantly find out about new business parks—areas of opportunity you never knew existed.

# Step Three: Stick Pins In 'Em

No, this isn't some variety of sales voodoo. Use pushpins to identify your current customers (if any) within the territory. I suggest you use a color-coded system here, too: Green for active customers who represent a great deal of revenue and/or currently purchase add-on services; yellow for customers who are not currently buying from you but are likely to do so in the future; and red for former customers you hope to win back. (You can adapt the same color system for non-geographical territory notes you keep track of in a binder.)

By identifying who is—and isn't—a customer in your territory, you give yourself an "at-a-glance" advantage...and you make it that much easier to target the people you should be talking to next.

# Step Four: Link Everything Up

Ask yourself which of the businesses in this territory could buy what you have to offer? Mark the answers on your map or in a separate notebook. If you sell a single product or service, this will be a fairly easy process. If your product line is diverse, you may need to take some time with this step. Do this step according to your own best instincts, then see the instructions on developing the *Template of Ideal Prospects* that appear in the next chapter. When you're done, you'll have, in one place, an accurate (and dramatic) representation of your territory. This, of course, is an ever-changing resource you should incorporate into your "plan of attack"—the personal sales plan you learned about in Chapter 2. As you learn more, you should be comfortable with the idea of constant re-evaluation of the companies in your territory.

# Step Five: Show Off What You've Done

Take the board you've put together, and the notes you've assembled, and show them to your sales manager. Then hang the board up in an impossible-to-miss spot in your office. Don't skip this step! By letting the world (and yourself) know that you're in charge of this group of customers and potential customers, you will be exhibiting social proof of your ownership of the territory.

Many salespeople never take the time or invest the energy necessary to show their colleagues (and the world at large) that they've assumed full ownership of a particular territory. It is probably no coincidence, then, that these people are often perceived as intruders by the people they contact. In fact, they consider themselves intruders or solicitors!

# Don't Start Calling Potential Customers Yet!

Even if you've researched your territory thoroughly, there's a very good chance you don't know as much about it as you should. Before you consider your basic research complete, you should talk to one of your own colleagues about customer habits and predispositions.

Pick out the strongest consistent sales performer in your organization. (You're only interested in talking to someone who's developed a system that has delivered results over time.) Once you've located this person (and bear in mind that he or she may be working on the other side of the country, for all you know) ask for a brief meeting, by phone if necessary. If the person is willing and able to meet with you in person, so much the better.

You're going to ask this sales rep some very important questions about three specific areas of business for you and your company:

1. Finding new potential customers.

2. Exploring in-process sales opportunities.

3. Servicing existing customers and accounts.

Mark my words, the answers you receive are going to prove far more valuable than anything in your company's orientation manual or sales training session.

Once you're in the meeting, ask your colleague questions like the following about finding new potential customers:

➤ What type of industry/company/individual usually turns into the biggest sale?

➤ What type of industry/company/individual usually turns into the fastest sale?

➤ Whom do your colleagues usually contact during their initial sales call?

➤ What aspects of our product/service/solution do people get most excited about?

➤ Who's our biggest competitor? Why do you consider that company our main competitor? Have you found any weaknesses in their approach that I should know about?

➤ What opening line do you rely on most when you're trying to win someone's attention?

➤ What do you do when someone asks you to send information?

➤ What's the biggest time-waster you think I should watch out for?

➤ What's the typical length of your sales cycle? Do you have any ideas about shortening it that you'd like to try someday?

➤ What's the biggest complaint you hear about our company, products, or services?

➤ If you could change one thing about your sales approach to new suspects and prospects and make it even better, what would that be?

Ask your colleague about in-process sales opportunities:

➤ How long is your typical sales cycle?

➤ In what portion of this cycle do you lose most of your opportunities?

➤ In what portion of this cycle do you seem to get really bogged down?

➤ What are some of the biggest time-wasters suspects and prospects ask you to do?

➤ If you could change one thing about your in-process activities what would that be?

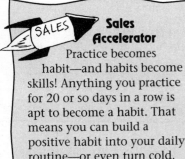

**Words, Words, Words**
The average elapsed time it takes you to convert a prospect into a customer is called the *sales cycle*.

Ask your colleague about existing customers and accounts:

➤ Do your existing customers give you referrals?

➤ How and when do you ask for referrals?

➤ How much add-on business do you feel you deserve but are not getting?

➤ What are the biggest problems our existing customers have with our products, services, and solutions?

➤ How often do you telephone or visit your existing customers?

➤ If you could change one thing about your interaction with your existing customers and accounts, what would that be?

**Sales Accelerator**
Practice becomes habit—and habits become skills! Anything you practice for 20 or so days in a row is apt to become a habit. That means you can build a positive habit into your daily routine—or even turn cold, hard facts into background information you can use "on demand"—simply by consciously repeating a few simple steps day after day.

Write down everything you hear in response from this person. Review it carefully every night before you go to bed for at least 20 days.

Remember, you're posing these questions to the strongest consistent sales performer in your organization. Unlike the new kid on the block, or the last member of the hero-of-the-month club, sales reps who fashion careers that are successful in the long term have endured the ups and downs. They've worked hard over a long period of time. They usually have a great deal of class. They're almost always team players who are eager to help others succeed, and they usually have the very best information. So take full advantage of their knowledge and experience!

# High Visibility and Access Within Your Territory

What's the best way to win superior visibility? Join an organization like Toastmasters—and stick with it!

Toastmasters will help you make a quantum leap in your ability to make presentations and communicate with others. Find an appropriate Toastmasters chapter in your territory. Join and participate for one full year. Attend every meeting. Give it your all. At the end of that year, you will, I promise, have made significant advances in developing your rapport building and presentation skills, and you won't have done your Rolodex any harm, either. This is a pretty reliable principle, unless, of course, your territory is large—say, the entire state of Ohio—in which case the benefit of Toastmasters will be centered on development of your communications skills. Even if your sales work requires extensive travel, you should look up the local chapter of Toastmasters, attend their meetings, and (gasp!) get ready to give a speech. (As a general rule, this group loves to schedule guests from faraway places.)

There are other organizations you may want to consider joining. You may, for instance, choose to find a non-profit cause or organization to which you can devote your time and energy. Join up! Volunteer, and be sincere in your contributions, and you'll meet those movers and shakers in your sales territory outside of their office settings and away from their gatekeepers.

## The Wide, Wide World of Visibility

There are plenty of other avenues to consider if your territory is not geographically defined. You may, for instance, want to consider joining national industry-specific organizations (such as the Association of Realtors if you're in real estate sales) and make occasional contributions to their publications. You could also work with your tech people to create a page on your company's Web site to respond to customer questions and concerns. Or you could decide to pursue lead-sharing opportunities with sales reps in organizations that don't compete with yours.

## "I'm an Expert!"

Ultimately, what you'll want to do to gain visibility is pretty simple: Make the most of your status as an authority on a topic about which you are knowledgeable. Take full advantage of print, broadcast, and public speaking opportunities that will appeal to prospective customers within your territory, whether or not that territory is defined geographically. The topic you develop for yourself should be related to what you sell, and it should be near and dear to your heart.

When you're the authority on a particular topic—using widgets to increase productivity, winterizing your car, getting the best deal on a tropical vacation package, whatever—you can win coverage in media potential customers pay attention to. And that visibility always helps your cause. Remember, you don't have to know everything about the topic(s) you choose, just enough to benefit someone less familiar with the subject than you are.

The key word in such a targeted campaign, of course, is "you." Your company's marketing department couldn't possibly do as good a job as you can when it comes to filling the needs of the hungry folks whose job it is to track down content for appropriate periodicals and broadcast outlets. Help them out, mention your company affiliation and contact data and turn your exposure into new contacts within your territory. The exposure you receive will also help you establish yourself as a speaker at relevant clubs and civic organizations, another fantastic source for business leads.

Pursue these and other "outside" opportunities to heighten your visibility and access, and you'll quickly build up a contact network that will be the envy of your colleagues.

# An Ongoing Process

Establishing and maintaining ownership of your territory is the job you never finish. Assume personal responsibility for learning about the economic comings and goings in the territory. Life in your territory isn't static. That means you shouldn't be either.

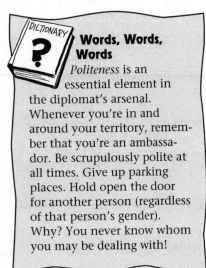

**Words, Words, Words**

*Politeness* is an essential element in the diplomat's arsenal. Whenever you're in and around your territory, remember that you're an ambassador. Be scrupulously polite at all times. Give up parking places. Hold open the door for another person (regardless of that person's gender). Why? You never know whom you may be dealing with!

When in doubt, just remember that you're the ambassador. That means you have to do your homework, show both confidence and precision in your dealings with others, and accept ongoing accountability for making progress toward key goals happen in your little corner of the world.

You never really exit the "research phase" when you own your territory. Measure the progress you make in your efforts to develop your sales territory. Commit to going the extra mile and learning anything and everything of relevance within your base of potential customers. Accept the fact that territory development doesn't really end. It's like a diplomatic post: You must constantly keep an ear open for the best ways to solidify new relationships, develop new ones, and use a tactful, polite, persistent approach to resolve pressing problems.

In the next chapter, you'll find out how to bring your research work into the next phase by setting up a *Template of Ideal Prospects*.

# The Least You Need to Know

➤ Your sales territory may or may not be defined geographically—or as a particular category of customers or potential customers.

➤ Complaining about your sales territory will earn you a reputation you probably don't want—and it will waste time and energy you should be devoting to the development of your customer base.

➤ When you assume ownership of your territory, you take full responsibility for learning everything about the potential customers in it and determining which ones are likeliest to benefit from what you have to offer.

➤ You should talk to a leading salesperson in your field about the best strategies to pursue in your territory.

➤ Join a local chapter of Toastmasters or a similar organization or find other ways to reach out to prospective customers within your territory.

➤ Never forget—you're a diplomat!

# Chapter 6

# The Template of Ideal Prospects

## In This Chapter

➤ What your best customers have in common

➤ The questions you need to ask

➤ Where to go to find the answers

So, you've done the research about your territory. Because you know that true sales excellence involves thinking in the long term and developing the capacity to highlight creative solutions, you've started thinking about yourself as less of a "sales rep" and more of an ambassador for your organization. You've decided to focus on learning everything you possibly can about your territory as a whole. You've filed all your old complaints about your sales territory under "waste of time and energy." You've committed to complete ownership of your territory.

And you've completed at least one interview with a high-achieving colleague whose methods (and performance) you want to emulate.

Now you're ready to get out there and start tracking down potential customers, right?

Well, not quite.

Of course, if you're already making your living as a salesperson, odds are you've got an established routine when it comes to establishing connections with people who may buy from you. In this chapter, I'm going to ask you to change that routine—and take full advantage of a powerful sales tool, the *Template of Ideal Prospects*.

The *Template of Ideal Prospects (TIP) Sheet* is a list of characteristics shared by your company's best customers. It will point you toward the most promising suspects—people whom you have not yet contacted about your product or service, but who may benefit from what you have to offer.

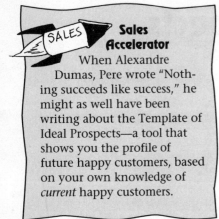

**Sales Accelerator**

When Alexandre Dumas, Pere wrote "Nothing succeeds like success," he might as well have been writing about the Template of Ideal Prospects—a tool that shows you the profile of future happy customers, based on your own knowledge of *current* happy customers.

**Sales Accelerator**

Among the resources you should probably ask for at the library are the *Million Dollar Directory*, the business directory for your state, *Thomas's Directory of Manufacturers*, *Dun's Directory of Service Companies*, and *Standard & Poor's Register of Corporations, Directors, and Corporate Executives*. Another source that can help you make sense of the often-confusing world of business-entity relationships is the *Directory of Corporate Affiliations*.

# On the Road Again

Grab your company's current customer list, a notebook (or perhaps a small personal tape recorder), the notes from your interview with that strikingly successful colleague of yours, and a pen or pencil.

Then head for the door.

As you may have already gathered, you're not going out to make a sales call. Nope. You're bound for the library, perhaps for the second time, but in any event toward the biggest one in your area with a business research department worthy of the name.

Experienced Internet users may be able to use the many and varied resources of the "information superhighway" to adapt the ideas in this chapter as part of an inspired Web search. As long as you eventually track down the information you need—and your sales manager knows that you're checking out research sites, and not the latest hard-drive-clogging adventure game—that's great! You may find that you have access to more up-to-date information that way.

I don't have anything against the Internet (although I would, from bitter personal experience, caution Net surfers to beware of the possibility of downloading viruses unintentionally). For the sake of clarity and accessibility, though, and for the benefit of readers who still track down their information the old-fashioned way, I'm going to assume that the main branch of your local public library is going to be the primary resource you'll be using to track down the facts you need. (Many of today's larger libraries, of course, feature terminals that will allow you to access the Internet on-site, which can certainly be a convenience!)

# What You Need to Know

Once you're at the library, take a good, long, look at that customer list you brought along. Then ask yourself the following question:

What do my company's best current customers have in common?

Success leaves clues, and so do your best customers. You'll be using the library resources at your disposal to find answers to the key questions about your organization's existing customer base—by working your way through the Template of Ideal Prospects (TIP) sheet later in this chapter.

The customer list you'll be reviewing may need to be broken down into subgroups. If you're selling a new magazine that is of interest to both public libraries and medical computer system administrators, you'll find that the specifics of each group should be taken into account. Fill out a different TIP sheet for each of the industries or niches to which you'll be selling.

# How You'll Answer That Question

What do my company's best current customers have in common?

That question may seem breathtaking in its simplicity. It may seem like the kind of question you can answer with an "I know 'em when I see 'em" response. Don't fall into that trap! You owe this question—you owe your own career—the fullest possible answer.

Take a look at the blank TIP sheet that follows. Make several photocopies for your own use. If you take the time to use the library's resources to develop detailed, meaningful first-draft answers to each of the sections of the TIP sheet, and then transfer your work into a duplicate of this form for a second draft, you will also know what your best future potential customer looks like.

Read the TIP sheet carefully before you do anything!

---

**Template of Ideal Prospects (TIP) Sheet in the _____ Industry/Business Area**

Fill in every slot thoroughly. Check the notes you made during your interview with your successful colleague, or see the appropriate company directories, annual financial reports, trade magazines, or industry reports in the library.

1. List all relevant titles of the typical decision maker within the target organization, as well as any third-party contact that may be necessary to formalize the sale.

    _____

    _____

    _____

*continues*

---

*continued*

2. My best customers in this area are likely to use my organization's product/service/ solution to solve the following problem(s):

_____

_____

_____

3. My best customers in this area are likely to enjoy the following specific (and quantifiable) benefits by working with my organization:

_____

_____

_____

4. My best customers in this area are likely to purchase my organization's product/ service/solution through the following channel(s):

_____

_____

_____

5. My best customers in this area are likely to have between _____ and _____ employees.

6. My best customers in this area are likely to use between _____ and _____ remote facilities.

7. My best customers in this area are likely to take in between_____ and _____ dollars in annual revenue.

8. My best customers in this area are likely to reach their own customers by means of the following marketing techniques:

_____

_____

_____

9. Other key industry/group/individual-specific data (include key factors that your product/service/solution affects):

_____

_____

_____

Taken together, all of this information will provide you with a reliable portrait of the "ideal" potential customer.

This portrait will help you compare your company's best customer's new prospect to new business leads, show you where your best opportunities are likely to be, and save you lots of time you would have spent rushing down blind alleys.

# The Ultimate Time-Saver

Even if you "hate research" and "don't have time for paperwork," spending a day in the library to develop your TIP sheet(s) may be the best investment of time and money you could possibly make. When it comes time to identify your list of suspects (potential customers) and determine which are the most deserving of your time and effort, all you'll have to do is ask yourself a simple question:

> How well does this opportunity match up with my company's TIP sheet in this area?

You'll always pursue the best matches first, of course! And you'll almost always streamline your selling efforts.

There will be some exceptions, of course, but as a general rule, you'll want to avoid making a time commitment to potential customers whose profile is radically different from the information you assemble in your TIP sheet. You guessed it! You'll be compiling research based on your TIP sheet for each and every prospect you'll be calling. When I tell salespeople this in my seminars, they tend to get a little agitated: "But Tony, won't that take forever?" Nah. Once you figure out that a prospect doesn't match up with your Template of Ideal Prospects, you'll simply move on to someone else, another candidate that presents a better potential match. What *really* takes forever is trying to sell your products, services, and solutions to the wrong prospects.

As you'll see a little later on in the book, the information in your TIP sheet will help you pre-qualify the people with whom you come in contact, so you'll spend less time spinning your wheels. The TIP sheet will also help you create attention-getting opening statements for your written materials; what's more, it will allow you to develop other tools you can use to get the attention of key decision makers.

# What It Looks Like When Complete

Following is an example of a TIP sheet that has been completely filled out.

Read it for reference, and to get an idea of the kind of information you'll be tracking down in the library or by means of consulting materials you've already gathered. Don't assume that the answers that appear in the sample TIP sheet below will have anything whatsoever to do with the answers that make sense for customers in a particular category in your own business!

---

### TIP Sheet (Template of Ideal Prospects) in the Manufacturing and Distribution Industry/Business Area

Fill in every slot thoroughly. Check the notes you made during your interview with your successful colleague, or see the appropriate company directories, annual financial reports, trade magazines, or industry reports in the library.

1. List all relevant titles of the typical decision maker within the target organization, as well as any third-party contact that may be necessary to formalize the sale…
   *Divisional Manager; Shop Floor Supervisor; Front Office Manager; Parts Expediter*

2. My best customers in this area are likely to use my organization's product/service/solution to solve the following problem(s):
   *Inventory control; shipping and receiving log; shop floor control*

3. My best customers in this area are likely to enjoy the following specific (and quantifiable) benefits by working with my organization:
   *One-stop shopping; customization to match specs on work site; on-site user training confirmed with post-training tests*

4. My best customers in this area are likely to purchase my organization's product/service/solution through the following channel(s):
   *Directly from our office with additional devices from Devices Unlimited*

5. My best customers in this area are likely to have between *100* and *250* employees.

6. My best customers in this area are likely to use between *4 domestic* and *6 domestic* remote facilities.

7. My best customers in this area are likely to take in between *$250, 000* and *$1 million* dollars in annual revenue,

8. My best customers in this area are likely to reach their own customers by means of the following marketing techniques:
   *Direct sales force / distributors*

9. Other key industry/group/individual-specific data (include key factors that your product/service/solution affects):
   *Typically used as job cost accounting add-on; production control often a major issue.*

---

So, let's say that's your BEST customer. In evaluating a new prospect, you could make use of an analysis similar to the following. The more matches, the higher the quality of your prospect!

| MY BEST CUSTOMER | THIS PROSPECT |
|---|---|
| 1. Relevant titles: | |
| Divisional Manager; Shop Floor Supervisor; Front Office Manager; Parts Expediter | Division Manager, Shop Floor Assistant Supervisor, Buyer |
| 2. Problems: | |
| Inventory control; shipping and receiving log; shop floor control | Inventory control, shop floor control |
| 3. Benefits: | |
| One-stop shopping; customization to match specs on work site; on-site user training confirmed with post-training tests | Potential for on-site user training and on-site support |
| 4. Procurement: | |
| Directly from our office with additional devices from Devices unlimited | Unknown |
| 5. Employees: | |
| 15 to 250 | 225 |
| 6. Remote Facilities: | |
| 4 to 6 in US (no international) | 6 in US, 2 in Mexico |
| 7. Annual Revenue: | |
| $250,000 to $2 million | $150,000 |
| 8. Marketing Style: | |
| Direct sales force, distributors | Distributors only |
| 9. Other Key Data: | |
| Typically used as job cost accounting add-on; production control often a major issue. | Already have job cost accounting |

From this analysis, you can see that the prospect you're evaluating matches up in most, but not all, areas with your TIP sheet specifications. All things considered, though, it's a pretty good lead. If you have to choose between setting up an appointment with this company, and setting up an appointment with a company that employs 5 people and has annual revenue of $100,000—guess who should get the first crack at your day?

The more you use it, the sooner you'll recognize that the TIP sheet is a valuable tool. Use it regularly to learn what you need to know about the prospects you're trying to reach!

# The Least You Need to Know

➤ You should hit the library (or the Internet), and develop the fullest possible answer to that question.

➤ You should ask yourself: What do my company's best current customers have in common? The Template of Ideal Prospects (TIP) sheet that appears in this chapter will help you fill in all the blanks.

➤ Even if you "hate research" and "don't have time for paperwork," taking the time to develop your TIP sheet(s) is among the very best time investments you can make—so make the time!

➤ Once you know what your best current customer looks like, you'll be able to prioritize your time in such a way as to spend most of it with prospective customer who most closely match that profile.

# Chapter 7

# Goal Setting and Time Management

## In This Chapter

➤ Short-term and long-term sales goals that work

➤ Managing your work day intelligently

➤ Benefitting from the 75/125 rule

➤ Filling the sales funnel to become a more effective salesperson

So, by this point, you have a better sense of what your territory is, how you should approach the job of gaining more information about that territory, and what your ideal prospect looks like. What about your own time managment—and the goals that support your day? In this chapter, you learn how to make the most of your day, how to use your daily schedule to mirror your entire sales process, and how to make sure you end up comfortably above your end-of-year quota when the dust settles. That's a lot to cover in one chapter, so let's get going!

# The Blinking Light

Several years ago, while on a nine-hour flight aboard a 747, I struck up a conversation with one of the flight attendants. He invited me to take a peek into the cockpit.

There were hundreds of gauges, dials, buttons, and switches. I was fascinated. As I sat there, I noticed one particular dial that seemed a little unusual. It looked similar to a compass, but it had a red light under it. Every second, that red light would flash several times. Neither the pilot nor the co-pilot seemed to notice the light flashing on and off, on and off. I wondered: Was the light of any importance? Had I discovered an emergency? Do these people know about the "red light" situation I've run into here?

After several minutes of small talk, I couldn't contain myself any longer. "Hey captain," I asked casually, "what's that compass-like thing with the red light?" He looked at me and smiled. "Oh, that's the automatic pilot," he answered. "It flashes every time we go off course." So, were we headed for Barbados rather than Piscataway, New Jersey? Was the pilot simply trying to get a rise out of me?

Gleam in his eye or no, though, he was telling the truth. The captain explained everything to me. It turns out that during a normal flight, a Boeing 747 SP400 spends 99 percent of its time heading in the wrong direction. The vast majority of flights are successful, though—not because the autopilot is never wrong, but because the corrections all take place very, very quickly, so that the plane's consumption of fuel, like the amount of time it actually spends off course, is minimized. ("Say," I thought to myself, "that's a pretty good analogy for the advantage of constant reviews of one's personal plan in sales work!") The captain went on to explain that the two most important pieces of information the computer receives are—you guessed it—where the plane is and where the pilot wants it to arrive. ("Say," I thought to myself, "that's a pretty good analogy for the work that has to come before you set up your personal sales plan!")

> **SALES** ➤ **Sales Accelerator**
>
> If your "computer" doesn't know where you're going, the trip may be a difficult one. Research has proven time and time again that people who achieve significant levels of personal, career, or social success share one key trait: They commit their goals to writing. It was true of Mahatma Gandhi; it was true of Thomas Edison; it was true of Henry Ford; it should be true of you.

# The Circle at the Center of the Bull's-Eye

What goals should you be setting for your sales career—and what should you do before you set them? There are two critical aspects of goal-setting you should know about when it comes to achieving success in your chosen field of sales. Here they are.

1. Knowing where you are right now (or, to be more specific: knowing your territory demographics, understanding your Template of Ideal Prospects, meeting all of your existing customers, and so on).

2. Knowing where you want to be in the near- and long-term future (or, to be more specific, setting goals for the period one to six months from now; setting goals for longer than six months from now; knowing your quota; having an intimate knowledge of your company's market plan, and so on).

Phrases like "knowing where you are" and "knowing where you're going" can easily lead to vague pronouncements that are less than useful to you. To get the most out of the planning process, you're going to have to get a lot more specific. Here's how.

There are (at least!) five separate areas in which you must "program your computer" with meaningful information about where you are and where you want to be. They are:

1. Quota performance

2. Product knowledge development

3. Industry knowledge development

4. Professional and career development (This is an essential component of any long-term personal sales campaign.)

5. Personal skills development (Ditto.)

The list I've just given you is subject to reordering; you may decide that it makes sense to add certain elements to your goal development list. But the five elements you've just seen must form an important part of your planning process.

If you're like the vast majority of salespeople, you're already focused to a certain extent on time-specific quota performance.

Although this aspect has a way of commanding attention in a very dramatic way from time to time, meeting a sales goal or quota doesn't happen in a vacuum, and it often doesn't happen at all if there is no formalized goal-setting and goal-monitoring plan in place.

I've been fortunate enough to hit the yearly winner's circle sixteen times over the course of my career; each and every time I've done that, I've had written goals in each of the five areas outlined above.

These written goals were in concert with my organization's objectives, and they were accompanied by a time management strategy that supported those goals.

Take a moment now to add subtitles to each category listed above. What would you like to accomplish in each area? Each goal should be specific and clear in

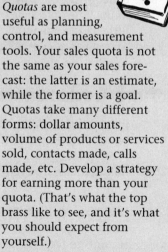

**Words, Words, Words**

*Quotas* are most useful as planning, control, and measurement tools. Your sales quota is not the same as your sales forecast: the latter is an estimate, while the former is a goal. Quotas take many different forms: dollar amounts, volume of products or services sold, contacts made, calls made, etc. Develop a strategy for earning more than your quota. (That's what the top brass like to see, and it's what you should expect from yourself.)

purpose, and it should be stated with reference to some specific time period. Make sure you have an easy way to measure and provide feedback as you make progress toward your goal.

Your personal sales goals and quotas set by your management should be:

➤ Understood thoroughly by you and your sales manager.

➤ Both realistic and optimistic.

➤ Attainable, based on past performance of the territory or on responsible market research.

➤ Connected to a substantial and satisfying reward for you, the overachieving salesperson.

# Time Management

Goals must drive your daily schedule, just as the autopilot computer directs a big jet airplane. The super-achievers in the sales world have the same number of hours to work with as the subpar performers: 24 per day, 128 per week, 8,736 per year. The superstars, the underachievers, and everyone in between all get exactly the same amount of this vitally important resource. Of course, what we do with each hour depends on many, many, factors, but I would argue that your attitude toward time—that is, the way you look at it, the state of mind you hold while interacting with it, the amount of respect you grant it—will have the most profound influence on whether time is your daily ally or your daily enemy.

You can't hold on to time. You can't stop it. You can't accelerate it. Contrary to popular belief, you can't save it. You and I, like everyone else on this spinning globe, simply have to use it, every single bit of it. To do that with maximum efficiency, you have to get a little bit jealous about your own time. You have to start asking it a lot of nosy questions. And, when you're selling, you have to use your time only on the tasks that directly support the overachievement of your goals.

## Time Tracks: Short-Term Goals

Everything is relative, and time is no exception. Some short-term goals simply won't be worth devoting your time to. My advice is simple: Make a list of all your short-term professional goals, then delete or revise the ones that aren't in sync with your company's objectives for quarterly time-frames. (If you don't know what they are, you should find out—see Chapter 2 for more details.)

Even a quarterly review of the ways your company's goals intersect with your own may not be frequent enough. Remember, that 747 doesn't take hours or minutes or even seconds to respond to a mismatch. It takes fractions of a second, and is constantly correcting the course. Otherwise it would take the plane days to reach its destination—and the jet doesn't have that much fuel. (Neither do you!)

So—what are your short-term sales goals—the goals that support your long-term goals, the goals you're willing to measure in the shortest feasible time frame? Write them down. The fastest and easiest way to develop this list is to ask yourself a simple question: "What's expected of me?"

Break everything down into the smallest, simplest, easiest-to-describe chunks you possibly can. If you're in retail sales, for instance, what's your quota? Is it expressed in dollars or by sales of a particular item or items? Are you judged by customer satisfaction ratings? Do you have complete control of all aspects of customer service—and, whether you are or not, what aspects of customer service are you responsible for? Or suppose you're selling consumable industrial supplies. Are you required to train your customers in the use of your products?

Sample short term goals might look like the following:

➤ Make 20 cold calls each day.

➤ Schedule six new in-person appointments each week.

➤ Close four new sales each week.

> **Watch It!**
> Short-term goals must support your long-term goals, and they must be monitored closely and constantly. If you forget to do this, you may be heading for a fall. Let's say you figure out that your annual cold-calling target has to be 1,612 initial calls in order to hit your income goal. You should monitor this goal monthly—not quarterly! By the time three months go by, you may be too far behind to make a difference!

Short-term goals have four important functions:

1. They provide a benchmark for ensuring that you achieve your long-term goals.
2. They offer you immediate feedback on stuff that works. This positive feedback will help keep you motivated; you'll know when you're on the right track.
3. They allow you to pinpoint any problems with your current plan or direction.
4. They allow you to validate your long-term goals, and they give you the opportunity to modify them if necessary.

# Long-Term Goals

Any meaningful list of short-term sales goals is part of a bigger picture. These are your long-term goals. Most organizations today are using a calendar year or other twelve-month period to establish long-term sales goals for their reps. Make no mistake: If you're a salesperson at one of these organizations, you'll be expected to be on (or ahead of) your quota at the end of each year.

At the beginning of your year, it may seem safe to assume that if you meet or exceed all of your short-term goals, your long-term target will be a cinch. Alas, this may not be the case. Why? Well, for one thing, every sales organization will have intangible (or "soft") goals that are hard to schedule, but that definitely take away from time and attention you would otherwise point toward more formal goals. Such soft goals might include:

➤ Becoming involved in quality circles.

➤ Participating in the "suggestion of the month" contest.

➤ Furthering your formal education.

➤ Furthering your informal education (by, for instance, becoming familiar with new products or services).

➤ Attending suppliers' conferences or other industry events.

➤ Taking part in charitable or community outreach programs.

**Watch It!**
Don't make the mistake of dismissing subjective, intangible goals are sometimes as "just office politics." Your job is to make things happen for your customers, and attaining goals related to your company's internal functioning support your ability that. If the CEO thinks occasional updates about quality control are worth two hours of your time each quarter, that's an important part of your job description!

When you're formulating long-term goals, like...

➤ Beat quota by 20 percent

➤ Develop a newsletter for customers

➤ Clean up your prospecting database

➤ Mentor a new salesperson

...you'll also have to take account of all the "soft-goal" expectations your company has of you. Don't get taken by surprise here; be ready to do a little digging.

Your sales manager may be very helpful on this front, as may senior-level executives and anyone who's climbed the corporate ladder and remembers the sales department as a point of origin. You may never find a formal list of "soft" goals, or at least nothing in print.

Don't let that stop you. Take a good, long look at the company directory and call on those who can help you figure out what you're going to have to do, how long it's likely to take, and how it benefits your customers.

# Beyond the 80/20 Rule: Making the Parinello Principle Work

In the world of science there is something called Pareto's principle, also known as the 80/20 rule. This rule says, in essence, that the vast majority of your outcomes are brought about by a small fraction of your efforts. In other words, most of what people try in the laboratory doesn't work—but scientists don't know which 20 percent will produce the corresponding 80 percent of desired outcomes.

Applied to the world of sales, the 80/20 rule would seem to dictate that about 80 percent of your sales dollars would come from about 20 percent of your activities. To be sure, there are any number of salespeople whose efforts and results are accurately described by Pareto's principle: The vast majority of what they try doesn't work.

But the truth is that for superior performance in the world of sales, you're better off following something I modestly call Parinello's principle.

The *Parinello Principle*, or the 75/125 rule, states that 75 percent of your sales activities will yield a 125 percent quota performance—if 75 percent of your work time is managed properly, and directly supports the sales process. (You'd be amazed how much work some salespeople do on things that have nothing to do with moving the sales cycle forward with suspects and prospects, or with keeping current customers happy.)

When was the last time you saw a retail display or advertisement promoting some time management system or other—a new personal calendar design, new piece of software, or new book that promised to help you turn your messy, disorganized work and personal life into a seamless, well-coordinated whole? If you're like me, this happened within the past 24 hours.

Time management is a multimillion dollar industry. You can buy all sorts of electronic gizmos with special function keys that allow you to "tag" key records, or issue "wake-up" buzzers that help you make your call, or keep your appointment. If one of these tools works for you, that's great. In my humble opinion, though, the most important factor in the success or failure of any time management system isn't the new organization philosophy, the layout of a daily planning sheet, or the name you give to an "activity transaction group" (whatever that is). The most important factor in your time management system is you—the time manager, as it were!

The Parinello Principle—the 75/125 rule—says that you must manage your time with extreme precision at least 75 percent of the time.

This means focusing only on issues that support your goals and move the sales process forward with any given customer or potential customer. This means you must become an expert time manager on your own. That means learning to make the most of your own time resources—and not relying on anyone else (like your sales manager) or anything else (like your palmtop organizer) to do that for you.

Experts know exactly where and how they are spending their time. To become a time management expert, you must be willing to ask, "How am I spending my time?"

**Watch It!**
Salespeople who spend the majority (or even a sizable chunk) of their time on dubious "administrative work"—bonding with photocopiers, cleaning out drawers and files that are already clean, catching up on old times with outside acquaintances who have little or nothing to do with their sales work—generally don't meet their quotas.

# What Happened to the # $!! Day?

Do you ever feel as though you're not getting enough done at work? Do you ever feel as though you're unfulfilled, guilty, rushed, and generally overloaded by the time you make it home? If you answered "yes," you owe it to yourself to look into how to turn things around.

Let's say you're just starting out in sales. Your product training is complete; your territory has been assigned; you're at 0 percent of your year-to-date quota. Or let's say you've been selling for a few years.

You're more or less accustomed to the pressures associated with ever-high quotas, ever-smaller territories, ever-increasing competition, and ever-slower administrative systems. You need to apply the 75/125 rule in both situations, and in every situation in between. Here's how you can do it.

# Captain's Log, Stardate 125, from the Beatquota Quadrant

To become an expert time manager, you must first know where you're spending your time now. This will require a time log. Make a list that uses time slices of no longer than 30 minutes. (See the model Time Log that appears on the next page.) Complete this log every day for a period of at least one week, but at the very least, estimate the length of time it takes you to perform all the important functions of your job.

Review your completed time logs closely! How much work does it take you to deliver the revenue that brings you closer to your long-term sales goal?

The sample time log that follows next illustrates a daily routine that almost certainly spells trouble. It belongs to a sales rep who works for the XYZ Office Supply Corporation. This rep's name is (gulp!)—Will Perish.

Will's organization has some short-term goals for him. The sales manager wants Will to make five presentations in which suspects turn into prospects (active, realistic leads); this five-good-presentations-with-new-people thing is supposed to happen each and every week. The sales manager also wants Will to nurture and grow the existing XYZ customer base by performing two account reviews (face-to-face meetings with current customers) per week.

Here's what Will's most recent time log looks like:

Time Log:

Will Perish, XYZ Office Equipment

| Time | Task |
|---|---|
| AM | |
| 1:00-1:30 | Created final pricing and proposal for Apex Mfg. |
| 1:30-8:00 | Drove to Apex Mfg. |
| 8:00-8:30 | Drove to Apex Mfg. (cont.). |
| 8:30-9:00 | Made presentation at Apex. |
| 9:00-9:30 | Made presentation at Apex (cont.)—got the sale! |
| 9:30-10:00 | Drove back to office. |
| 10:00-10:30 | Drove back to office (cont.). |
| 10:30-11:00 | Returned calls to prospects needing additional information. |
| 11:00-11:30 | Returned prospect calls (cont.). |
| 11:30-12:00 | updated sales forecast. |
| PM | |
| 12:00-12:30 | updated sales forecast (cont.). |
| 12:30-1:00 | Ate lunch at desk while reading industry trade magazine. |
| 1:00-1:30 | Prepared new proposal for Applegate Publishing. |
| 1:30-2:00 | Prepared new proposal for Applegate Publishing (cont.). |
| 2:00-2:30 | Prepared new proposal for Applegate Publishing (cont.). |
| 3:00-3:30 | Drove to customer's site for account review. |
| 3:30-4:00 | Drove to customer's site for account review (cont.). |
| 4:00-4:30 | Performed account review. |
| 4:30-5:00 | Checked and cleared voice mail messages. |
| 5:00 | Drove home; called it a day. |

Even if the day looks familiar to you—even if you're tempted to consider that sale of Will's to be a sign of victory—let me assure you that our friend Will is no time management expert. If Will's day sounds like yours, guess what? You need to take control of your time.

**Watch It!**
If events are driving your day, if your time log shows that most of the events on your calendar are reactive, if there is no significant conscious time allocation, then you're headed for mid-range sales peformance or worse.

Even though he is on track to meet or exceed his sales manager's requirements, Will is not getting the most out of his day. Will needs to group his activities, so that the Parinello Principle is working for him, and 75 percent of his time is allocated to work that is directly related to income-producing activities involving interaction with suspects, prospects, and customers.

Here's an example of a salesperson who makes a great many more conscious choices about the way her day is spent and consciously allocates at least three-quarters of her day to tasks directly associated with tracking down likely new customers and keeping current ones happy. Meet Ima Success, who also works for the XYZ Office Supply Corporation, and who has the same sales targets as Will does.

Time Log:

Ima Success, XYZ Office Equipment

| Time | Task |
|------|------|
| AM | |
| 1:00-1:30 | Created final pricing and proposal for Beepex Mfg. |
| 1:30-8:00 | Prepared proposal for Peargate Publishing Company. |
| 8:00-8:30 | Prepared proposal for Peargate Publishing Company (cont.). |
| 8:30-9:00 | Updated sales forecast. |
| 9:00-9:30 | Updated sales forecast (cont.). |
| 9:30-10:00 | Returned calls to factory regarding delivery schedule. |
| 10:00-10:30 | Returned calls to factory regarding delivery schedule (cont.). |
| 10:30-11:00 | Drove to Beepex Mfg. |
| 11:00-11:30 | Drove to Beepex Mfg. (cont.). |
| 11:30-12:00 | Made presentation at Beepex—got the sale! |
| PM | |
| 12:00-12:30 | Ate lunch while reading industry trade magazine. |
| 12:30-1:00 | Drove to customer's site for account review. (Note that her drive takes less time than Will's—she saved herself a trip back to the office!) |
| 1:00-1:30 | Performed account review. |

| | |
|---|---|
| 1:30-2:00 | Made cold calls while in territory, getting new leads for next week's presentations. |
| 2:00-2:30 | Made cold calls while in territory, getting new leads for next week's presentations (cont.). |
| 2:30-3:00 | Made cold calls while in territory, getting new leads for next week's presentations (cont.). |
| 3:00-3:30 | Drove back to office. |
| 3:30-4:00 | Drove back to office (cont.). |
| 4:00-4:30 | Returned calls to prospects needing additional information. |
| 4:30-5:00 | Checked and cleared voice mail messages. |
| 5:00 | Drove home; called it a day. |

Hey, wait a minute! Sure, Ima got more revenue-focused work in—but she cheated! She moved appointment times around, queued up office tasks that could be done in succession, and grouped key activities together!

Yep. She cheated. (Not that anyone minded.) And as a result, she won another one and one half hours from the day, and pointed that time directly toward the overachievement of her goal. Notice that session of cold calling she did while on the road!

Ima, you see, has learned to be an expert time manager. She's learned to use the one word that most other salespeople hear all too often, but hardly ever use themselves. Can you guess what that word is? You guessed it, "No." She knows that she doesn't have to agree to any appointment time, even when it's suggested by a hot prospect.

Learn to say no. When a prospect or customer calls up and says something like, "Ima, can you make it out here at 8:30 tomorrow morning?", be prepared to respond with this: "No, but 11:30 would work great for me—does that make sense for you?" Be proactive...not reactive. Set up your own schedule, and don't alter it until and unless you run into a legitimate emergency or a prospect who simply won't budge. That will happen a lot less often than you think. Take this approach to your day, and you'll make the 75 percent half of the 75/125 rule a reality: 75 percent of your day spent in work that is directly related to income-producing activities involving interaction with suspects, prospects, and customers. Once you do that, the 125 percent of quota part of the rule has a way of taking care of itself.

Here are nine easy-to-follow "golden rules" that will help you become an expert time manager. They work for me—I think they'll work for you, too.

1. Keep a daily log of your tasks. Write down the where, what, when, and who of your sales day. Review it often; keep an eye out for areas of improvement.

2. Group together your sales activities (cold calling, presentations, follow-up meetings) as much as possible. Remember: Activities like driving can take a big chunk out of your day.

3. Minimize administrative paperwork; try to schedule this work for before or after your selling time.

4. Use as many "productivity boosters" as you can afford and use easily: pagers, cell phonse, prospect tracking software, and so on.

5. Every lunch should be a working lunch.

6. Learn to use the word "no" when people ask you to give any of your sales time to activities that do not support your sales goals.

7. Keep a daily "to do" list.

8. Know when your peak energy times are. Make sure you're performing your most intellectually challenging work during these times.

9. Use your drive time as productive time. Listen to motivational and inspirational tapes.

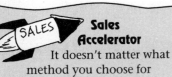

**Sales Accelerator**

It doesn't matter what method you choose for keeping track of your time—a personal computer with software that's easy for you to use, a yellow legal pad, a snazzy-looking personal planner. What matters is that you commit to monitoring your own time in the real world!

## The Sales Funnel

Many sales organizations, at one point or another, use the image of a funnel to represent the sales process. It's a useful model because it's very visual. If you choose to use a funnel, you'll be able to see the number of suspects, prospects, and customers you're working with instantly. A single glance will tell you exactly where you stand—and where you need to focus your sales activities.

*The Sales Funnel (basic structure).*

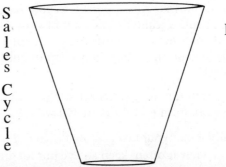

Sales Funnel

Suspects

Prospects

S a l e s C y c l e

Suspects (people who've never heard of you before) hover above the top of the funnel, waiting for a nudge from a salesperson to nudge them into the next group or confirm that they don't belong in the cycle.

Just inside the funnel are prospects (people who are interested in learning more about what you have to offer). These people have taken part in some form of sales outreach effort; the closer they are to making a commitment, the deeper inside the funnel they go. The fact that the funnel gets narrower, of course, reflects the fact that a good many prospects are removed from the sales cycle, for any number of good reasons: lack of money, lack of interest, industrial downturns, new management philosophy, whatever.

Finally, some prospects appear as new customers—coming out of the funnel. (Eventually, customers can turn into long-term allies, or partners.)

Whether or not your organization promotes the funnel model, I want you to use it to analyze the way you work with suspects, prospects, and customers. Why? The funnel model is an extremely effective method of visualizing the transitions these people make. Lots of suspects turn into a smaller number of prospects, who eventually turn into a still smaller number of customers.

Just as important, the sales funnel is a great tool for your time management system. This model allows you to pinpoint exactly where you need to spend the time. Let's see what effective funnel management looks like.

## Your Sales Cycle

Your organization may not know how long your sales cycle is, which may be a bit of a hurdle if you're new to sales. If necessary, consult your sales manager, or a more experienced salesperson, and find out what the typical sales cycle in your company and your industry is.

Let's say, for the sake of argument, that your sales cycle is two months long. Using the funnel form shown on the following page, write down all the steps that are necessary during that two months to move suspects to prospects. Illustrate each step in chronological order from the top of the funnel to the bottom. Then divide your funnel into three regions: the top third, the middle third, and the bottom third.

*The Sales Funnel (blank).*

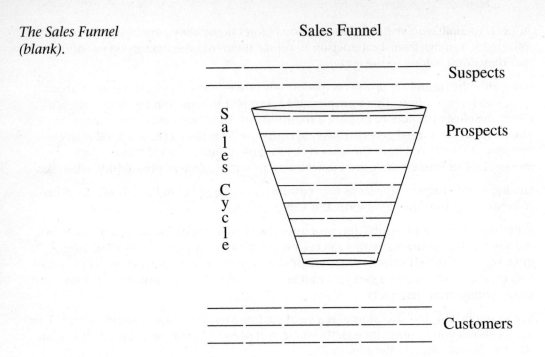

Here's an example of what your form might look like when completed:

*The Sales Funnel (including sample companies).*

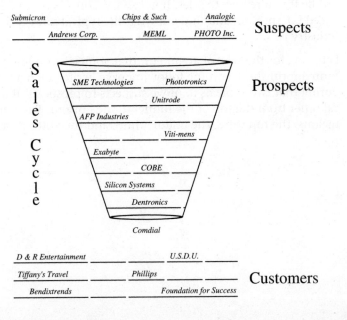

Sound "funnel management" is really the same thing as sound time management. Day after day, you must tackle your funnel—and schedule time for each group—in the order of each third's priority, without skipping any group. That priority list is as follows:

➤ **Priority one.** Look at the bottom of the funnel. Take the steps that are necessary to bring closure and commitment to each and every prospect currently in the bottom of the funnel.

➤ **Priority two.** Look at the top of the funnel. Take the steps that are necessary to convert as many suspects into prospects as you can.

➤ **Priority three.** Look at the middle of the funnel. Take the steps that are necessary to move these prospects down—or out—of your funnel. (Typically, you'll do this by providing agreed-upon information and determining the next step, or responding to requests from prospects with whom you've met previously.)

Taken as a whole, your work in these three areas should account for 75 percent of your working day—day in and day out!

Take a look at Will and Ima's time logs one more time. You'll see that Ima followed the model perfectly.

First, she went out to Beepex Mfg. to make a presentation and the sale. (That's the bottom of the funnel.) Later on in the day, she worked in some vitally important cold calls. (That's the top of the funnel.) Finally, she returned calls to her mid-range prospects, providing them with the additional information they needed. (That's the middle of the funnel.) She took on each of these tasks in the correct sequence, and she devoted at least 75 percent of her working day to them.

Will, on the other hand, skipped the top of his funnel altogether (a decision that will almost certainly come back to haunt him down the line). What's more, he spent a heck of a lot more time driving than Ima did…and, as a result, devoted less than 75 percent of the hours in his day to "funnel work!" Will may or may not make quota, but it's a pretty good bet he won't be exceeding it in any dramatic way if he keeps spending his days this way.

Ima, on the other hand, is well positioned to reach 125 percent of her quota. That's my personal opinion, of course—but it's an opinion based on my work with thousands of salespeople over the years.

## Make 75/125 Work for You!

If you follow this bottom, top, middle, sequence, day in and day out, and if you make sure that activities in these areas constitute at least 75 percent of your working day, you'll have a robust funnel, and you'll almost certainly beat your quota in a way that makes everyone sit up and take notice.

If you don't follow the system I've laid out, however, your performance will probably look like a rollercoaster that swings up and down, or, at best, leaves you either a little bit above quota or a little bit below it. You'll feel like you're never really getting ahead. You'll make your sales manager question your future as a top-performing salesperson. And you'll probably work harder than you have to, because you'll have to stop constantly to "prime the pump" and track down new suspects. (Whether you're new to sales or a seasoned veteran, you'll probably admit without much prodding that cold calling is the part of the job that's easiest to put off.)

Don't skip any steps. Don't cheat yourself out of any income. Work the funnel and your calendar in the way that I've suggested here.

You'll be glad you did.

# The Least You Need to Know

> ➤ There are two critical aspects of goal-setting: knowing where you are right now, and knowing where you want to be in the near- and long-term future.

> ➤ Your personal sales goals—both short- and long-term—should support the company's quotas or sales targets, as well as your own career goals.

> ➤ Goals must drive your daily schedule, just as the autopilot computer directs a big jet airplane.

> ➤ The Parinello Principle says that you must schedule at least 75 percent of your day to focus only on issues that support your goals and move the sales process forward with any given customer or potential customer.

> ➤ Identify where your contacts fall in the sales funnel, then attend, each and every day, to the bottom, top, and middle of the funnel—in that order!

# Chapter 8

# Your Stuff, the Competition's Stuff

**In This Chapter**

➤ Using product knowledge intelligently

➤ What people want to hear (and what they don't)

➤ The network of influence and authority

In the last chapter, you learned how time management is related to your goals, both short-term and long-term. In this chapter of the book, you'll learn about another key to sales success: product knowledge. What kinds of information should you share during the sales process? With whom you should share particular chunks of information? How much should you know about the competition's offerings? By learning the answers to these questions, you'll be in a better position to turn your goals into realities.

## What Should You Know?

How much do you need to know about the products, services, and solutions you sell—and the position your stuff occupies in relation to other products, services, and solutions in the marketplace? That's a tough question. I think the best short answer I can give you is summed up in this saying: "People won't care about how much you know...until they know how much you care." In other words, all the product knowledge and competitive intelligence in the world won't overcome a significant people-skills problem.

And yet...

## Tricky Questions

Talk about your chicken-and-egg situation! How can you show a suspect, prospect, customer, or business partner how much you care about him or her, until you show how much you know about the stuff you sell?

And here's another question: How can we keep all that product and service knowledge from coming across as intimidating?

I don't mean to imply that all salespeople are stuck up, or that they routinely talk down to others. By the same token, though, I've had my fair share of encounters with salespeople, and in a good many cases I've walked away feeling like one of us was from a different planet.

Techno-babble, industry jargon, buzzwords, unfamiliar product names—all of these can add up to some pretty confusing conversations. Conversations that may leave the other side both puzzled and paralyzed. That's bad news, because people who are puzzled and paralyzed usually don't make buying decisions. (At least, they don't if they're smart!)

**Watch It!**
It's possible that your company makes the common mistake of failing to invest in product/service training sessions, or assumes that the session you took four years ago is sufficient today. If this is the case, update your knowledge of the product/service to ensure that you can answer any question regarding the product.

Here's another tricky question: Exactly how much time should you spend getting ready to approach your target audience? My answer: Less than you think! Sometimes we salespeople get so wound up in "getting ready" for our encounters with suspects, prospects, customers, or business partners, that we never seem to make it over to the actual "doing" part of our job!

Those are some of the problems associated with the area of product knowledge—that is, knowledge of your own products, services, and solutions. And now that you've gotten a good look at the problems, it's time to take an in-depth look at some possible answers.

## Getting the Right Word Out About Your Stuff

The right word is the word that your suspects, prospects, customers, and business partners can understand. It's entirely possible that, as part of the "getting-up-and-running" phase of your job, you went through your fair share of product/service training sessions. Whether or not they used the same terminology I do, those product/service training sessions, if they were worthy of the name, introduced you to the Functions, the Features, the Advantages, and the Benefits (F.F.A.B.), of what you sell for a living:

➤ **Functions.** How does someone use—or function by means of—your product? Will what your customers are doing today change after they begin to use your product? How? Is the care that they must give their product different from what they are used to doing?

➤ **Features.** What are the components, pieces, and parts of your product? What are the characteristics of each of these individual pieces? Features are easily understood... perhaps too easily. In many cases, product training and advertising/marketing materials focus too heavily on the "feature set" of what we sell. (In the real world, few of your discussions with suspects, prospects, customers, and business partners will be centered on features.)

➤ **Advantages.** How will your product, service, or solution be tailored, modified, customized, or otherwise changed to fit the precise need or needs of this individual or organization? How is what you have to offer going to offer an advantage over any other product, service, or solution your customer or potential customer might choose?

➤ **Benefits.** What good things happen when someone uses your stuff? What will this individual or organization feel, see, or hear that will make a difference in either a tangible or intangible way? As a general rule, when can this impact or result be expected to happen or be realized?

**Sales Accelerator**
At a loss for information? You can complete a "function-feature-advantage-benefit analysis by turning to your customers. Call someone who's happily using what your organization sells and interview them! If that's not an option, talk to another salesperson...or your own sales manager.

Let's put this F.F.A.B. model to work for a particular product. Say you're selling high-grade saw blades to industrial mills and furniture manufacturers. You're at—ready?—the "cutting edge" of current technology in this product area. (Sorry about that.)

What are the functions, features, advantages, and benefits of the product you're bringing to customers? You should write them down for each product you sell. The following example shows an F.F.A.B. analysis for saw blades.

---

### F.F.A.B. Analysis: High-Grade Saw Blades

➤ **Function.** When users feed wood into the blade, they have to let the blade pull the material. Only a light pressure is needed—much lighter than the pressure required by conventional blades. Cutting cannot begin until the saw is completely up to speed. When replacing the blades, the user must install a clutch nut and torque it to 125 foot-pounds. At the end of each day, the user must spray the blade with a protective silicon coating to inhibit rusting while the blade isn't in use.

➤ **Feature.** Each blade has 178 cutters, each made of a diamond/tungsten composite. The customized profile of the blade (see below) has a tolerance of less than .01128 of a percentage point; a special laminate is used to taper the hub to the cutting

*continues*

---

*continued*

edge. Each blade has a life-cycle of 679.5 cutting hours. Sharpening is part of the scheduled maintenance procedure; only a factory-authorized representative may sharpen blades.

➤ **Advantage.** Each blade is profiled to the specific cutting application of the user. Factory-trained personnel measure the speed and application of the user's environment and select the proper blade.

➤ **Benefits.** Less noise than leading competitor, which makes the unit easier to work with; reduced "high-pitched buzz" sound. Less arm strength is needed to perform each cut; therefore, the user will experience less fatigue at the end of the day. Longer overall product life and less frequent blade failure than leading competitor means that each sawmill using the equipment will maintain the highest cut time possible at the lowest possible price.

# Who Needs to Know What?

Okay, with a little research, it's easy to see and understand the differences between functions, features, advantages, and benefits. The question remains: What do you do with all this information?

Does everyone who's interested in what you have to sell get the full F.F.A.B. treatment? Nope. Why not? Because a great many of the people you'll be running into simply won't care about some of the stuff you know. They'll be operating under the W.I.I.F.M. principle: What's In It For Me? The trick is learning to filter the information you have so that it matches up with the answers that any individual member of your audience is seeking.

Every product, service, and solution has its own unique "sales aids"—collateral we can use when we explain or demonstrate whatever it is that we sell. Earlier in this book, I suggested that you collect any and all materials that your marketing department created. (Instant refresher course department: This material includes, but is not limited to, advertisements, TV or radio spots, brochures, pictures, and the like.) Now it's time to add to your collection.

Get your hands on every bit of product samples and support information you can track down: demos, loaners, samples, owners' manuals, updates, summaries, the works. Review it all closely, but do this after selling hours—at the end of the day or on the weekend—so you don't feel rushed.

Sort all of the written material you've got according to the four categories you've learned about in this chapter: function, feature, advantage, and benefit. Don't get too high-tech during this phase. (My information management system of choice for this job is scissors, a glue stick, and a stack of construction paper!)

However you choose to segregate your information, you're going to end up with "collateral" information that's divided into four distinct categories: functions, features, advantages, and benefits.

Now then—how do you make educated guesses about which members of your contact group should receive which information during your calls and visits?

In many situations, of course, you won't be certain about whether the people with whom you'll be interacting will be using your product, service, or solution. For your present purposes, you're going to divide all these folks into two categories.

# Counselors

A counselor is an individual or group of individuals who are going to make a recommendation, or otherwise have significant influence over, the decision to buy your product.

These people may not ever see or come in contact with whatever it is you're selling, much less use it or help anyone else use it. If you sell books to corporate markets, for instance, you may interact with a purchasing agent who handles the procurement of books and periodicals. This person may never read—or even see—the books you're selling to this organization. Nevertheless the counselor is likely to have significant influence over the person with the final buying authority.

Another example of a counselor would be the committee that has been established within an organization to review all potential product purchases affecting the automation of the accounting department. This committee may be made up of individuals from the accounting department, but it may also include people from the headquarters' office, the order entry department, the credit department, and the customer service department. It may even boast a consultant or two for good measure; if you're really lucky, the CEO's brother-in-law, who's never before set foot inside any building having anything to do with any organizational initiative whatsoever, will be granted a seat of influence and honor. Whether or not that brother-in-law has even the vaguest clue about what you have to offer and how it can benefit the organization (and he may not), he's likely to have an impact, direct or indirect, on the final purchase decision.

As you'll see a little later in this chapter, there are three varieties of counselors. You'll highlight different elements of what you have to sell, depending on the type of counselor you're dealing with.

> **Words, Words, Words**
> *Influence* means the ability to change the minds of others. *Authority*, on the other hand, can be defined as having the control to make decisions, and the final power to spend the money that is associated with making the sale—whether or not others agree with your proposed course of action.

## Authority Decision Makers

An *authority decision maker* is the individual or group of individuals who will actually make the final decision to purchase (or not to purchase) whatever it is you're selling.

These folks usually (but not always!) have some experience with the environment within which your product, service, or solution will operate. They can generally be counted on to take a more hands-on approach to the decision-making process, but they, too, may not ever come in direct contact with what you have to offer.

In most situations, the head of the accounting department would be an authority decision maker when you're selling a new accounting system.

Mom and Dad are usually the authority decision makers if you're selling a new car that their daughter plans to use as her primary vehicle. You may find out that the board of directors of the local school district represent the authority decision makers if you're selling new science lab equipment.

As a general rule, the benefit of what you have to offer—that which makes it better than competing options—is most appealing to authority decision makers.

## Combining Counselors with Authority Decision Makers

So, who has the most power, the counselor or the authority decision maker?

Let's take the case of the wife and husband who are purchasing a new car for their daughter. The daughter is the influencer; Mom and Dad are the decision makers. As salespeople, we're tempted to ask: Who do you sell to? Who has the most power?

Unfortunately, there's no clear one-way-or-the-other answer to that question. You've got to appeal to *both* parties. Leaving either out of the picture is a huge mistake that will probably cost you the sale.

What you've got to do is adapt your F.F.A.B. information properly, and begin the journey that will allow you to influence the counselor and get the decision maker to make a decision in your favor. As luck would have it, each of the four elements of the F.F.A.B. model matches up with a category within the target organization.

## Appealing to Influence and Authority

Here are some other labels for people you might sell to:

➤ **Leaders.** At the top of every organization I've ever sold to there is a leader, someone who can override the directives of any committee in the structure—even (especially!) those he or she has personally set up. This is the person who writes the mission statement, who has the vision, who has the ultimate levels of influence and authority. When I say "ultimate levels of influence and authority," I mean that this person can be counted on to change the minds of others (that is, influence them), and make or override any decision and spend any amount of available money (that is, exercise authority). These folks, as we have seen, may be accurately described as authority decision makers.

➤ **Directors.** One level down from our authority decision makers, you'll find the directors. These are the individuals who are held responsible for the timely completion of the goals, plans, and objectives of the leader. Their titles may or may not be "director"—actually, they can be (and are) assigned such titles as office manager, regional manager, or some variation on a title including the words "vice president." Whatever title they go by, these people are held directly responsible for the direction of the workforce—a workforce with which our authority decision maker may have little contact. Directors are *not* authority decision makers—they're a type of counselor.

➤ **Influencers.** One level down from the director, you'll find the influencers, the trusted advisors to the directors. Their job is to influence and advise the directors on critical issues. Their titles might include (but are certainly not limited to): purchasing agent, head administrator, head engineer, head scientist, data processing manager, telecommunications manager, etc. Influencers are *not* authority decision makers. They're a type of counselor.

➤ **Consumers.** And one level down from the all-important influencers, there are the occupants of the largest (and lowest) level of the company, that of the consumers. These are the worker bees: factory floor workers, marketing and sales personnel, office personnel, fulfillment workers, and so on. In short, just about everyone who doesn't fit into one of the other three levels falls into this category. Consumers are *not* authority decision makers. They're a type of counselor. (Note that consumers are often invited to sit in on selection committees, and thus may have indirect input into recommendations that are forwarded to authority decision makers.)

# Mix and Match: The Complex Sale

In a complex sale—which, you'll remember, is one that generally requires contact with more than one person and a longer selling cycle marked by several presentations or demonstrations—the consumer community usually represents the individuals who will use what you sell. You may be asking yourself a question right about now: If you sell, say, office supplies, does that mean that the leader of the organization turns into a consumer (from your company's point of view, at any rate) every time he opens a box of paper clips?

Yes, it does! It's important to note, however, that, while a leader can certainly play the role of a consumer, a consumer can never step in and play the role of the leader!

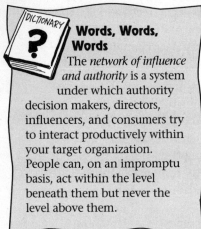

**Words, Words, Words**

The *network of influence and authority* is a system under which authority decision makers, directors, influencers, and consumers try to interact productively within your target organization. People can, on an impromptu basis, act within the level beneath them but never the level above them.

The same principle applies for all four levels: Everyone on the list—which I call the *network of influence and authority*—is capable of assuming, on a short-term basis, a role in one of the categories beneath him or her, but nobody can "transfer up." In other words, a leader may, at any given moment, act as a director, an influencer, and a consumer; a director may, at any given moment, act as an influencer and a consumer; and an influencer may act as a consumer. But nobody can award himself or herself an on-the-spot promotion!

I think of the network as being similar to a bottle of Italian salad dressing. A tenth of a second after you shake the bottle, the oil and vinegar begin to separate and return to their customary (and separate!) relationships.

## So, What Do You Pitch to Whom?

Use the list below to help arrange your F.F.A.B.-sorted product and service materials for use in a complex sale. This is a summary of what the players in a complex sale want to see:

➤ **Leaders want to see benefits.** They want to see exactly how what you have to offer will bring them closer to important goals.

➤ **Directors want to see advantages.** They want to see exactly why what you have to offer makes more sense than other options, or how you can customize what you offer in a way that no one else can.

➤ **Influencers want to see features.** They want to see all the details they possibly can about the "bells and whistles," the technical ins and outs that might, for instance, show up on the specification sheet.

➤ **Consumers want to see functions.** They want to know what it is about what you have to offer that will make their jobs easier.

Keep separate files for each group—and put the focus on what each group wants to hear.

When you're meeting with leaders, grab the file with information about the benefits, the "what happens that's good"—and be prepared to talk over the specifics of exactly how your product, service, or solution will move the organization closer to a key goal the leader has identified.

When you're meeting with directors, grab the file with information about advantages, about how your product or service is (or can be) distinctively configured to a particular situation. You should also be ready to talk to this person about advantages you have over your competition. (You'll be reading more about handling comparisons with your competition in just a moment.)

When you're meeting with influencers, grab the file that talks about features—the bells and whistles. If you've been selling for more than a month or so, it will probably come as no surprise to you to learn that these folks often have a voracious appetite for information about all the product doodads and special service plans your organization offers.

When you're meeting with consumers (a group whose blessing has saved many a sale), you should grab the file that talks about functions. These people want to know about practical stuff: How will it work in the real world? So focus on that for them.

If you follow these simple guidelines, you'll reduce to a bare minimum those complex sales visits when you can't seem to "speak the language" of the various people you'll be meeting with. You will have learned to speak the right language, and you won't fall into the trap of believing that all the members of a group focus on a problem from the exact same vantage point. (Trust me. They don't.)

# The Simple Sale

This is, as you will recall from Chapter 1, a sale that is made swiftly. It's the result of a single sales call or an in-person visit that involves one person or perhaps two people. When the visit involves one person, you may be talking to the sole proprietor of a small business.

Yes, you guessed right. During the brief period of time in which sales activity is taking place within this model, you'll have to shift gears quite a lot, focusing, in succession, on various elements of the F.F.A.B. analysis of your product, service, or solution.

Let's go back to our example of the new car sale. Mom and Dad are out to buy their daughter a new automobile. If I were the salesperson lucky enough to have this three-some walk into my showroom, I'd consider the daughter to be my consumer, and, as a result, I would sit the owner-to-be right in the front seat, invite her to adjust the seat, play with the mirrors, and tune the radio to her favorite station. You guessed it—I'd acquaint her with the specific "how" of the vehicle—the functions, the things she'll actually be coming in contact with day in and day out.

Then I'd have to do a little guesswork. Based on the body language and general demeanor of the parents of the owner-to-be, I might conclude that Mom represents the decision-making authority, while Dad is the counselor—specifically, a features-hungry influencer. Once I assign these categories, my approach is clear. I'm going to try exposing Mom to the "benefit data" by passing along warranty information, consumer magazine studies, and cost comparisons from authoritative studies. (Of course, if I get clear signals that I've got the roles backward, I'm going to change my approach in a hurry!)

Then I'm going to pull Dad over to the side of the car. After I ask his daughter to pop the hood, I'm going to launch the best summary of this vehicle's end-of-the-millennium, state-of-the-art auto engineering that anyone's ever heard. I'm going to give this influencer all the information about technological features that he can handle. (As for the personalized advantages of the car, I might decide to take a Polaroid snapshot of the whole family by the car and pass it on to the family, and then follow up by asking all the relevant questions about customizing the vehicle with specific options and color choices during the final phases of the sale.)

To a certain extent, the simple sale represents an adaptation of appeals you'll find within the complex sale. But remember: The minute the interview moves beyond "one-contact-to-close-the-sale" category, you've moved out of the simple sale and into the complex model.

### Bet You Didn't Know

You can apply the function-features-advantages-benefits model to everything, and I do mean everything, that your organization sells. Most salespeople persist in speaking a single language to each and every customer or potential customer; the system I've outlined for you in this chapter allows you to quickly and painlessly develop four languages that correspond to the four main interest groups you're likely to encounter on a day-to-day basis. With a little practice, you'll find yourself moving seamlessly from one group's viewpoint to another.

# What Does the Competition Have?

Being a top salesperson means developing a thorough understanding of your own products, services, and solutions—and an equally comprehensive understanding of what your competitor has to offer. Once you've got a good basis of information built up on your competitors, it will be pretty easy to keep the files current. You can make the job easy by teaming up with other salespeople in your organization and pooling your "upkeep" research efforts.

The rest of this section gives five sure-fire ways to get acquainted with, and stay on top of your competition's offerings. Why do you need to know about the competition? Because the different categories of customers will ask questions (to you, to others, or to themselves) about how what you sell compares to the other vendors who are out there. You need to be prepared to address these queries and concerns, and perhaps provide appropriate F.F.A.B. information.

## Look to Your Marketing Department

Marketing departments spend a whole lot of time studying the competition, researching the marketplace, and helping the product folks develop the very best stuff. Truth be told, they work like dogs. And after they've uncovered this critical competitive information, all the spreadsheets, analyses, and comparisons get filed away or forgotten. For some reason, no one thinks to fill the salespeople in about all this stuff. Once the competition catches up or moves ahead, the marketing people pick up from where they left off and the whole cycle starts over again.

If you run into a question that you can't immediately answer, it's usually a good idea to get in touch with a marketing person to see if there's new information that is applicable to the situation you face. Or, if a competitive issue puts you at a disadvantage with a number of customers or prospective customers, it might be time to ask that the marketing department gather new information or suggest a strategy for dealing with the problem.

The basic principle: Go out of your way to get your hands on all the research data your company has created thus far. And make no mistake: You're probably going to have to get out there and ask for it because the people in marketing often forget to volunteer everything they know—and you ought to know—about the market.

By the way, if your company distributes many different types of merchandise as, for instance, retail stores do, getting this information is going to be relatively easy—if you're willing to contact important manufacturers directly. (You should be!)

## Look to Your Existing Customers

Surprise, surprise: The vast majority of your existing customers have, at some point in the past, bought from at least one of your competitors. If you have a great working relationship with one of your current customers (you do, right?), ask your contact what his or her experience was with Brand X. No, this information isn't going to be the most recent you can track down, but it will still help you understand how your competition operates and how it's positioning itself in the market.

When should you bring up the subject of the competition? I see only two situations. The first is when you're talking to a current long-term customer with whom you have a great relationship (a business partner). If you're eager to find out this account's past history with your competitor, go ahead and ask. The other situation is when a suspect or prospect asks you about the competition, and/or makes it clear that he or she is about to go with the other side.

Speak as a reporter in this circumstance; show off independent evidence that demonstrates how well your outfit stacks up against Brand X. (You may also choose, in the interests of winning an up-for-grabs sale for the good guys, to share a pertinent and factual story about poor service or missed shipments.)

**Watch It!**
Don't go out of your way to badmouth the competition. It's classless, and it usually backfires.

**Sales Accelerator**
Do your best to approach competitive challenges with an open mind. If a new strategy of the competition's has the potential to change the way people buy what you have to offer—talk it over with your sales manager! Don't assume the other side is always wrong—they're not.

## Look to the Stock Market

Is one of your competitors publicly held? Great! Go out and buy a single share of the stock.

As a stockholder, you'll get all kinds of fascinating information in the mail: annual reports and interim reports (which often offer information about new and upcoming products and services you may be competing with), invitations to board meetings, and, yes, notifications that you're eligible to vote for corporate officers! What's more, you'll be asked if you'd like to be placed on the mailing list for the company newsletter. For my money, there's simply no better way to get inside the head of your competition than to become a (minority) stockholder.

## Look to the Library

Certainly, one of the best, most useful, and most up-to-date sources of competitive information is your local business library. Many industries are monitored by organizations that track and compare different providers of similar services. These independent assessments, which your reference librarian should be able to identify for you, are great tools that will help you determine the competition's true position in the industry—as well as that of your own organization. The information you dig up will be quite useful during your discussions with suspects and prospects.

## Look to Cyberspace

Is there anybody who doesn't have a Web site these days? Odds are that your competitors do, and you owe it to yourself to find out what they're saying about themselves to your potential customers. I'm constantly astounded by both the volume and the sensitivity of the information you can obtain on-line these days. It's as though no one believes the competition will ever visit the company's home page!

## The Least You Need to Know

➤ Leaders want to see benefits.

➤ Directors want to see advantages.

➤ Influencers want to see features.

➤ Consumers want to see functions.

➤ Taken together, these four groups constitute the network of inflence and authority.

➤ You must do what it takes to find out exactly what the competition is offering to your customers and prospective customers.

# Part 3
# Great Beginnings

*Building relationships with prospective customers is an art, not a science...but there are certain principles you can master, and certain basic questions you can address definitively, to increase the odds that you will be able to get the new relationship pointed in the right direction.*

*In this part of the book, you'll find out about what motivates buyers, what you'll want to find out before you initiate contact with a potential customer, and the detailed "battle plans" you'll need to develop before the first call or first meeting. You'll also learn how to make the first in-person appointment the success it ought to be...by listening, rather than talking!*

# Chapter 9

# Why We Buy

## In This Chapter

➤ How the hierarchy of needs affects buying decisions

➤ Buyer behaviors you can count on

➤ The Necessity mindset vs. the Choice mindset

➤ References, internal and external

➤ The buyer's goals and fears

In the last chapter, you learned about the types of product and service information particular buyers want to hear about. In this chapter, you'll take an in-depth look at the "why" of that fascinating phenomenon, the purchase decision. When the right information reaches the right buyer and is targeted to the right motivation, guess what happens? A sale!

Whether we like it or not, though, making sense of human motivations is more of an art than a science. The odds are that, as you master that art, you'll need more than one way of analyzing your buyer in order to get a reading on how he or she buys. That's why more than one method of evaluating buyers appears in this chapter. In the following pages, you'll learn how you can make sense of (and appeal to) the fundamental hierarchy of human needs. You'll learn how to identify necessity buyers (they're different than choice buyers). You'll learn what references are and how they can help you. You'll learn how to distinguish between goal-based buying and fear-based buying. And you'll also learn how the senses affect buying decisions.

No one of these tools will tell you everything you need to know about the "why" of each and every sale, but, taken together, they'll provide you with the start you need to make reasonably accurate motivational assessments second nature in your sales work.

# Some Basics

If you can fully understand the reasons your customers and potential customers decide to buy your product, service, or solution—and, perhaps just as important, the amount of time they take to make that decision—then you'll be in a good position to recreate those circumstances. Please understand, I'm not advocating "interpersonal cues," New Age psychobabble, subliminal messages, or any other variety of trickery to get your contacts to buy from you. All you'll be looking at in this chapter is honest, ethical sales work; the kind of sales work that brings you closer and closer to a living, breathing embodiment of the ideal buyer you identified on your TIP sheet (the Template of Ideal Prospects that you learned to develop in Chapter 6).

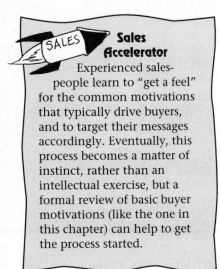

**Sales Accelerator**

Experienced salespeople learn to "get a feel" for the common motivations that typically drive buyers, and to target their messages accordingly. Eventually, this process becomes a matter of instinct, rather than an intellectual exercise, but a formal review of basic buyer motivations (like the one in this chapter) can help to get the process started.

**Sales Accelerator**

All the theory in the world won't change one simple fact: Everyone is unique. There are always going to be some buyers whose motivations pretty much mystify you. Although this group should become smaller and smaller as you become more adept at understanding the motivations that guide your customer base, confusing buyers will never completely disappear.

## Three Simple Ways to "Get It"

What do you do when you can't quite figure out where a buyer is coming from? There are three reliable ways to understand someone else's fundamental buying motivations. These should serve as a "backup" to the other tools and techniques you'll be reading about in this chapter. When in doubt, you can always:

➤ Put yourself in the other person's buying situation (literally or figuratively).

➤ Observe the other person as he or she progresses through that buying situation.

➤ Observe others in an identical buying situation.

Unless you're facing precisely the same set of circumstances as the person whose behavior you're trying to understand, the emphasis here is going to be on observing somebody else—either your target buyer or someone whose circumstances more or less duplicate those of your target buyer.

Take detailed notes on everything you observe. Reflect on what you learn about your target buyer. Review your notes, then sleep on 'em. When you return your attention to the buyer who's got you stymied, you may just find that you've got a better understanding of this buyer's behavior. Is a small business owner's obsession with cost, for instance, really a reflection of the shrinking market for his product? If so, ask yourself: What is there about your product, service, or solution that will help to attract or retain more and better customers?

## Count on These Buyer Behaviors

No matter what you sell, and no matter what the profile of your target buyer is, there are some things you can count on when it comes to purchase decisions. Over the past quarter-century, I've assembled a list of guiding motivations shared by virtually all suspects and prospects (that is, people who haven't bought anything from you yet). Here it is:

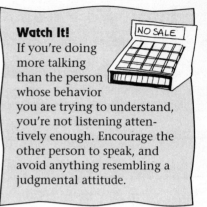

**Watch It!**
If you're doing more talking than the person whose behavior you are trying to understand, you're not listening attentively enough. Encourage the other person to speak, and avoid anything resembling a judgmental attitude.

➤ Decision makers buy for their own reasons (not ours); they always move away from unpleasant experiences and toward pleasant experiences. So emphasize that which is pleasant for your buyer and focus relentlessly on solutions and positive outcomes.

➤ Emotions have a strong, and usually primary, influence on buying decisions. Logic, on the other hand, does not always have a primary influence on buying decisions. So avoid the trap of confusing a presentation with a legal brief. Your aim is not to prove, but to persuade.

➤ If you offer alternatives, suspects and prospects will usually at least consider them. So make direct and unapologetic proposals once you've learned about the specifics of the suspect's or prospect's operation.

➤ The better-informed your buyer, the more likely he or she is to take an extremely cautious approach to decision making. So instead of fighting over "who's right," learn to become an information ally—someone who provides the buyer with key updates from the front, whether or not this results in a sale. Your objectivity will win attention, interest, and, eventually, trust.

**Sales Accelerator**
There's no escaping second-guessing—some form of remorse almost always sets in after any decision to buy anything. Ask your sales manager, or a veteran colleague, to help you identify the approaches that have worked the best in combating "buyer's remorse" in your field.

➤ People who buy out of necessity make purchase decisions more quickly than people who buy as the result of conscious choice. So learn to identify which is which (this chapter will help), and alter your income forecasts accordingly.

Those, then, are some of the specifics you can count on, and some advice on what to do in particular situations.

# Maslow's Pyramid

Another reliable tool with which you should be familiar has to do with the underlying needs that drive all purchasing decisions—and, indeed, every other human decision! The renowned psychologist Abraham Maslow (1908–1970) wanted to develop a thorough understanding of why human beings are motivated to satisfy particular requirements. He is remembered today for his highly influential "hierarchy of needs," an ascending five-stage grouping of need categories.

Maslow held that human needs must be satisfied from the base of the pyramid upwards. At the base, Maslow placed physiological needs (such as sleep, shelter, food, and drink). At the next level are "safety and security" needs (protection of ourselves, our loved ones, and our possessions). At the next level, you'll find the need for "belonging and recognition" (family, professional, and social participation). The fourth of the five levels reflects the need for "social status, self-respect, and the esteem of others" (a sense of value and rank within social systems). And at the very top of Maslow's pyramid is "self-actualization" (the experience of reaching one's full potential and experiencing life to the fullest).

Take a look at Maslow's pyramid, and ask yourself: What need grouping does your product, service, or solution satisfy?

*Maslow's hierarchy of needs.*

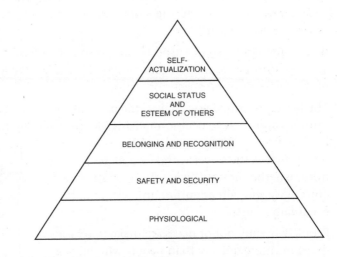

# Ratcheting Up

Maslow argued that human beings will always fulfill their needs from the bottom, or base, of this "needs pyramid," and move upwards from there. If a lower-level need isn't satisfied, Maslow argued, people will focus on that need before they address a higher-level one. That means that if you sell physical "essentials" (food or shelter, for instance), you'll have to contend with a different, and probably more intense, set of emotional responses and motivations than you will if you're selling alarm systems (a second-level need). The same principle applies to memberships in social clubs or other organizations (which correspond to third-level needs), high-status purchases such as luxury automobiles (fourth-level needs), and self-help products or demanding mountaineering trips (fifth-level needs).

The guiding motivations behind all these purchase decisions may be complex and overlapping, of course. For instance, someone may purchase a home both to satisfy shelter needs and to gain entry into a prestigious social grouping strongly associated with residence in a certain neighborhood. But, if Maslow was right (and most experts these days acknowledge that he was) you can count on this: When it comes to finding out what "lights a fire" under your target buyer, you're going to need to learn which need level(s), if any, he or she has already satisfied. The next one up is the one that's likely to make the most difference in a purchase decision.

> **Sales Accelerator**
> No, buyers are not all alike. Decision makers crave information suited to their individual needs. So give it to them!

## Your Ideal Prospect's Needs

Before you do anything else, ask yourself: Is your ideal prospect...

➤ Struggling to keep hearth and home together, to make ends meet, to keep the kids fed and the rent paid? (If so, appealing to second-level needs or higher probably won't get you very far. This prospect is interested in basic day-to-day survival, and highly motivated to find solutions in that area.)

➤ Eager to protect important people or possessions? (This is the sign of someone with second-level concerns in the needs hierarchy. Without second-level concerns there would be no such things as insurance policies or auto theft deterrent systems.)

➤ Trying to establish a sense of social belonging? (This reflects a third-level Maslow need.)

➤ Working to win status within a group, small or large? (Status and recognition are an important part of fourth-level Maslow needs.)

➤ Aiming to experience new levels of creativity, achievement, and mastery? (This fifth-level Maslow need arises among people who've addressed the pressing requirements of the four previous levels.)

> **Watch It!**
>
> Subjecting your contact to too much information can be just as damaging to your cause as providing too little information. Don't fall into the sale-killing trap of simply reading every line of the product catalog to your contact!

Don't get too hung up on product and service associations with particular Maslow needs. The person walking into your auto showroom may need to buy a modest car that makes possible the daily commute to a new job…a job that is the difference between renting an apartment and asking Mom and Dad how they feel about a new roommate. This buyer is going to be operating on the first Maslow level, and you're going to want to frame your benefits accordingly. ("This used vehicle has an excellent service record and won't give you lots of repair problems.") Another buyer might be interested in a car that establishes him as a member of a respected social class. (In that case, you'd appeal to this fourth-level need: "The president of the Anytown Bank just bought this model.")

Sometimes the prospect's answers to questions, like "Why are you in the market for so-and-so?" will give you all the clues you need about the Maslow category under discussion. At other times you'll have to observe closely and follow your own instincts and experience.

# "I Gotta" vs. "I Wanna"

Let's add some real-world sales experience to Maslow's theory so we can examine the "how" of buying. I think most veteran salespeople would agree that there are three factors to consider here. Let's look at the first factor in this section, and the next two in following sections.

Is necessity—or choice—driving your target buyer?

In the broadest sense, these two mindsets, necessity and choice, encompass the most important motivations underlying any purchase decision. In my experience, at any rate, one or the other of them is always playing a guiding role in anything you or I would be tempted to call a sale. (And as you read earlier, buyers who are motivated by necessity are generally at the center of sales cycles that move along more rapidly than those of other buyers.)

## Which Is It?

Is your target customer buying because of something akin to an emergency that's arisen— or because "it's time to look into such-and-such an area"? In every single sale I've ever made, this necessity-or-choice issue has eventually come up. And at the end of the day, one or the other of these forces has emerged as the guiding force for every single customer. At some point in our discussion, the prospect would always respond to a question in a way that let me know exactly which mindset I was dealing with.

Let's say I asked a prospect something like this: "Ms. Prospect, why did you select the system you're currently using?" The answer you get to a question like that will tell you a lot about who you're dealing with. See if you can tell which force, necessity or choice, serves as the driving force in the following two examples:

➤ "Well, at the time we didn't have much money, and we didn't have the time to take a really thorough look at our options, so we just picked the most affordable low-end system that would actually do the job for us. That's how we ended up, so we picked the Apex 102." (In this case, Ms. Prospect made her choice based on necessity.)

➤ "Well, I'll tell you. We did a really exhaustive search—it took about three months—because we knew it was time to upgrade, and we wanted to make the very best choice, a choice that would see us through for a while. We looked at each system on the market, we tested everything, we looked at all the demonstrations we could get people to come in and give us. After a good, long look at all our options, we made a recommendation to the president of the company that he authorize a purchase of the Zeepex 303 model. And that's what he did." (In this case, Ms. Prospect was part of a decision-making process guided by choice.)

## What It All Means

What does all this have to do with how someone might buy right now? Everything—and nothing. Everything if the circumstances are substantially the same now as they were the last time the choice/necessity forces were in play, and nothing if changes in financial status, geographic location, competition, or any of a dozen other areas have forced your target customer to move from one mindset to the other. But you should have some idea which viewpoint is emerging in your sale. Fortunately, it's not that hard to figure out which force is dominating the proceedings. (Always bear in mind, too, that necessity buyers do tend to reach their decisions more quickly than buyers driven by choice.)

# What Outsiders Say, What Insiders Say

Buying decisions, whether they're made by an individual or a group, are influenced by external and internal references. References are also known as "people proof" among some salespeople.

## "It Works for Them!"

Let's look at external references first—satisfied customers in another company, say, who are buying widgets for about the same purpose your target company is considering buying widgets. You say to your prospect, "Jack Wallace over at ABC Company just bought a similar product—would you like to talk to him about how it's working out for his organization?"

The closer the match the external reference has to the individual or organization making the decision, the greater that reference's potential influence. I say "potential" influence because some individuals and organizations simply shut down and refuse to evaluate any recommendation or feedback from an external reference. (Hey, tunnel vision happens, right?)

> **Words, Words, Words**
> *References* are the answers you can give to questions like: What are other people in a similar situation doing? What kind of results have they been getting? How would they deal with this issue? A reference who is willing to back up your claims with a prospective customer can provide a powerful incentive to buy.

In such situations, internal references—people inside the organization—carry even more importance than usual. To generate internal references, you'll have to work to build inside alliances, and that may take some time. I'll cover internal references next.

## "So What?"

I've done a lot of selling over the years, and I've met lots of people who couldn't care less what people in another company or another organization are doing. A good many of these folks have strong internal references: They know who they need to talk to before making a decision, and they don't need any more names from you, thank you very much. These people tend to have very strong convictions; they don't put a high value on your opinion, or, indeed, on the opinion of any outsider. Sometimes they'll even ask you for the names of your customers, and then never follow up and make the call.

All the same, you can—and should—routinely volunteer external references for your suspects and prospects. That is to say, you should have your list of satisfied customers handy, and you should be ready to refer to it regularly during your discussions with people who have not yet bought from you.

# Of "Onward!" and "Ouch!"—Goals and Fears

A compass has 360 points, or degrees. Each one of these tiny lines points to a direction a traveler can take. Now, a compass probably isn't something you need in order to travel down the streets of your sales territory, but if someone takes you off the familiar streets, and puts you in an unfamiliar area, one where you don't know the roads (or where there aren't any roads), a compass would be a pretty important instrument to have and know how to use.

There's a simple compass with just two "degrees" that you can use to navigate the un-familiar byways of a new suspect or prospect's world. Life in general, and the purchase decision in particular, offer two distinct directions for individuals who have to make decision. Here they are:

➤ Toward a goal.

➤ Away from a fear.

Say you're sitting with an authority decision maker who has just explained that she's expanding her operations to include the entire Pacific Northwest. Plans for expansion! That means she's going to need lots more of your widgets! You do your best not to start drooling on her desk. You can see the huge potential here, and your prospect can see that you see it. You're both in complete agreement: Growth is great! But you still need to ask an important question: Why is the growth occurring?

That's right. You need to ask your prospect, "Why is it so important to you personally to expand into the Pacific Northwest?" (The word "personally" is vitally important—use it, and restate your contact's goal when you do!) The answer tells you whether the prospect is moving toward a goal or away from a fear, so you can adapt your remarks accordingly.

## Goals

Suppose your prospect says something like this: "When my competition wakes up and sees my services offered throughout the entire Pacific Northwest, they're going to go into a coma. I can hear them now. They'll scratch their heads and ask, 'How on earth did she do it so quickly and so quietly?'"

If your prospect says something like that, you know she's moving toward a particular goal…and throughout the sales process, you're going to have to show how your widgets can turn that goal into a reality within her timeframe. You might consider talking about dramatic schedule improvements and reduced time-to-market.

## Fears

On the other hand, she might say, "If I don't shake my company loose from this downturning economy, I'll be out of business in one short year. I've got to get into a more solid, upbeat business base, and I've got to do it quickly."

If your prospect says something like that, you know she's moving away from a fear…and throughout the sales process, you're going to have to show exactly how your widgets can help make that fear go away. You might choose to highlight the higher levels of customer satisfaction—and customer retention—that will be likely to result from using your product.

Many salespeople make the mistake of assuming that a prospect is operating from a fear viewpoint simply because he or she expresses a general frustration with some aspect of the sales presentation. Actually, this kind of frustration is likelier to have its cause in the way you present information to your contact. The content, as you saw in the previous chapter, certainly matters—but the *way* you present that content matters a great deal, too! Read on, and you'll see what I mean.

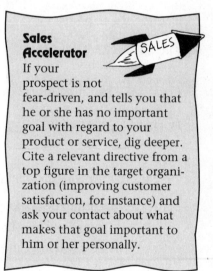

**Sales Accelerator**
If your prospect is not fear-driven, and tells you that he or she has no important goal with regard to your product or service, dig deeper. Cite a relevant directive from a top figure in the target organization (improving customer satisfaction, for instance) and ask your contact about what makes that goal important to him or her personally.

## The Prospect Has Three Senses

Forget what you learned in school. When it comes to selling, there are three senses, not five. They are:

➤ Hearing.

➤ Seeing.

➤ Feeling.

Any time you try to sell something to someone, you're going to be talking about your potential solution. That means the other person's going to have to hear what you have to say. You're also going to show the product or demonstrate the service—that is, make some sort of presentation. That means the other person's going to see what you have to offer in action. And finally, you're going to let your prospect come in direct contact with your product, service, or solution; you're going to let them use what your company makes or try the service your company provides. Whatever form this "test drive" takes, the other person is going to "try out" what your organization offers in order to experience, directly, the feel of it.

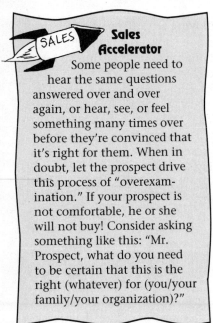

**Sales Accelerator**

Some people need to hear the same questions answered over and over again, or hear, see, or feel something many times over before they're convinced that it's right for them. When in doubt, let the prospect drive this process of "overexamination." If your prospect is not comfortable, he or she will not buy! Consider asking something like this: "Mr. Prospect, what do you need to be certain that this is the right (whatever) for (you/your family/your organization)?"

We use all three of these senses when we make a decision to buy, but we generally pick one to emphasize or favor.

Allowing suspects and prospects to learn, to become knowledgeable about what you have to offer, is critical to the process that turns them into customers. And everyone learns differently. Some of us respond better to seeing; others use hearing as the primary means of gathering information. Still others really need to "feel" information—physically or emotionally—before making an important decision. You need to find out which category your potential customer falls into, and target your sales presentation accordingly.

If you're not sure which style of learning your conversational partner favors, play it safe and use a combination of all three methods. Eventually, you'll pick up on the other person's references.

If you hear your suspect or prospect saying things like...

➤ "I want to hear about..."

➤ "Can we talk to someone else and get another opinion?"

➤ "I hear you loud and clear..."

...then the odds are that you're dealing with a person who favors a hearing (or "auditory") style of learning. You then need to emphasize verbal presentations.

If you hear your suspect or prospect saying things like...

➤ "I don't see how..."

➤ "Can we see some more (pictures of the product in use/data/graphics/written testimonials/whatever)..."

➤ "You haven't shown us anything about..."

...then the odds are that you're dealing with a person who favors a seeing (or "visual") style of learning. You then need to emphasize displays and graphically interesting key-point summaries.

If you hear your suspect or prospect saying things like...

➤ "It just doesn't feel right..."

➤ "Can you leave it here so we can get the feel of it?"

➤ "Let me try it myself..."

...then the odds are that you're dealing with a person who favors a feeling (or "kinesthetic") style of learning. You then need to emphasize hands-on demonstrations.

## Lots of Tools

At this point, you've learned about a number of tools for evaluating the motivations and predispositions of buyers. These analyses can certainly overlap, and as I noted earlier, no one of these tools is "right," except in that it encourages you, over time, to develop an instinctive awareness of the forces that commonly guide the people who buy from you. You might want to make a list now of your top thirty or forty prospects or customers. Make an attempt to evaluate each according to the models you've just read about. Don't try to develop a master's thesis on these buyers; do brainstorm for half an hour to an hour and see which elements emerge as common motivators. Do more than half of your prospects typically operate from a first-level safety need? Are they necessity-driven, or choice-driven? Are they moving towards a goal, or away from a fear?

## "I Don't Have to Buy from You!"

Any discussion of why the buyer buys from you should address the very real possibility that he or she will decide not to do so.

Yes, it's true: Every suspect or prospect you talk to has alternatives to deciding to buy what you have to offer, and priorities that affect how he or she considers those alternatives. Not all of the alternatives are logical, and not all of the priorities are within your control. (If the budget's just been cut to shreds and all new purchasing has been put on hold for ninety days, it doesn't really matter how good your references are; your contact's priorities are going to dictate a "no-buy" decision.)

To a certain extent, understanding these alternatives is part of understanding the larger challenge of overcoming objections. What follows is a brief review of some strategies you can use to put the odds in your favor when you come up against two factors that play a huge role in the "why" of the sales decision. The topic of dealing with objections as a whole is the subject of Chapter 15.

## "Checking-Out-the-Competition" Alternatives

"We're trying to find a better price."

If there was ever a common sales roadblock, this is it. How do you deal with a potential buyer who tells you she has to track down the best possible price—and who lets you know, in one way or another, your organization is not on the short list?

There's no all-purpose remedy for the price dilemma, of course, but there is a way you can pull some of these nervous folks back into the fold. The technique I'm about to suggest is not for the faint of heart, but it does have the advantage of capturing your suspect's or prospect's attention and bringing a completely new perspective to the proceedings.

When your contact says something like, "I'm afraid the price is just too high for us," you'll respond by asking a simple question. "Mr. Prospect," you'll say, "can you define 'price' for me?"

At this point, you can expect the other person to start sputtering a little bit, or to give you a few funny looks. Wait this out. Eventually, he or she will probably say something like, "Define price? Well, okay: It's what I pay. It's what shows up on the invoice."

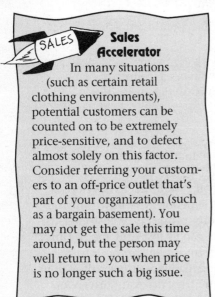

**Sales Accelerator**

In many situations (such as certain retail clothing environments), potential customers can be counted on to be extremely price-sensitive, and to defect almost solely on this factor. Consider referring your customers to an off-price outlet that's part of your organization (such as a bargain basement). You may not get the sale this time around, but the person may well return to you when price is no longer such a big issue.

You'll respond with something like the following:

"Mr. Prospect, of the (six/twelve/thirty/two hundred/whatever) customers and business partners we have in your industry, each and every one of them have reminded us at some point that they are now getting (and here mention some appropriate, accurate functions, features, advantages, or benefits of what you are offering) without really paying for those items. Those things never show up as a line item on any invoice, and so I suppose you could say our customers don't really pay for (and here repeat the functions, features, and benefits)—but they do get these things as part of the value we deliver. Mr. Prospect, do you think that what I'm talking about could make a difference to your organization this (week/month/quarter/year)?"

In other words: If you offer free follow-up diagnostic service, or dry cleaning, or oil changes, make the case that the prospect is really comparing apples to oranges.

# Time, Time, Time

Timing is the second major prospect alternative you may have to address. Remember the "simple" and "complex" modes of selling? The first is based on a pressing problem that needs to be solved in the short term; the second is usually more deliberative.

Sales decisions in the "simple" mode are, by definition, fairly brisk; the decision maker usually wants to wrap things up in short order. Still, some prospects do manage to delay, even in this mode of selling. Fortunately, virtually every product, service, or solution represented by the simple sales model can be offered for limited time frames: specials that are going to conclude, sales that are going to end, factory rebates or limited-time offers that won't last forever, owners of homes who are getting ready to leave the country. For as many reasons as a prospect can find to delay, the simple sales model can help you supply a valid reason for him or her to take action.

The buyer in the complex sale, on the other hand, is not so easily motivated. Actually, though, the problem here has less to do with the prospect's time than with your own. If there's no realistic chance that you're going to be able to do business with this person, you want to know that—and fast—so you can get back to making the Parinello Principle a reality by talking to someone else in your funnel. Your time is too valuable for you to spend it with people who aren't really interested in what you have to offer. (And so, for that matter, is your prospect's time!)

## Bet You Didn't Know

Have you ever noticed that suspects and prospects use both their lack of time and their abundance of it to put off decisions?

"I've got no time to look into this further right now."

"I'm in no rush...let me think about it and talk everything over with the members of my team, and I'll call you back later."

Many times, suspects and prospects who are not truly interested in what we have to offer will use the time alternative as a convenient way of getting themselves off the hook, and "letting salespeople down easy." At least, they think they're letting you down easy. Take the hint: A suspect or prospect who consistently takes a pass on decision-making, and routinely appeals to time to justify this activity, is almost certainly telling you "no."

As the salesperson, you must bring the time element into the spotlight when your contact says, "I've got to think this decision over." At this point, you've got to ask another question that takes a little courage—but trust me, once you realize how much it helps you avoid spending time running down blind alleys, you'll wonder why you never asked it

**115**

before. You've got to look your delaying prospect in the eye and say, "Ms. Prospect, if you had to make up your mind right now about doing business with us, what would that decision be?"

Suppose your contact says something like, "Well, if I had to make up my mind right now, I guess I'd have to say we'd pass. I just don't have the information we need to justify this expense. I'd defer the decision—say no for now and look at it again after we'd gathered some more facts." In this situation, you're not dealing with a buck-passer; you've hooked up with a real, live decision maker—one for whom time is not an issue, and who's going to exercise her interest in exploring all the choices available. Follow the prospect's lead and supply all the information you can, in the form that is most accessible to your contact. But don't expect a "yes" answer tomorrow morning.

Beware of investing lots of time and energy in meetings with prospects who flatly refuse to consider any aspect of a hypothetical "What would you decide if you had to decide right now?" question about purchasing your product or service. In all likelihood, this person lacks the authority to turn your sale into a reality. Try to get your contact to introduce you to others in the organization.

In a great many cases, when you ask this question, your contact will give you a surprisingly direct answer. "Gee, if I had to make up my mind right now, we'd go with Brand X." This is a decision maker who wants to work with someone—maybe you. Whether your contact realizes it or not, you've just moved the decision making process along and helped to accelerate the tempo. (A little later on in this book, I'll show you exactly how to ask for the business when you get this response—whether or not you sell Brand X!)

## What's Next?

Now that you've got an idea of the motivations that guide buyers, you're a step closer to putting what you've learned into practice. In the rest of this part of the book, you'll find out what you need to know before you make that first call to your suspect or prospect and the kinds of questions you should be prepared to ask people who have already bought from you.

## The Least You Need to Know

➤ People buy for their own reasons, not yours.

➤ Maslow's pyramid of needs offers important insight into human motivation, including purchasing decisions.

➤ Life in general, and the sales decision in particular, offers two distinct directions for individuals who have to make decisions: toward a goal or away from a fear.

➤ When it comes to selling, there are three senses—not five—decision makers tend to favor hearing, seeing, and feeling in evaluating your message.

➤ Every suspect or prospect you talk to has alternatives to deciding to buy what you have to offer and priorities that affect how quickly he or she considers those alternatives.

# Countdown: Pre-Contact Work

## In This Chapter

➤ Proactive selling

➤ What you should have down cold

➤ What you should be ready to ask

Now that you've gotten an idea of why people buy, you're ready to start preparing for your contact campaign. In this chapter, you'll learn why it's best to take the initiative, what you need to know before you make your first contact with a suspect or prospect, and what you should be prepared to discuss with your current customers and business partners.

## What's That Sound?

It was my very first day on the job as a salesperson; I'd landed a job with one of the world's largest (and, at that time, one of the world's only) big-time computer firms. I'll never forget that day, because that's when something extraordinary happened, something I would never have expected in a million years. Something that taught me a tremendous career lesson.

The telephone on my desk rang.

Panic city! My first reaction was to run and hide. Then I stopped in my tracks: Suppose my mother was calling me at work, reminding me to be careful if I decided to drive out into my territory? I froze. All I could do was stare down at the phone. No one had prepared me for this during my product training. I was the one who was supposed to be making the calls...wasn't I?

By the third ring, all the other salespeople in the "bullpen" had gathered around to watch me watch a ringing phone. Everywhere I looked, eyebrows were starting to go up, so I figured I'd better answer the call and pray it was my mother after all.

I took a deep breath, picked up the receiver, and said, "Help desk, this is Tony, how can I make your day a brighter one?"

## A Bad Connection

There was a pause, and then the person on the other end of the line said, "I thought the receptionist was going to connect me to the sales department. I don't need help. I need prices! Can you give them to me?"

Prices. Prices. I knew that somewhere in, on, or near my desk, perhaps in a box I had not yet unpacked, was a price sheet. The trick was to track it down. I started looking around frantically, and the tried to stall for time with a suave-sounding "probing" question, the first of my young sales career: "What will you be using the system for, sir, once you buy it?"

**Watch It!**
Keep up-to-date marketing materials and price lists handy at all times. You never know when you're going to need to refer to them!

Bad move. My conversational partner almost shouted his reply: "I didn't say I was going to buy anything. What I said was that I needed PRICES!"

I eventually tracked down the information my caller needed, but I honestly don't know whether he ever bought from us. After the call, I was too shell-shocked to jot down any notes. What a way to start a career!

## Who's in Charge Here?

I learned two important things from that experience.

First, salespeople who are proactive (that is, take the initiative and make the calls) generally have an easier time of it than salespeople who are reactive (that is, wait for the telephone to ring). Being proactive gives you choices. From that first day on the job to the present, I've tried, wherever possible, to put my emphasis on taking the initiative in relationships with suspects and prospects—although I've certainly grown more comfortable with the job of supplying customers who contact me with the information they need.

The second thing I learned from my traumatic telephone experience was actually pretty simple: Always answer a direct question when one is posed to you, and don't try to pose your own question until you've done so. Only after you've answered the other person's query do you have the right, privilege, and influence necessary to ask a question of your own.

Now then, which salesperson has the right to ask that all-important first question of the relationship? You guessed it, the proactive one.

## Gather the Facts

You're ready to play Sherlock Holmes! What do you need to know before you make (or take) your first sales call? Almost everything.

These are the facts you've got to have "down cold":

➤ How, when, where, and why your company was started.

➤ What your mission statement or vision statement is.

➤ What your company's current year-to-date performance is.

➤ What your products, services, and solutions are, what they do, and how they do it.

➤ The individuals and/or industries you serve—and exactly how you serve them. (In other words, you must know the functions, features, advantages, and benefits of everything you sell.)

➤ The names and industry affiliations of your other customers.

➤ The number of customers you serve and precisely what it is that you help them to do.

You must also know:

➤ The various options available to people who want to buy whatever it is that you sell.

➤ What those options cost.

➤ Lead times, delivery considerations, and options.

➤ Who the competition is, and how you stack up against it.

Depending on who you're calling, there will be other preliminary research you'll need to conduct. But the list above applies equally to your contacts with suspects, prospects, customers, and business partners.

## Don't Evade the (Potential) Customer!

As my experience indicates, you must always be able to answer important questions directly! Here are some specific questions to prepare for.

## "How Many Customers Have You Got?"

When anyone asks you how many customers your organization has, give a number! Never say simply "lots" or "a whole bunch" or any other vague phrase. As a salesperson, you need to quantify how many customers your company has, although you don't have to get hung up on issues of precision. You can express the number as a rough figure or a percentage—but you have to have some idea of what the number is, no exceptions. Your answer might sound something like this:

> "We have approximately 80 customers in the corporate arena, and I'd estimate that 15 percent of them are routinely interested in travel to the same destinations you're interested in examining."

## "What'll It Cost Me?"

The same principle holds true for people who ask you vitally important questions—for instance, any variation on "How much is it going to cost me to do business with your organization?" These questions are usually phrased with laser-like precision. When your customer asks, "What will it cost me to get three reams of your 80-pound card stock, special ordered for overnight delivery?" you need to be able to respond with something like this:

> "If the destination is in North America, three reams of that item will not exceed $76.30, assuming that there are no corporate or other discounts."

## Tailoring the Specifics You Prepare

A moment ago you saw a list of things you absolutely, positively have to know if you plan to work as a professional salesperson. If you want to be an above-average salesperson, and I assume you do, you'll need to pay a little more attention to the specifics of what your organization offers. You'll need to dig deeper about exactly what it is you do, so you can relate to the individual or industry on the other side of the desk.

The keyword here is "relate." If you don't relate to someone, there's no relationship! And in order to relate to your suspect, prospect, or customer, the questions you ask must be directed to the concerns your contact person faces daily.

So, who exactly are you dealing with, and what are their concerns? It's time to take another look at the major groups of people you'll be dealing with in your sales work—a group that's made up of suspects, prospects, customers, and business partners. Taken together, this group is known as "buyers." Let's look at each category in greater depth right now, and find out about the predispositions, and the specific requirements, of the various types of buyers.

# Prepping to Approach Suspects

You'll recall that suspects are individuals or organizations you suspect of being able to use what you have to sell. As a general rule, they fit your Template of Ideal Prospects, that you developed using the guidance in Chapter 6. (If you find out that a suspect does not match your TIP sheet, you should think long and hard before committing any time or energy to trying to turn this person into a customer.)

No contact has yet been made—either proactively or reactively—with the suspect. So what's the game-plan for your first conversation? What do you need to know before you pick up the phone? What information is critical if your call is to be an effective one?

Use a copy of the following worksheet to develop a partial list of the information you should have "down cold" before interacting with a prospect. Take a moment now and fill in the blanks in a copy of the worksheet as they relate to your selling situation.

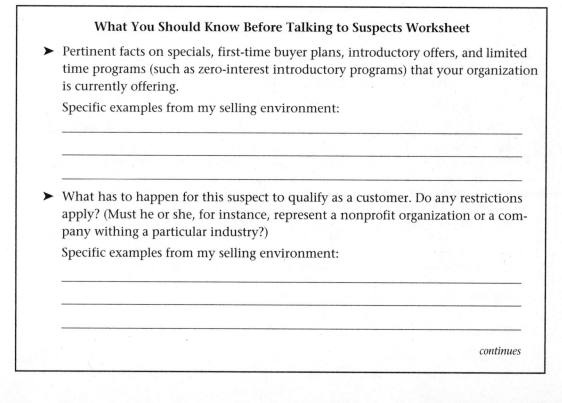

**Words, Words, Words**

*Buyers* are the people who could conceivably buy from you or are buying from you now. When you make a cold call to a referral you've never met before, you're interacting with a buyer. When you sit down for a meeting with your organization's biggest customer, you're interacting with a buyer.

---

**What You Should Know Before Talking to Suspects Worksheet**

➤ Pertinent facts on specials, first-time buyer plans, introductory offers, and limited time programs (such as zero-interest introductory programs) that your organization is currently offering.

Specific examples from my selling environment:

_____

_____

_____

➤ What has to happen for this suspect to qualify as a customer. Do any restrictions apply? (Must he or she, for instance, represent a nonprofit organization or a company withing a particular industry?)

Specific examples from my selling environment:

_____

_____

_____

*continues*

---

121

*continued*

➤ The categories of information the suspect will need to give you. (Will you need to know something about the suspect's phone bill? Next attendance at an industry convention? Size, color, or style preferences? First or second choices of a vacation destination?)

Specific examples from my selling environment:

_____

_____

_____

➤ The typical problems you've helped people in this industry or area of activity solve. (Be certain, however, that this individual shares the same types of problems before you start making massive generalizations about what you can and can't do in this case.)

Specific examples from my selling environment:

_____

_____

_____

**Watch It!**
Prospects are, by definition, active participants in the sales process. Failing to ask your prospects to take action or responsibility for the decisions that lead up to a choice to buy from you is risky business! Play it safe: Make sure your contact knows that you know he or she is responsible for the purchase decision—or at least part of that decision.

## Prospects

These are individuals or companies that have already shown some interest in what you have to offer. Perhaps you've already spoken to this person or company, or perhaps you've received a "give me more information" coupon from a direct-mail promotion your company has sponsored. Some interaction—typically, some form of conversation—has taken place between you and this person or organization.

Use a copy of the following worksheet to develop the important information you will need to acquaint yourself with before interacting with a prospect.

**What You Should Know Before Talking to Prospects Worksheet**

➤ What's the next step for you and/or you and the prospect to take? What will you be suggesting as the next step? Will you need to perform a demonstration, presentation, or other formal display of your organization's capabilities?

Specific examples from my selling environment:

_____

_____

_____

➤ What decisions must typically be made before your prospect commits to becoming a customer? Will he or she have to request a purchase order, authorize a delivery date, or obtain a peer review?

Specific examples from my selling environment:

_____

_____

_____

➤ What other parties must typically become involved in the purchase decision? (A top manager? A satisfied customer whom you provide as a reference? Your credit department?)

Specific examples from my selling environment:

_____

_____

_____

➤ How do prospects express urgency about your product, service, or solution? Do they highlight approaching deadlines, ask to speak to your manager, or bring you in for a special face-to-face meeting? What have you done in the past that has helped to intensify that urgency?

Specific examples from my selling environment:

_____

_____

_____

*continues*

---

*continued*

➤ How can you tell when a prospect understands what's happening as a result of not taking action in a particular area? Does he or she start talking about lost sales, lost calendar days, or regulatory problems? How have you succeeded in the past in convincing prospects that the passing of time is costing money, time, risk, or value? How have you succeeded in the past in dramatizing what could be happening instead if a prospect took action? (Some individuals and companies will respond better to the risk of not taking action than they will to the potential reward of taking action.)

Specifics from my selling environment:

_____

_____

_____

---

## Customers

Yes, you should take the time to contact current customers on a regular basis. Why? Add-on sales—and the increased loyalty that results from maintaining good relationships with the people with whom you do business. What's more, *failing* to follow up on existing customers provides your competition with an opportunity to win business from you.

**Sales Accelerator**

Current customers are a superb source of referrals for new business. Ask openly and unapologetically for them, along the following lines: "Ms. Prospect, is there anyone you know here in (geographic area) whom you might be able to introduce me to, someone we might be able to help in a similar or even greater way?" Don't be nervous about asking for referrals; the vast majority of the people who work with you will be happy to supply you with new prospects.

Information from your *current* customers should support your efforts to prepare for contacts with *prospective* customers. You should, of course, keep a customized file on each customer in your territory, a file that lets you know how this group makes its money or fulfills its mission, who makes the most important decisions, and what the recent trends in the industry are that your contacts are monitoring. (If you can, of course, you should review your customer's industry trade magazine. The questions you ask during periodic (and regularly scheduled!) calls to these folks should arise out of the specific information you collect on each of these vitally important contacts, and should also include the following:

➤ What one single word would you use to describe our (product/service/solution)?

➤ If we changed our (product/service/solution), so that it was (smaller/faster/less expensive/a different color, style, or configuration/more responsive/whatever), would you purchase more of them?

➤ Is there anything about our (store/showroom/factory/service/procedures/whatever) that we could change to make you happier?

➤ Have your plans, objectives, or needs changed in the past (period of time)? If so, how?

➤ What can we do for you right now, or in the future, that we're not doing now, and that would make this relationship work better for you?

➤ What other products or services can we help you obtain? (Be ready to offer your customer help in any and every area that doesn't result in dollars going to the competition!)

## Business Partners

You may not be able to turn every customer into a business partner, but that's no reason not to try. Too many salespeople settle for a client base that consists entirely of short-term relationships. They never make the effort to emerge as a partner, someone who helps both sides manage important strategic questions. Don't be one of those salespeople.

Usually, business partners help each other co-develop products, or assist in the design and development of emerging technology. The most loyal customers have a way of winning input into the selling organization's decisions. Recently, a friend of mine was flown to Italy to assist in a test drive market survey for Ferrari automobiles. No, he's not a race-car driver; he happens to be a loyal (to say the least) Ferrari owner. There are eight different models in his garage!

It should go without saying that you must be even more familiar with the unique business profile presented by your business partners than those of your customers. In addition, you should be ready to ask the following questions:

➤ What's your main organizational goal for (period of time)?

➤ How can we help you meet or beat that goal?

➤ What (information/experience/background/support) can we supply right now for your?

➤ Would you consider testing our new (product/service/solution)?

## Now That You Know All That...

If you've followed the advice in this chapter, you now have the critical information you need to deal with suspects, prospects, customers, and business partners. You're ready for a look at the strategies you'll be using to contact real, live potential customers.

In the next chapter, you'll get an overview of the methods available to you when it comes time to connect with these people—and in the chapter after that, you'll start assembling a script you can use or adapt in virtually any first-time encounter.

# The Least You Need to Know

➤ Being proactive (taking the initiative and making calls) gives you more choices.

➤ Know the basics about price and startup for your product, service, or solution.

➤ Gather the specific facts outlined in this chapter before you contact, or are contacted by, suspects and prospects.

➤ Review the questions outlined in this chapter so you know what to ask customers and business partners.

# Getting in the Door (and Staying There)

## In This Chapter

➤ How you can contact potential buyers

➤ Pros and cons

➤ Using these techniques to stay in touch with people who become customers

Finally! It's time to take all the information you've gathered thus far and start making some decisions about your campaign to get in touch with prospective customers. In this chapter, you'll take a look at the "keys" available to salespeople who want to open the doors to new business. This is where you start learning about the contact options that will allow you to reach out to those suspects and prospects who match your Template of Ideal Prospects.

## Knock, Knock

The biggest challenge salespeople face, whether they're new to sales or seasoned hands, is the age-old struggle of "getting in the door." How do you hold the other person's attention for long enough to ensure an honest, open-minded look at what you have to offer? What avenues are open to you that will allow you to attain this goal on a regular basis, and with a minimum of embarrassment, aggravation, and wasted time and energy?

Take a look at the various strategies now, and consider the advantages and disadvantages of each as they relate to your unique selling environment.

# Face to Face, Door to Door

**Sales Accelerator**

The potential advantage of employing a customized "personal touch" with buyers is a major factor in all face-to-face selling work, not just that which involves people you've never had any contact with before.

**Sales Accelerator**

Selling in person (whether or not you use personal visits as an initial contact method) requires:

➤ Immaculate personal grooming

➤ Inspired improvisational ability (because you must adjust instantly to the culture and style of the person/organization to whom you're selling)

➤ Preparing and circulating critical sales materials that look almost as good as you do (for example, business cards, brochures, and the like)

Many Fortune 500 companies require their sales reps to make in-person cold calls.

Knees in the breeze, feet in the street—this is the classic, and literal, "getting in the door" technique strongly associated, in years past, with vacuum cleaner and encyclopedia sales pros. Those who rely on this method for their initial contact with buyers certainly have the opportunity to showcase the greatest differences between themselves and the competition— themselves!

## Initial Contact Strategies

If you know that everyone you contact in a certain geographic area is a likely candidate for your products, services, and solutions, this option may well make sense for you— assuming you know how to make a great first impression in person and follow through on that first impression.

Some products and services are quite well suited to this method of initial contact. I know of an enterprising mechanic who scouted up all sorts of local business by introducing himself to the receptionists at each and every one of the businesses in a local industrial park! The receptionists then told the big boss about the mechanic, and the big boss often realized that a mechanic who visits a work site means lower rates of absenteeism in the work force. This mechanic got some pretty high-powered endorsements from presidents and department managers, and he won a great deal of business. Are you surprised to learn that he was neatly dressed during his visits, impeccably polite to the support staff, and willing to provide written references to each new contact? I wasn't, either.

Selling in person can be both fun and rewarding if you pursue creative strategies like the following:

➤ Know what you plan to say at the outset of each contact with a new person. (You'll be discussing this aspect later on in the book when you learn how to craft a high-impact opening statement.)

➤ Expect to hear the word "no" more than you'd like.

➤ Remember—in some settings, any sign of interest—even, say, a skeptical examination of some claim of yours—is a win. Don't set your expectations for a one-call close unless that's precisely what your sales model calls for (and it's been done before with this type of prospect).

➤ Focus on the personal. People buy from people, so take any and every opportunity to show that you're not "just another salesperson." Some successful salespeople do in-person cold calling on the days when the weather is lousiest—simply because they know the competition won't.

➤ Let the written word establish a positive image for you. Two of my favorite examples of this: postcards that feature your product, service, or solution on the front; and brief, personalized, *handwritten* notes left for prospects whose schedule made an in-person meeting with you impossible.

## And Once You're Dealing with a Customer...

Whether or not you initiate contact with your customer by means of an in-person meeting, you will definitely want to support and extend the relationship, if at all possible, by means of an ongoing series of face-to-face meetings. Yes, I said, "if at all possible." It's true that, in this multifaceted marketing world of ours, there are some selling situations (such as telemarketing) in which you may be able to close the sale without ever coming in direct contact with the person to whom you're selling.

I believe that some kind of personal contact with customers—or, at the very least, with the most important customers—is essential to building business partnerships. If you accept the partnership relationship as your ultimate goal, and I believe you should, then you'll make an effort to convince your sales manager, or anyone else who needs convincing, of the importance of your meeting in-person with key customers. Once you're in front of them, plan to add value to their day by:

➤ Offering new product information. Customers love to find out about your new offerings. Just be sure to observe the rules about what gets emphasized to whom: functions for consumers, features for influencers, advantages for directors, benefits for leaders.

➤ Making a commitment to help improve the bottom line. If you know of any ancillary service that is related to your product, service, or solution—something that could be of importance to your prospect—make sure your customers know about it. Even if you don't sell it, if the option makes your

**Watch It!**
Don't try to get current customers excited about "future" releases or service options. A new product or service is available right now—a future product or service is a gleam in a designer's mind! If your customer mistakes one for the other, there may be disappointment if things don't materialize.

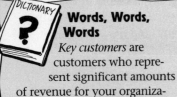

**Words, Words, Words**

*Key customers* are customers who represent significant amounts of revenue for your organization. They're the people you should be meeting with face-to-face on a regular basis.

**Sales Accelerator**

The telephone is an essential sales tool. If you're going to reach your full potential as a salesperson, you're going to need to become an expert at developing a "telephone persona" that's immediately appealing. You can do this by role-playing with fellow salespeople, recording the results, and then (here's the hard part!) listening to your own vocal delivery and asking for constructive criticism.

customer's pursuit of profit easier without putting your organzation at a competitive disadvantage, you should be willing to talk about it. If you sell industrial lubricants, consider finding out who sells the best cleaning solvents and/or disposal systems.

➤ Showing unfailing respect for your prospects' time. Get to the point! Avoid, at all costs, "just stopping by" for an unscheduled visit in order to pass the time with idle chitchat.

A review of the strategies that should guide the beginning phase of your first scheduled appointment with a buyer appears in Chapter 13. Information on handling questions, dealing with objections, and winning commitment during the appointment appears in Chapters 14, 15, and 16. Advice on in-person presentations appears in Chapters 17 and 18.

# On the Telephone

Most of today's selling begins on the telephone. Today's salespeople use the telephone to make introductions, uncover initial needs, set appointments, and, at times, actually get a final business commitment.

Scheduling in-person appointments with interested new contacts is the way most, (but not all) salespeople develop fresh revenue sources. There are lots of different ways to get appointments, but the method that's most likely to deliver good results for you is to contact a suspect—someone who's never communicated with you before. Another term for this type of call is "cold call." If you're like most salespeople, you're going to be making a lot of them!

## Initial Contact Strategies

What will you sound like when you contact your suspect by phone for the very first time? Magnificent—assuming you follow all the relevant advice laid out in this book. In the next chapter, you'll be learning about a pretty sophisticated, high-performance model for an opening statement that will form the basis of your telephone cold calling campaign. For now, remember that the most important rules for telephone contact in general, and initial contact in particular, are:

➤ **Controlling your voice.** That means making sure that your tone is varied and appealing, and that your rates of speech and volume are appropriate.

➤ **Controlling your dialogue.** That means selecting transitional words and phrases carefully, and delivering your pitch in such a way that it sounds natural, not memorized.

➤ **Controlling your emotions.** That means staying calm, even in the face of adversity, and never making the prospect feel that he or she is under attack.

➤ **Controlling your environment.** That means doing whatever it takes to eliminate background noise. If there's a problem here, talk to your sales manager about it!

**Words, Words, Words**
A *cold call* is a sales call you make to someone who's never interacted with you in any way. Unless you're in telemarketing, the aim of the cold call is not to finalize a purchase commitment, but to get the other person to agree to work with you to move the sales process forward.

Here are some additional ideas on the best ways to find more suspects and prospects to fill your sales funnel:

➤ Set up a lead sharing program. If at all possible, create alliances with other noncompetitive salespeople. If you sell custom-tailored suits, your target audience is wealthy business executives. Contact the salespeople who work for travel agencies, investment firms, prestige auto dealerships, and so on. Offer to share customer lists!

➤ Ask your sales manager about resuscitating "dead" leads from elsewhere in the organization. Perhaps there's a few "unproductive" leads that you can pass along yourself. Sometimes a change in approach is all that's necessary to awaken new interest in a prospect.

➤ Share appropriate out-of-territory leads with colleagues. If one of your customers has divisions that are outside of your territory, pass along those leads and share them with your peers. Ask for the same in return.

## And Once You're Dealing with a Customer...

No surprise here: Good telephone skills are, in most selling situations, essential to maintaining a good relationship with your customer. Periodic "phone checks" are a must, because they let you keep up with new developments in your prospect's business. Just make sure your follow-up calls are:

➤ Respectful of your customer's time, and

➤ Part of a broadly scaled "continuing contact" campaign that includes face-to-face meetings, too.

In addition, you should:

➤ Always ask your customers when they would like to be contacted (that is, what week of the month, day of the week, and time of day).

➤ Be ready to augment and support your telephone contact with other appropriate contact methods (such as personalized, written correspondence; newsletters; and e-mail).

➤ Use teleconferencing when this makes sense for the situation. If your product, service, or solution is supported by factory personnel, you may want to arrange for periodic teleconferencing calls that let your customers dial in and ask specific questions of the "technical guru."

Use the telephone to pass along good news about what your organization has accomplished for the target company—don't just call when a crisis arises. At the same time, be careful not to abuse your contact's time or attention with frivolous or irrelevant "updates."

# Written Communication

For centuries, people who make important business decisions have relied on and been influenced by those who write well. If you already know how to develop a powerful written message, you're in a great position to take advantage of that fact in your sales work. If you're a little uncertain about your written communication skills, fear not: You're about to learn about a simple, but incredibly effective, letter model you can adapt to your situation that will set you apart from the vast majority of salespeople.

## Initial Contact Strategies

Yes, the right letter, aimed at the right person, and presented in the right way, can "get you in the door." You can use written appeals to gain access and influence with buyers at your target organization—sometimes, very powerful buyers indeed. A certain amount of inspired telephone and in-person follow-up, however, is a necessity. But trust me: The letter itself is a very powerful weapon, assuming it's composed with care and executed flawlessly. Neatness definitely counts in your written communications.

Here's an example of a letter I've used literally thousands of times to reach, and win appointments with, CEOs, presidents, and other important types. (Talk about a great opportunity for a power referral! When these folks say "jump," the rest of the organization says "When do you want us to stop floating in midair?") This letter can be adapted to virtually anyone in the organization, of course, but it has been shown to work miracles with authority decision makers.

> ### *Boredom is a source of illness. You're holding the cure in your hands.*
>
> Date
>
> Mr. Vito Benefito
> President, Suncare Systems
>
> Disengaged, unhappy people get sick more, and hurt themselves more often, than people who do things they enjoy. And when residents are occupied with enjoyable activities on their own, they're less dependent on a critical resource: your nursing staff. Residents who are engaged in absorbing, enjoyable, self-sufficient activity aren't bored...and that means they're going to be happier, stay healthier, and make fewer attention-motivated calls to your nursing staff.
>
> The ABC oversized, double-sided widget is the only recreational widget devoted exclusively to people with large print needs. The magazine was born when someone with large-print needs told us, "My eyes may need help, but that doesn't mean my mind is gone!" This widget:
>
> - Lets your critical resource—your nursing staff—get more done during the course of the day.
> - Increases the quality of the health care you deliver...by keeping residents engaged, happier, and, healthier.
> - Makes busy nursing home staff members say things like "Thank you! We've been looking for something like this!"
>
> Can we make the nurses and residents at Suncare as happy as the people who are already using our widgets? Well, we certainly hope so. But only you can decide whether this resource makes sense for your organization. Together, we should work to determine whether or not our program for industry leaders is right for you.
>
> Sincerely,
>
> Will Prosper
> 999/555-1212
>
> P.S.: I will call your office at X:XX am on June XXth. If this is an inconvenient time, please have Toni advise me as to when I should return the call.

There's a lot to be said about the use of the letter format you've just seen—more than I can fit in here, in fact. Let's just address the basics. If you decide to adapt this letter to

**133**

your own purposes in contacting top officers (and I recommend that you do), bear the following points in mind:

➤ You must be sure to state a compelling, direct benefit (or a credible, verifiable endorsement) in the headline, and use no more than 30 words to do it. If you're targeting the letter to someone other than a leader in the organization, focus on something besides benefits—advantages for directors, for instance.

➤ The first paragraph of your letter must take the theme of the headline and carry it into the letter.

➤ The bullets section of your letter should contain information of high interest to the reader.

➤ Make the P.S. time-specific. (Don't write, "I'll call someday next week" or "I'll call Tuesday morning.")

➤ You need to do phone research to determine the name of the top officer's secretary or assistant.

➤ When you make your follow-up call at exactly the time you specified, you must be ready to treat the secretary or assistant as though he or she were the most important and influential person in the organization. (You won't be far from the truth when you do.)

➤ You must—without fail—include your phone number at the end of the letter.

➤ You must use plain white paper—not company stationery—for the letter—unless, of course, you're in an industry where there is some government regulation to the contrary. Ideally, your logo should not appear anywhere on this correspondence. Logos cause pre-judgment, and at this stage of the sales game, pre-judgment is the kiss of death. Save the stationery with logos for your customers.

➤ You must mail the letter in a large (9" × 12") envelope. That helps you stand out from the rest of the pack when the mail gets opened!

There is room for some variation within these guidelines. If your industry, person style, or target customer base point toward a more casual approach, you might want to consider an upscale personal type of stationery (but again, no logos), a handwritten note, a stylish font, or even a photograph of yourself placed in the lower right-hand corner of the letter.

In addition, for your follow-up call, you'll want to review all the advice on initial phone contact that appears in the next chapter.

## And Once You're Dealing with a Customer...

Written updates are important—and positive—parts of your relationship with a customer, but they shouldn't assume central importance in your contacts with the people who buy from you. Strike a balance. I like to give new customers a binder at the outset of a business relationship, then supply regular written updates on the solutions I've provided. The sheets I pass along fit neatly into the binder I've supplied. Always follow the rules: Highlight functions for customers, features for influencers, advantages for directors, advantages for directors, and benefits for leaders.

You should strongly consider using such an approach as part of a keeping-in-touch strategy that involves personal and phone contact.

Remember, you're a salesperson—not a writer. Unless you're considering changing jobs and developing direct mail or advertising sell copy, your focus needs to be on maintaining your own relationship with the person you're selling to. Don't expect your correspondence to take your place. It can't.

**Watch It!**
In correspondence you draft for suspects, prospects, customers, and business partners, stay away from any technical industry jargon your contact will not understand. Test the piece on a "guinea pig" outsider who will give you honest feedback on your message's accessibility. Edit out or revise confusing or unfamiliar terms.

# E-Mail and the Internet

If you've ever used e-mail, you know that it's a truly remarkable means of communication. It combines breathtaking speed (in both directions) with a certain "nowhere-to-hide" quality: If people want to get through their e-mail, they have to take at least a cursory look at some part of your message.

## Initial Contact Strategies

These days, there are a lot of outfits that will promise to blanket cyberspace with your e-mail message for next to nothing. This means that if you compose a reasonably compelling appeal, you can expect to hear from some interested prospects via return e-mail. My advice is to use e-mail a little more selectively. Either conduct your e-mail campaign yourself, picking out contacts from the World Wide Web or particular newsgroups who seem to fit your ideal prospect profile, or work with an established bulk e-mail firm that will allow you to be choosy about the group you're appealing to.

You want to be as efficient as possible, of course. You also want to avoid adding any more than you absolutely have to to the staggering levels of "junk e-mail" most computer users must now contend with. This problem has grown so immense that some regulators are now trying to figure out ways to track down salespeople who use tiny bulk e-mail outfits to send the same message to, say, all five million members of a particular on-line service.

If you're careful with your time management (see the following cautionary notes), and if you target your message carefully to people who are likely to fit your Template of Ideal Prospects, e-mail may make sense for you as one method of reaching out to potential customers.

You should pattern your e-mail after the written correspondence I showed you a little earlier in this chapter: include a date and time you'll be calling, or explicitly provide a way for suspects to contact you. If you choose the latter option, always give specific dates and times that you'll be available to take calls.

Your correspondence "schedule" should look something like this:

➤ Day One: Send your first e-mail.

➤ Day Four: If you've gotten no response by this point, place a phone call and leave a voice mail message (see the special section on voice mail messages at the end of the book).

➤ Day Seven: If you've gotten no response by this point, leave a different voice mail message.

➤ Day Ten: If you've gotten no response by this point, leave a different voice mail message.

➤ Day Thirteen: If you've gotten no response by this point, make a last-ditch effort to win a response from this prospect by formulating another e-mail message, one that follows the same format as the first one, but that addresses additional areas where your organization has a proven track record for success in delivering results for other individuals or organizations facing problems similar to the prospect's.

## And Once You're Dealing with a Customer...

**Watch It!**
Offensive or careless e-mail messages are easier to send than you think. If you're communicating with suspects, prospects, and customers, you'll want to be sure your message is composed carefully, and reviewed closely before it's zapped off into cyberspace. On particularly important messages, consider composing the text on your word processor and pasting it into your e-mail manager's message box.

These days, e-mail is more than a medium of communication. It's a culture unto itself. Once you join the "wired nation" (by, for instance, including your own e-mail address on your business card), you'd better be willing to check your own mail at least once a day and respond promptly to any and all customer queries you find there. E-mail can be particularly tricky because the person to whom you're responding will always know how long you waited before responding to a message!

Think long and hard before you pass out your own e-mail address as a means of keeping in touch with customers. You'll probably undermine some relationships if it turns out that you can't live up to the mile-a-minute communication commitments e-mailers often expect. If you do decide to use this medium to keep in touch with current customers, be prepared for another tricky time management problem. When there are 25 or more messages to wade through every day, allocating time to respond to them all can be quite a challenge.

# What's the Right Mix?

Only you and your sales manager can make the final decision about the best ways to make initial contact with prospective customers in particular fields. As someone who's been training salespeople for 26 years, however, I can tell you that the superstar reps I've worked with have had in common, among other things:

➤ The ability to make cold calls over the telephone (or, if appropriate to their industry, via in-person visits) to set up later face-to-face appointments, and

➤ The ability to compose striking written appeals that serve as the basis for later telephone contact requesting in-person appointments.

What do I get from that? Well, if I were a betting man, I'd wager that cold calls and customized mail pieces, or a combination thereof, are your best options—assuming that your objective is to contact, and set up appointments with, promising buyers. The other contact methods discussed in this chapter are, I think, likely to be most useful to you as backup or secondary strategies, or approaches to experiment with carefully.

**Sales Accelerator**

If you decide to use e-mail as a method for keeping in touch with current customers, be prepared to invest some extra time to keep up with all the message traffic. It will grow more quickly than you expect. Consider getting up a half-hour earlier, and/or going to bed a half-hour later, to manage message traffic without disrupting the rest of your schedule

# Next Stop: Dialogue!

Now that you've got a good idea of the techniques available to you to make contact with buyers, it's time to look at what you'll say to them during your first encounter. In the next chapter, you'll explore the best strategies for ensuring that the first eight seconds of your relationship with a prospective buyer go as close to perfectly as you can make them—whether you've contacted that person by phone or in person.

# The Least You Need to Know

➤ You're probably going to need a combination of superior cold calling skills and strong written appeals in order to get in touch with new suspects and prospects.

➤ Phone skills, written communication skills, and the ability to interact persuasively in person, will all help your cause once your prospect turns into a customer or business partner.

➤ Consider using the model letter in this chapter to reach top officials within the organization, or adapting it to reach others in the network of influence and authority.

➤ Always show respect for the time of your key customers.

➤ E-mail is more than just a means of communication; it's a culture unto itself.

# Opening Statements

---

# Chapter 12

## In This Chapter

➤ Making the most of the first eight seconds

➤ Developing your statement

➤ Adapting your statement to different audiences

➤ Handling receptionists and assistants

---

So, you understand what motivates people to buy; you know the relevant specifics about your product, service, or solution; and you have a good idea about the strategies at your disposal for contacting people who may give you new business. When you finally find yourself in a discussion with someone who fits your Template of Ideal Prospects, what do you say?

In this chapter, you'll craft your opening statement—the first thing you say to the prospective buyer with whom you haven't yet spoken. You'll also get some invaluable advice on dealing with receptionists and administrative assistants—the "gatekeepers" who stand between you and your contact.

As an added benefit, note that all of the strategies and tacits in this chapter can be used to construct opening statements for use with *any* prospect or customer, in *any* setting, whom you have not yet met.

# "Let's Get Together"

In this chapter, I'm going to assume that your current goal is to develop new business, and I'm also going to assume that:

1. You've decided to use the telephone to do this, either by means of a follow-up call on a written communication, or as your first contact with the target organization.

2. Your aim is to get an appointment with someone who has partial or full responsibility for purchase decisions in your area.

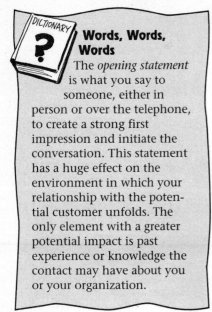

**Words, Words, Words**

The *opening statement* is what you say to someone, either in person or over the telephone, to create a strong first impression and initiate the conversation. This statement has a huge effect on the environment in which your relationship with the potential customer unfolds. The only element with a greater potential impact is past experience or knowledge the contact may have about you or your organization.

In other words, the goal of this call is not to "close the sale," build relationships, establish commonalties, improve your company's image, or anything else, no matter how high-minded. You want to find suspects who will take over the conversation, and then turn themselves into prospects by committing a particular chunk of their schedule to a face-to-face meeting with you. To the extent that your call helps you accomplish those things, it's working; to the extent that it doesn't help you accomplish those things, it's not working.

By the way, the opening-statement principles you're about to review can (and should) be applied to situations where you're meeting in person, for the first time, with an important contact who's never had any significant interaction with you. Remember, in such a situation, you're not out to sell. You're out to win attention and interest—make a good first impression—and get the other person to take over the conversation. After that, your objective is to learn!

## Toast!

When you think of opening statements, think of a hyperactive toaster oven. If things don't go right in eight seconds or less, you're toast.

I use this eight-second standard not because there's unanimity among the sales experts about exactly what constitutes the length of time necessary to leave a good first impression (there isn't), but because my own experience is that this is the outer limit for sales professionals. Believe me, I've made every mistake it's possible to make when it comes to opening statements. Eight seconds is all the time you have to get things off on the right foot. I have yet to run into a veteran salesperson who disagreed with me on this point.

Not long ago, one of my employees and I were driving to an important face-to-face meeting with a contact who'd never spoken to either of us before. Daniel, the salesperson who was accompanying me on this visit, was skeptical about my eight-second standard.

He looked at me and said, "Boss, eight seconds is too short a period of time! That's hardly enough time to take a deep breath, let alone make a meaningful opening statement!"

We happened to be waiting at a red light when he said this. As the light turned green, I kept my foot on the brake and started counting: "One thousand one, one thousand two…" People started honking. By the time I got to "one thousand four," Daniel was begging me to get moving. By the time we hit the sixth second, the guy behind us was starting to get out of his car, and Daniel was looking for a place under the floorboards to hide. When I finally hit eight, the intersection was a symphony of honking horns and shouting mouths. I hit the gas.

**Watch It!**
Launching an opening statement that doesn't let the other person "cut in" is a classic beginner's sales mistake. Stop talking when your contact wants to make a point. If you're not willing to be interrupted, you cannot deliver an effective opening statement.

Daniel never questioned me again on how long eight seconds really is, or whether you can make an impact in that length of time.

## Goals for the High-Impact Opening Statement

Your three big goals with regard to the opening statement are:

➤ **Make it sound conversational.** Once you develop an opening statement, read it into a tape recorder. Then play it back and transcribe it—write down every word of it. Then read it back into the tape recorder. Repeat this process five times! If you do, you'll sound much more natural when you deliver it in real life.

➤ **Deliver it with confidence.** Butterflies? Everyone gets 'em. But you have to learn to reach down deep inside and say it like you mean it—because you do!

➤ **Get a favorable interruption—one that puts your contact in control—as soon as possible.** That's what lots of the people you'll be dealing with, especially leaders and directors, are used to doing, being in control.

## The Five Key Ingredients of Your Opening Statement

Let's set the stage. You've been handed a list of leads. You're picking up the telephone to call a suspect. For right now, assume that you actually do get through to the person you're trying to reach. (Yes, I know that's a big assumption; later on in this chapter, you'll learn how to deal with the gatekeepers whose job seems to be to keep you from getting in touch with the people you want to reach.)

## Step One: The Introduction

Usually, when someone picks up a direct line, that person will say his or her name: "This is Sally," or "Sally Jones speaking." Your first step will be to repeat this person's name—or, if the person doesn't say it upon answering the phone, say it for the first time. Keep things formal for now—use Mr. or Ms., then the contact's last name.

> Prospect: This is Sally.
>
> You: Ms. Jones?
>
> Prospect: Yes.

Or:

> Prospect: Hello? (Or: "Production." Or: "4527." Or: "Can I help you?")
>
> You: Ms. Jones?
>
> Prospect: Yes.

At this point, you have Sally's undivided attention. Whatever she was doing prior to your saying her name, she's now stopped doing. She's paying attention to you.

Be very careful hereabouts! What you say next will make all the difference.

What most salespeople do now—despite ample and endlessly repeated evidence that they shouldn't—is say something like this: "Hi, Ms. Jones. This is Will Perish, with the ABC Insurance Company." Unless your name is, say, Garth Brooks, or your company affiliation is, say, the Prize Disbursement Division of Publishers Clearing House, I can tell you what's going to happen next in the vast majority of such calls. The contact will respond to this self-defeating "verbal handshake" by tuning out, asking you to send written information, pretending that the building just caught fire, or otherwise disengaging from the call. In other words, you will have only been on the line about a second and a half, and you'll be done. You'll be a smoking English muffin.

## Step Two: The Pleasantry (Not Your Name!)

Here's an alternative plan. What I'm about to tell you to do may well contradict what you've been taught to do during your sales training. Do it anyway.

When Sally Jones says "Yes," you're going to respond with something positive and enthusiastic, something that does not directly identify you, your company, or the product or service you eventually want to discuss. It's too early in the relationship for you to pass along that kind of information. Instead, you're going to use a pleasantry, something like this:

Prospect: This is Sally.

You: Ms. Jones?

Prospect: Yes.

You: It's great to finally speak with you!

Here are some other pleasantries you can use in this slot, lines that have been shown to help salespeople sustain momentum in opening statements.

➤ "Thanks for picking up the phone!"

➤ "Thanks for taking my call."

➤ "It's an honor to finally speak with you."

➤ "Your time is important. Let me cut to the chase."

➤ "It's such a surprise to get you on the phone; you're a very busy (man/woman)."

➤ "It was a pleasure to read about (pertinent, positive news event relating to target company)."

You get the idea. Each and every one of these pleasantries will do a far better job for you than simply volunteering your name and company affiliation at the outset of the conversation.

What happens on the rare occasions when your contact says something like, "Hey, wait a minute, who is this?" That's easy. Just say, "Oh, sorry, forgot to tell you. This is Will, Will Prosper, with the XYZ Insurance Company."

Then move on to…

**Words, Words, Words**

The *pleasantry* is the upbeat transitional phrase you use immediately after you've gotten your contact to say "Yes" in response to his or her name. It's unique, it comes from your heart, and it sounds both happy and interested.

**Watch It!**

Never use "small talk" in the pleasantry slot of your opening statement. Queries like, "How are you today?" or "Did you get those thunderstorms down by your place last night?" or "How about those 49ers?" will cause your suspect to disconnect from the conversation instantly.

# Step Three: The Hook

Immediately after your pleasantry, you're going to catch the person's attention by using a hook that's keyed directly to something likely to be of interest to your contact—who falls, as you remember, into one of four very different groups.

Remember:

Leaders want to learn about benefits.

Directors want to learn about advantages.

Influencers want to learn about features.

Consumers want to learn about functions.

For instance, let's say you know that your contact is a director. What are directors inter-ested in? Advantages. That's what your hook will address. Or say you're talking to a leader. What are leaders interested in? Benefits. That's what your hook will address:

Here's what a hook for a leader in the widget industry might sound like:

> You: We've helped ABC Widget Corporation reduce its overhead costs by twelve percent this quarter—and they did it without laying off staff or sacrificing product quality.

Now, there's a tangible benefit if ever there was one! Keep your hook focused and one or two sentences long, and you can't go wrong.

When talking to leaders, the people who identify the big organizational goals, wrap your hook around benefits that directly support those goals.

When talking to directors, the people entrusted with the job of turning those goals into reality, wrap your hook around advantages—that which leaves the competition in the dust:

> You: Right now, ABC Widget Corporation is enjoying a shorter production cycle with fewer defects and rework—while they increase worker safety.

When talking to influencers, the people who know the technical stuff backwards and forwards, wrap your hook around the features, the bells and whistles:

> You: Our latest widget compressor seals any angle lids with two-tenths of a percent-age accuracy—while drawing less current than older methods.

When talking to consumers, wrap your hook around functions—the "what happens and how it works":

> You: If your eyes are irritated at the end of a long day from straining to inspect lid welds, you'll love our new inspection system. It's as easy as watching TV!

## The Interruption

More often than not, around here is where you'll get interrupted if your hook is doing its job. Your contact is likely to cut in and say something like:

> "This sounds interesting—tell me all about it."

Or:

> "I think I read something about your company."

Or:

> "I haven't heard of this before, but I must admit it sounds vaguely interesting."

Or:

> "I have absolutely no interest."

Don't worry. You'll be learning how to deal with all of these interruptions, including that scary-sounding last one, later on in the book. For now, just remember that cold calling is a numbers game, and that your objective is to keep the other person talking. If that's not happening after one or two attempts at initiating person-to-person discourse, say thank you and move on. (You may decide to use the final element of your opening statement, the question, to respond to objections during the cold-calling phase.)

As I said, you'll almost certainly get interrupted by this point. For the sake of completeness, though, you need to complete developing your opening statement, so you know what to say in those cases where you don't get interrupted at this point.

## Step Four: Naming Names

Once you've shared your hook, the other person knows the reason for your call. The cat's out of the bag. This is the perfect time to identify yourself and, if you'd like, your organization. If you choose to identify your employer, give it a brief "commercial." What you say will fit in one sentence. It should sound like this:

> You: This is Will, Will Prosper, with ABC Insurance Company—the hardest working company in the insurance industry today.

## Step Five: Your Ending Question

If you don't get interrupted by this point, you're going to conclude your opening statement with an ending question that incorporates some element of time.

> **Watch It!**
> Never sully your own image—or that of your company—by engaging in pointless conflicts during your telephone prospecting. When in doubt about your ability to maintain composure on the line, take a break. Cold calls are your opportunity to play the consummate professional. Take advantage—and remember that the majority of these calls, by definition, are going to fall into the "no thanks" category.

> **Words, Words, Words**
> Your opening statement's *ending question* is a thought-provoking query that gets your contact thinking about what you've said, and encourages him or her to make a comment. Don't get too concerned by a negative response to your ending question; you'll be learning how to deal with that soon.

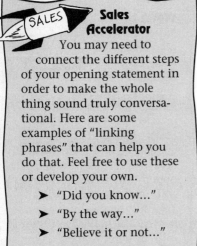

**Sales Accelerator**

You may need to connect the different steps of your opening statement in order to make the whole thing sound truly conversational. Here are some examples of "linking phrases" that can help you do that. Feel free to use these or develop your own.

➤ "Did you know…"
➤ "By the way…"
➤ "Believe it or not…"
➤ "In a recent discussion with Widgetco, we learned…"

**Sales Accelerator**

If you're uncertain about the category your contact falls into, build your opening statement around an advantage hook. It's the most accessible to everyone. If you're calling the head of the organization, though, it's a pretty solid bet he or she will be most interested in benefits.

Just before you deliver your ending question, which should run no longer than two sentences, you'll probably want to say the contact's name. Here's what it might sound like:

You: Ms. Prospect, does this touch on issues that are of concern to you this (month/year/quarter)?

Here are some other examples of ending questions that would work in this slot.

➤ "Are you trying to accomplish something like this by the end of this (quarter/year)?"
➤ "Is this something you'd like to explore further?"
➤ "What are your thoughts right now?"
➤ "Have I touched on an issue that affects your day-to-day operations?"
➤ "Who besides yourself would you like for me to talk to about our ideas before the end of this week?"

## What It Sounds Like

Here's an example of an opening statement that works. Yours shouldn't sound exactly like this one, but it should be about this long, and it should, like what follows, hit all the bases you've been reading about.

This opening statement is directed toward a leader in your target organization. Remember, your aim is to use your statement to *win interest and attention,* typically by eliciting some significant comment or interruption within the first eight seconds. You're *not* trying to compete with the prospect for the right to talk, so you can "finish" your statement.

Your Suspect's Name: Ms. Importanto? (Your suspect replies: "Yes?")

Pleasantry: It was a pleasure to read that your company has successfully expanded into the European marketplace. By the way…

Hook: After studying another client's operation, we suggested an idea that provided revenue gains of over $25,000 per year. The real surprise is that we did this without taking one bit of Acme's hard-earned capital.

Your Name: "This is Will Prosper at Zenith."

Ending Question: "Acme's impressive results may be tough to duplicate. But would you be open to taking the next step between now and the first of the year?"

**Watch It!**
Never use the words "I," "me," or "mine" in your opening statement, or any of their forms. These words turn off suspects. Other words to edit out of your opening statement: afraid, anxious, disappointed, failure, fear, maybe, perhaps, possibly, and stupid.

Again—you shouldn't try simply to insert your company specifics into the script you see above. You should use all the ideas I've given you in this chapter, combine it with your function, feature, advantage, and benefit material, and make it yours.

Take a moment to develop your own opening statement right now, using a copy of the Opening Statement Worksheet.

---

**Opening Statement Worksheet**

Your Suspect's Name (and Group or Type):_____

_____

Pleasantry: _____

_____

Hook: _____

_____

Your Name (and Title): _____

_____

Ending Question: _____

_____

---

Of course, not everyone you talk to will give you an appointment; that's simply the nature of sales. But everyone you talk to by means of this script will give you a good idea about whether or not he or she is interested in making the transition from suspect to prospect.

Don't get overly concerned about the specific responses to your contact's interruptions just yet. The idea is to let the other person take control of the conversation. Sometimes that will turn into an appointment. Sometimes it won't. Don't cajole, don't push, and don't attempt to change the person's mind. Ride the wave and conclude the call promptly and politely as soon as it's appropriate to do so. You'll learn all about dealing with specific objections—both on the phone and in person—in Chapter 15 of this book.

# A Few Words About Gatekeepers

If you're planning to make telephone calls or in-person visits to suspects and prospects, you'll be running into two very different types of gatekeepers. It's vitally important that you learn to distinguish between

➤ Receptionist gatekeepers, and

➤ Administrative assistant gatekeepers.

## Receptionist Gatekeepers

These people are the front line of the organization's "defense." However, their goal is not, as you might sometimes think, to make the salesperson's life a living hell. It's to make sure calls are routed quickly and efficiently to the proper individual.

**Sales Accelerator**
These days, many organizations employ electronic call management systems that allow you to skip human receptionists altogether. Do some re-search; call ahead and ask (briefly!) for confirmation on the spelling of your contact's name. Then, on your second call, you can try to spell your way through the company's electronic directory.

For the most part, receptionist gatekeepers are pleasant, helpful individuals who are truly interested in making sure the right people get connected with one another. Over the years, salespeople have given these folks more than their fair share of grief by:

➤ Asking endless questions

➤ Trying to engage in long-winded discussions

➤ Stretching the truth (or worse)

➤ Claiming to know people they don't

➤ Adopting a smug or condescending manner

Don't do any of that stuff! These activities undermine your career growth in both the short and long terms.

Instead, follow these two simple rules in your dealings with receptionist gatekeepers:

➤ Always tell the truth.

➤ Don't get huffy if the person asks "What's the call about?"

In fact, the fastest way to get connected to the person you're trying to reach is to tell the gatekeeper receptionist exactly what the call is about. All you have to do is deliver a (slightly compressed) version of your hook, the one you've prepared for your opening statement. Let's be honest: A hook that will make sense to your ultimate goal, the suspect, may or may not make sense to the gatekeeper receptionist. This gives us two possible scenarios.

➤ The busy receptionist understands exactly what you're talking about. (In the majority of cases, your call will go right through to your target person.)

➤ The busy receptionist will have no idea what you're talking about, but will understand who you want to talk to. (In the majority of cases, your call will go right through to your target person.)

What's to whine about? Be honest and up-front with receptionist gatekeepers who ask what the call is about. They're only doing their job!

**Sales Accelerator**
When receptionist gatekeepers say, "Would you like to leave a message?" say this: "Yes, thanks for asking, but it's a rather long message. I have an idea. Let me save us both some time. Please give me Ms. Bigshot's fax number. I'll fax my message; your switchboard sounds busy." You'll usually get the number. (I like to fax notes on an oversized "While You Were Out" form—this gets great results!)

## Administrative Assistant Gatekeepers

If you're trying to reach directors or leaders, you'll most likely spend some time talking to the trusted administrative assistant gatekeeper.

The vast majority of salespeople make a fatal mistake here. They turn these people into enemies. Don't do that. The administrative assistant, as a general rule, knows all, sees all, and controls all access. (Truth be told, many of them are better informed, and more on top of things, than their bosses are.) The administrative assistant is not a person you want to get mad!

There is one simple rule to keep in mind when dealing with the administrative assistant who works for a director or leader. Here it is.

Treat this person exactly the way you'd treat the director or leader.

No exceptions, no variations, no kidding. It's a bit of a mistake to say this person is the "power behind the throne." The administrative assistant is, not infrequently, the power ON the throne, in that he or she takes over and runs the work group, department, or company when the leader isn't there! (Quite a few of them run the show when the director or leader IS there.) Treat these people with the respect they deserve.

Whenever an administrative assistant answers the phone, you have, for all intents and purposes, reached your contact. Launch into your opening statement; the only change you'll make will be to use the administrative assistant's name instead of the director's or leader's. (You'll want to confirm both names—that of your target person and his or her administrative assistant—before you make this call.)

The downside to this approach? The administrative assistant can reject you. But guess what? He or she can do that anyway, so you might as well be nice. The upside? By making your statement to this all-important gatekeeper, you'll…

➤ Win rapport with the administrative assistant,

➤ Convince the administrative assistant that your ideas are sound, and

➤ (In the vast majority of cases) earn the right to speak to the boss.

## Try It!

Most salespeople make no distinction between the two types of gatekeepers, and simply try to bully their way through. My approach to dealing with these two (very different) members of the target organization takes all the conflict and misery out of interactions with gatekeepers and lets you get where you need to be: on the gatekeeper's good side. That's a desirable destination, since these people control your access to key players, and thus, control your income!

## The Least You Need to Know

➤ The first few seconds of your opening statement are absolutely critical.

➤ Your opening statement should contain: Your suspect's name, a pleasantry, a hook targeted toward your contact, your name, and an ending question.

➤ Be honest when dealing with receptionists and assistants.

➤ Treat assistants as though they were their boss—you won't be far from the truth.

YOU MAY GO RIGHT
IN MR. CONNER...

# Chapter 13

# Getting (and Showing Up for) In-Person Appointments

> **In This Chapter**
>
> ➤ Your image
>
> ➤ Meeting and greeting
>
> ➤ Handling the preliminary stages of the appointment

So, you've developed an opening statement, one that (we'll assume) you'll use on the phone to reach a number of suspects, prospects, and yes, even customers who represent that all-important add-on business. You've taken some time to develop a customized message that appeals to particular players (typically directors or leaders). In the vast majority of your calls, you'll be interrupted by someone before you finish your statement; in a few, you'll get all the way through to your ending question. In this chapter, you'll learn what happens next.

## "No Thanks!"

Some of the people will take a pass on the option of talking with you in depth about your product, service, or solution. (Hey, that's no problem. The name of the game in cold calling is removing people who don't belong in the funnel, right?)

**Sales Accelerator**

For most successful salespeople, cold calling is a regular part of the daily and weekly sales routine. Don't let complacency get the better of you. Even if you're ahead of quota, even if you've got plenty of sales today, if you want to have income tomorrow, you'll usually need to devote time—perhaps five to six hours a week—to prospecting by phone.

If you put to good use all of the suggestions, tactics and strategies for listening and asking questions that are addressed later in this book, you'll be able to pick up on the other person's impatience or unwillingness to talk. Hey—it's possible that your call is not a timely one for the other person. If you get these "bad vibes" over the phone, it's time for you to terminate the call and leave the door open for later contact. What you say could sound like this:

➤ It appears that I've caught you at an inconvenient time. I'll call you back some other day. Have a pleasant [morning/afternoon]. (Click.)

➤ I'm so sorry—I didn't mean for the call to interrupt your [morning/afternoon]. You seem busy. I'll call back at a later date. Have a productive day! (Click.)

## "Tell Me More"

Some of your contacts, though, will express an interest in what you have to offer. They'll turn themselves from suspects into prospects. They'll say things like, "That sounds interesting," or "What other companies have you worked with?" or "What's your circulation?" Or, perhaps, if your ending question features some reference to future contact, "What's this 'next step' you're talking about?"

**Watch It!**

Some sales managers may expect you to "go for the close" at each and every face-to-face meeting. (Mine used to bark "Don't come back without a contract!" when he saw me grabbing my briefcase and heading for the door.) This approach may work for some industries and settings—but if it doesn't work for yours, it may be time to either a) have a heart-to-heart talk with your manager, or b) update your résumé.

Typically, your objective is going to be to get these folks to tell you to show up for an in-depth meeting of some kind. Most of the time, when your hook has truly aroused someone's interest, that's what will happen: You'll be summoned to appear before the Wizard. Leaders, in particular, are very good about issuing orders to people about attending meetings. They love telling people what to do, so you're going to let them do just that. In a few cases, you may want to nudge your contact ever so slightly by saying something like this:

You: Ms. Prospect, do you think we ought to set a time to discuss this in detail sometime next week?

When the prospect says "yes" to that question, or tells you to drop by for a meeting, take down all the relevant information, confirm the date, and stop talking. Don't try to sell. Don't try to convince. Don't repeat yourself. Just double-check the specifics.

A prospect who agrees to a meeting doesn't want you to try to "close" him or her over the phone. Once the meeting is set, continue to follow the prospect's lead and back off the moment he or she seems to want to conclude the conversation.

> ### Bet You Didn't Know
>
> Face-to-face meetings aren't just for suspects and prospects. The head person in any organization you currently sell to is, in all likelihood, a great coach waiting to give you support and advice. You should meet with this person, too!
>
> Just about every sales job requires you to keep existing customers happy. Make sure you meet in person, or at the very least speak by phone with, the directors at each and every one of your current accounts. Your existing contacts should be able to help you get in touch with these folks; the letter you saw in Chapter 11 will help, too. Demonstrate how you add value to this person's organization!

## Where Are You Going?

Let's say you've set up a meeting with a contact you haven't yet met. What should you do?

Don't waste your prospect's time, but do call the reception desk well before the appointment to confirm the address and directions you'll need. Plan on showing up at least ten minutes early. When confronted with unfamiliar or challenging sites, consider a "trial drive" the day before that will allow you to make absolutely sure you've got the directions right.

Don't be late to the appointment!

## How Should You Look?

Your wardrobe selection and overall appearance will, of course, have a major impact on the first visual impression your prospect receives from you. You'll want to send signals of competence and professionalism during the first meeting—and every meeting thereafter!

What is appropriate attire for the in-person sales call? Your company may have guidelines here; ask your sales manager or immediate superior if he or she has any suggestions. If the issue is left up to you to resolve (and it may well be), you may find the following suggestions on dress, grooming, and accessories helpful:

**Watch It!**
Your image is your livelihood, so make sure your clothes are pressed and clean for each and every sales visit you make. If that means a quick pit stop somewhere for a change of clothes at midday, so be it.

➤ Dress to match or complement the individuals or companies you'll be calling on. For three years, I sold to the U.S. Navy. No, I didn't wear an admiral's uniform, but you can bet I didn't wear a business suit, either! That would have screamed "outsider." Instead, I wore a blue sport jacket (which I removed at the earliest opportunity), a well pressed Oxford shirt, a sharp-looking pair of beige slacks, and some casual shoes polished to a high sheen.

**Sales Accelerator**

One good all-purpose "uniform" for men selling in a commercial environment: Dark business suit, white shirt, stylish tie, shined business shoes, and no flashy jewelry. For women: Conservative business suit, limited accent jewelry, polished shoes. Use moderate makeup and perfume. For both genders: Make sure your look is conservative and business-oriented!

➤ Your grooming should, of course, be immaculate. Every hair should be in place; every fingernail should be appropriately trimmed and cleaned. Men: Avoid the five o'clock shadow syndrome!

➤ Your briefcase should be attractive and professional looking, inside and out. Trade in that bumped, battered model for a new case. Make sure that people who happen to look inside the case come away impressed by how well organized you are.

It should go without saying, of course, that you must pay sufficient attention to personal hygiene issues before going on a sales call. If you have any doubts about body odor or breath order, do whatever you have to do to make those doubts disappear. Pop a breath mint or quickly brush your teeth before the meeting.

## Study the Surroundings, Sherlock

If you have a scheduled apppointment, and if you follow my advice about showing up early, you're probably going to spend some time in the lobby.

Take a look around. Are there plaques on the wall celebrating high achievements in quality, customer service, or sales? Are there lists of famous clients, or letters from satisfied customers? Pull out a notebook from your briefcase and write down all the pertinent information. (Some salespeople carry small pocket tape recorders and dictate this information discreetly while they're waiting for a contact.) Is there a company newsletter you can read—and keep?

Do you notice any of your competitors' names? Are there any product boxes lying around bearing brand names that look familiar? For that matter, did you see any trucks unloading the competition's wares in the loading dock? Jot everything down in your notebook, including any evidence you've spotted that offers you insights on the company's financial situation. (Are people working out of temporary offices? Does this mean there's construction going on?)

# "Come On In"

Eventually, your contact (or someone who represents your contact) is going to tell you to come into the Inner Sanctum. Once you do, you're going to engage in some kind of social interaction, and you're going to need an ice-breaker statement.

A winning ice-breaker statement is:

➤ **Sincere.** That smile is essential—as long as it's genuine!

➤ **Relevant, but not too personal.** Don't, for instance, compliment a contact of the opposite sex about his or her looks or wardrobe.

➤ **Unapologetic.** Say what you have to say and wait for the response that is a natural part of social discourse.

➤ **Something you can come back to again comfortably at the end of the meeting.** In other words, as you head out the door, you want to be able to say something like, "I'll be keeping an eye out for you on the tube, now that I know you've got those season tickets!"

Here are some examples of less-than-effective, and effective, ice-breaker statements. Not that, in the last case, a longwinded, "I"-heavy icebreaker fails the test!

Less-Than-Effective: "Nice lobby."

Effective: "Nice lobby! It was a real treat to read about all of your company's accomplishments in the newsletter. By the looks of the plaques and trophies up on the wall, this is a very rewarding place to work! How long have you been part of the team?"

Less-Than-Effective: "That's a beautiful picture. Is that your family?"

Effective: "That's a beautiful picture! Was that actually taken outside, or is that a studio shot?"

Less-Than-Effective: "What beautiful plants you have in your office. I'm a grower, I guess you could say. I love the way gardening lets you forget all about the pressures of life. My good friend Noriko is helping me to grow bonsai. I could tell you all about the fundamentals of that ancient art..."

**Words, Words, Words**
Your *ice-breaker* statement is the first sentence or two you say to a new acquaintance during a face-to-face meeting. It's usually issued in an effort to build rapport and ease any tension you or the prospect (most likely you) happen to be feeling.

**Sales Accelerator**
At some point during your initial face-to-face encounter with your contact—perhaps right before your ice-breaker statement—you'll want to deliver a strong handshake and look the other person in the eye with confidence. Avoid the "wet fish" or "bonecrusher" handshake variations at all cost.

**155**

Effective: "What beautiful plants you have in your office! They add a real sense of serenity and purpose."

# Assuming Responsibility

Don't get too hung up with the small talk. Use it as a transition. When you're making an in-person sales call, you'll be working against the clock. (In most cases, your prospect will have agreed to see you for a limited period of time, such as 15 minutes.) Be prepared to pull the conversation (tactfully but firmly!) back to the business world with a question that shows you're assuming professional responsibility for a successful meeting.

Say your ice-breaker question took the form of a brief comment about a beach volleyball trophy in your contact's office, and your contact has decided to launch into a long discourse about volleyball. At an appropraite break in the conversation, your question could sound like this:

> "So—(little pause, little smile)—Mr. Prospect, do you feel that your assembly line team on your factor floor has the same focus on zero-defect performance that your volleyball team obviously did?"

It's part of your job as the salesperson to keep the conversation on track. Don't apologize for doing your job. Smile and wait for the prospect to follow your lead.

# Phase One, in Which You're Invited to Ramble On

You've shaken hands—confidently but not overpoweringly. You've exchanged some small talk with your contact. You've made it into the other person's office. Now what?

There will come a point at the beginning of the meeting proper where your contact will look at you expectantly. He or she may say something along the following lines:

➤ "So—tell me all about what you do."

➤ "Give me all the details."

➤ "I want to hear everything you have to say."

➤ "What's on your mind?"

➤ "What did you want to talk to me about?"

As tempted as you may be, upon hearing such stuff, to launch into a seven-minute monologue about the miracles you've wrought for your legions of happy customers, don't do it.

Repeat (or, if you've never spoken with this person before, deliver for the first time) the "hook" portion of your opening statement, complete with targeted function, feature, advantage, or benefit for your contact's benefit, and then get ready to ask a question that will tell you about your contact's position and mindset. (You'll find out exactly what kind of question makes sense in the next chapter.)

The truth of the matter is that you simply do not know enough about your contact or his or her target organization yet to start discoursing about the solutions you can offer. Even though a lot of prospects (particularly directors) would like to believe that you can offer instant analysis and implementation plans after 30 seconds of discussion, you can't, and it's not in anyone's best interests for you to pretend that you can.

That "take-it-from-the-top" moment is when the real work of your first meeting with the buyer starts. In the next chapter, you'll learn how to win the right to ask the questions you need to ask—even if the other person doesn't seem to be interested in answering questions yet. You'll also learn how to target your questions, so that you can find out exactly what you need to know about this buyer, this department, and this organization.

# The Least You Need to Know

➤ Make sure you look sharp.

➤ Double-check your directions, and consider making a trial drive, to the target organization where your first appointment is scheduled.

➤ Use your "lobby time" to learn about the target organization.

➤ Use effective ice-breaker statements to make the initial meet-and-greet stage flow smoothly.

➤ Don't accept the invitation to ramble on about your product, service, or solution. Instead, run through your hook again, and prepare to ask key questions.

# Part 4
# In Depth

*Preliminary discussions. Presentations. Committees. Questions. Objections. Reviews. Technical analyses. Revisions and re-presentations.*

*Depending on whom you ask, this is either the part of the sales process that really tests your mettle, or the part where you get to do what you love to do most. In this part of the book, you'll find out about the best sales strategies for negotiating the occasionally intimidating territory that lies beyond "Yes, we'll talk to you about such-and-such."*

# Chapter 14

# Any Questions? (Well, Yes...)

**In This Chapter**

➤ What your questions should accomplish

➤ The five questioning scenarios

➤ Designing effective questions

➤ The preliminary suggestion

So, you've gotten to a critical point in your initial contact with your suspect or prospect. You've been ushered into the other person's office, you've had a little small talk, and perhaps, after things have gotten sidetracked, you've pointed the conversation toward the business at hand: business.

In one way or another, silently or overtly, the contact (who may be a suspect, a prospect, or a new contact in an existing organization) has asked you to "take it from the top"—to start expounding on all the solutions you can deliver. Problem: you probably know next to nothing about the challenges this person faces on a day-to-day basis. The truth of the matter is, you *can't* make any recommendations yet, but you don't want to waste precious minutes of your sales call explaining that to your contact!

In this chapter, you learn what to do next—and how to pose the questions that will help you make recommendations that will benefit everyone.

# Your Objectives

The next phase of your discussion is going to focus on your questions about the person and the organization you're dealing with. The results you want from these questions are pretty straightforward.

➤ You want your questions to build rapport and establish your business credibility.

➤ You want your questions to show that you're interested, that you have empathy.

➤ You want your questions to get the prospect to think (or say), "Great question! You've really got an understanding of what I'm all about."

➤ You want your questions to shine some light on which of these contacts are most likely to buy from you, and to accelerate the sales process with likely buyers you identify.

➤ You want your questions to help you track down critical information.

Before you can start asking questions that point you in the right directions in these areas, however, you've got to find out some more about your prospect.

# Beyond "Take It from the Top"

You'll recall that, in your initial attempts to contact this person or discuss what your organization has to offer, you won his or her attention and interest by focusing on a particular elements of your product, servce, or solution. You made an inspired guess about where this person fell in the network of influence and authority, and then you tailored your message to this person accordingly.

For leaders, you highlighted benefits.

For directors, you highlighted advantages.

For influencers, you highlighted features.

For consumers, you highlighted functions.

Right now, you know, or at least have some idea, of what this person does. To get out of the "take-it-from-the-top" trap, you're going to have use a question that allows you to highlight the benefit, advantage, feature, or function again. And, based on what you hear in response, you're going to gather some crucial information about the personal style of this buyer.

So, when you reach "take-it-from-the-top" phase, you're going to give a brief (and I do mean brief) description of your company or organization's history. This, after all, is what your conversational partner expects to hear. And then you're going to repeat—or, if you're talking to this person for the very first time, introduce—the hook you developed for your opening statement. Once you've done that, you're going to pose a simple version of your ending question—one that asks your conversational partner, in essence, what he or she things about what you just said. At that point, you're going to listen very carefully to what you hear in response—and make a decision about how this person operates.

Assume, for the sake of argument, that you're meeting with a leader. The dialogue is going to sound something like this:

> Leader: So, Will, you asked for 15 minutes, and I'm giving you 15 minutes. What have you people to tell me about widgets?

> You: Mr. Prospect, we're XYZ, the nation's fastest-growing widget retooling company. We've helped ABC Widget Corporation reduce its overhead costs by 12 percent this quarter—and they did it without laying off staff or sacrificing product quality.

**Watch It!**
Debates kill sales. Don't get hung up on the specific, literal truth or falsehood of what you say or the prospect says in response to your question. The true "meaning" of your exchange will be dictated by some subtler interpersonal cues. Keep an eye out for *how* your prospect responds, and stick with the question types that produce engaged, positive interactions.

If your prospect interrupts you at this point, great! You don't even need to ask the next question. Disengage and listen carefully to what he or she has to say. If you don't get an interruption, continue with...

> You: Mr. Prospect, what do you think about the possibility of reducing your overhead costs with a program similar to ABC's?

# Then What?

There are, in my experience, five possible ways for the conversation to proceed at this point.

➤ The prospect can stonewall you and provide you with no meaningful feedback. This is no fun, but it tells you something! Either you're talking to the wrong person, or there's only a minimal potential for a good match here than you might have hoped.

➤ The prospect can start picking apart some aspect of what you've just said—a process that may occupy a fair chunk of time!

➤ The prospect can start talking about himself or herself in an energetic way.

➤ After appearing to enjoy your statement, the prospect can start fidgeting slightly, or otherwise show some discomfort about the direct question you've just posed.

➤ The prospect, in your response to your "What do you think about X?" question, can immediately deliver a concise, direct, and decisive response outlining exactly what he or she thinks about X.

# Five Different Scenarios

Once you've got an idea of how your prospect operates, what do you do next?

Following, you'll find some vitally important strategies for dealing with all five of the scenarios we've just identified. Once you've taken a look at these specific suggestions, you'll be ready to examine a few broader techniques for posing questions—techniques that are likely to help you make good progress with buyers in just about any selling situation.

# Stonewall

This is the first possibility. The prospect says nothing—or issues distracted grunts, or curt responses, to your question. (Examples: "I don't know," or, "What should I think?" or, "It's not my area," all followed by a vacant stare.)

If you get no meaningful response whatsoever to the question you've posed, guess what? You're not talking to someone who's interested in moving the sales process forward with you. At this point, you should explore the possibility of talking to someone else in the organization, and perhaps secure a referral:

> "Is there someone else in the organization you feel would benefit from talking about this?"

The stonewall approach doesn't reflect any particular operating style. In all likelihood, it simply means you've inherited someone whose interest is elsewhere, or who has no real involvement in or responsibility for what you're discussing. Don't invest significant amounts of time or energy trying to "convert" prospects who stonewall. If you can't move forward with a referral to someone else in the organization, and your contact doesn't make it clear he or she occupies one of the following four categories, simply say "thank you," leave your card, and move on to the next opportunity on your list.

# "Pick It Apart": The Analytical Approach

In this scenario, when you ask your prospect what he or she thinks about X, the contact tries to get you to define your terms, or somehow questions the specifics underlying your question. (Examples: "How did they measure overhead cost?" or "What's your definition of overhead?" or "How did you measure quality?") Perhaps the person launches a master class on how what you've been talking about should be evaluated and put into the proper perspective.

Don't get defensive—you now know that you've hooked up with a buyer who takes an analytical approach. This is the "see more" buyer, the contact who always wants to see more data, more charts, more data points, before making a decision.

The questions you pose from this point onward must:

➤ Be as detailed as possible. ("Mr. Smith, what is the specification you feel would serve the AC power requirements of your automatic grinding units?")

➤ Use numbers and percentages. ("Mr. Smith, of the five parameters you mention, what is your department's priority in solving them—and can any of the five go unresolved?")

➤ Help the buyer clarify his or her priorities. ("Mr. Smith, putting any concerns of price and delivery aside for amoment, does this system address the input-output ratio problem you raised a little earlier?")

➤ Appeal, where appropriate, to the endorsements of authoritative third parties.

➤ Be very narrowly focused.

➤ Use current products, services, and experiences as a starting point.

➤ Resolve one issue before proceeding to the next, because analytical buyers will not be interested in focusing on issues you raise if they violate strict logical sequence. Warning: They also won't take kindly to interruptions, and will view these as evidence that you don't really know their situation! ("Mr. Smith, before we tackle your supply problems—are we in agreement that the Splash 1,000 system handles all the rinsing problems you raised?")

**Words, Words, Words**
The buyer who takes an *analytical approach* is factual, serious, steadfast, hard-working, exacting, systematic, and critical. He or she can be an extremely valuable ally as the sales process moves forward. The analytical buyer lives for details, details, details!

**Watch It!**
"Gut feelings" won't cut it with buyers who take an analytical approach! Don't make statements to "see more" buyers if you can't back up what you say with hard data.

Words and phrases to use in your questions and preparatory statements for the analytical buyer:

| | | |
|---|---|---|
| ➤ Comprehensive | ➤ Total | ➤ Learn more about... |
| ➤ Exact | ➤ Sweeping | ➤ Match the capabilities of... |
| ➤ Exactly | ➤ Full-length | ➤ Leave no stone unturned |
| ➤ Extensive | ➤ Solution | ➤ We've confirmed all the information... |
| ➤ Exhaustive | ➤ Discover | ➤ I've personally confirmed all the information... |
| ➤ Researched | ➤ We are certain... | ➤ This is exactly where X fits in |

Words and phrases to avoid in your questions and preparatory statements for the analytical buyer:

➤ I'm not sure, but…

➤ Approximately

➤ Comfortable (these folks are never comfortable about work!)

➤ Maybe

➤ Perhaps

➤ Need

➤ I'll try to find out…

➤ I'll try to get it to you by…

➤ How do you feel about…

➤ I don't know

➤ There's no way to prove…

Your questions to the analytical buyer should sound something like this:

"What are the four most important characteristics you're looking for in your new office furniture?" This use of numbers can help you clarify priorities.

"All right: quality, guarantee, steel frames, and cherry wood were at the top of your list. How do these requirements compare to your existing office furniture?" Restate the answer for the analytical buyer, so he or she knows you've "got it." Then compare the criteria to a known source.

"What don't you like about the way your current office furniture layout affects traffic patterns in your department?" Allowing buyers who take an analytical approach to discourse on what doesn't work now is one of the best ways to get them to open up.

## Talk, Talk, Talk: The Expressive Approach

You've asked what your prospect thinks about what you have to offer, and your contact has started talking at great length. Your question hasn't resulted in a thumbnail sketch, but a detailed painting that takes up a huge canvas. When this happens, odds are you've hooked up with a buyer who takes an expressive approach.

Ask these people how they feel and then give them plenty of time to tell you! If you let them talk, they'll be convinced of your extraordinary intelligence, and they'll consider you an ally for life. Some people at work have an unfortunate habit of asking these folks to "summarize things briefly." They hate that. Let them get everything out—and remember, expressive buyers (like the rest of us) may view interruptions as an insult that indicates an uncaring approach.

Don't ask questions that carry even a hint of challenge. These buyers will go to great lengths to avoid being put on the spot. Talk in terms of reactions, feelings, and responses, not lists and requirements.

Ask questions that feature built-in compliments because stature and acknowledgment are very important to these buyers. Ask questions that allow them to imagine themselves using the product, service, or solution. (One of my favorite questions with this group is: "Can I take your picture next to the Model X widget?" Then I snap a Polaroid and keep it in front of the expressive buyer at all times!)

Buyers who take an expressive approach love to talk to people who love to listen. That's how they build alliances.

Words and phrases to use in your questions and preparatory statements for the expressive buyer:

> **Words, Words, Words**
> Buyers who take an *expressive approach* are a little like that fellow in the old joke who, when asked what time it was, started giving an explanation about how he chose the watch he wears. These buyers are friendly, enthusiastic, spontaneous, talkative, self-promoting, independent, commanding, and creative. They love to be the center of attention, and they can sometimes be a bit manipulative.

- ➤ How do you feel about...
- ➤ You're our first priority...
- ➤ Just between you and me...
- ➤ Can you imagine yourself...
- ➤ Have you ever thought about...
- ➤ Let's face it...
- ➤ You can join in...
- ➤ Everyone speaks highly of this...
- ➤ Have you ever stayed awake at night thinking about...
- ➤ What can I do to help you (take advantage of/seize the opportunity to meet X goal)
- ➤ Will you be in a position to...

Words and phrases to avoid in your questions and preparatory statements for the expressive buyer:

- ➤ We can't...
- ➤ Only larger/selected/major clients are eligible for (solution your buyer has expressed an interest in)
- ➤ You didn't...
- ➤ That's not available...
- ➤ You don't qualify
- ➤ I can only...
- ➤ That's outside my area of responsibility.

Your questions to the expressive buyer should sound something like this:

"Your office is so up and cheerful; your employees must really respect you. How do you keep the atmosphere focused so positively with such aggressive performance

levels?" (Your first question should incorporate some kind of direct, credible complement; if that means you have to stray from the business at hand for a moment, so be it.)

"I can tell you've got a lot of experience with automated systems; you don't win the manager-of-the-quarter award in your area without a strong background in that area. Tell me, what improvements do you feel are necessary within the next 90 days to keep your team focused, happy, and performing at above-target levels?" (Wherever possible, tie your questions to the particular achievements of the expressive buyer.)

"Between you and me, what are your feelings so far about the way our widgets might fit in with what your team is doing, given what you've heard from me so far?" (Keep the tone friendly and confidential.)

## "You Like Me!": The Amiable Approach

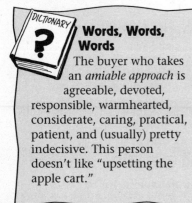

You asked a direct question, and your contact started acting as though you'd kidnapped the cat. It's time to slow down and take things one step at a time because you've almost certainly hooked up with a buyer who takes an amiable approach.

It may have taken a direct question for you to identify this buyer, but now that you know who you're dealing with, you should stay away from queries that require on-the-spot evaluations or assessments from here on out. Be prepared to invest some time with this buyer; he or she will usually make a point of avoiding snap decisions. (People might get mad if the decision isn't the right one!)

Be in agreement as much as you possibly can with the amiable buyer. Cite tradition and precedent wherever you can—highlight what's worked!

Words and phrases to use in your questions and preparatory statements for the amiable buyer:

➤ Together we can...

➤ Would it make your colleague/superior/ spouse/relative/ happy to know...

➤ Did you know that...

➤ Can I ask for your help?

➤ I'm confused; can you help me?

➤ Would you take just a moment and help clear something up for me?

➤ Don't gamble/take chances with…

➤ What's the safest way to…

Remember: The amiable buyer doesn't like change. Your questions should not point toward dramatic shifts or startling new initiatives. Words like "new" and "revolutionary" may scare off the amiable buyer.

Other words and phrases to avoid in your questions and preparatory statements for the amiable buyer:

➤ Can you…

➤ Should you…

➤ Shouldn't you…

➤ What would you like for me to do next? (or any variation thereof)

➤ Do you want me to…

➤ When will you (finalize this/make up your mind/reach a decision)?

➤ I'll leave it up to you

➤ If you don't (take action/make a decision/finalize) you'll miss out on…

> **Words, Words, Words**
> Buyers who take a *driver approach* are determined, tough, efficient, assertive, dominating, decisive, direct, and, not infrequently, hungry for power and authority. Driver buyers have a way of delivering "yes" and "no" answers crisply and quickly—and sticking to their guns.

Your questions to the amiable buyer should sound something like this:

"Can you help me understand what your feelings are about the office furniture you've been considering for your employees?" (Focus on feelings, not facts.)

"If you were to picture yourself and your team selling a new line of educational books, what would be the most important topics related to meeting customer needs?" (Emphasize the team; emphasize happy end users.)

"Do you feel that our mailing station is the kind of resource you want your team to have, or shall we look at other ways of addressing their needs?" (Keep the options open—don't pressure for yes-or-no answers.)

> **Sales Accelerator**
> It's a good idea to avoid, whenever possible, using the words "I" and "me" in your dealings with suspects, prospects, customers, and business partners. It's a *great* idea to avoid these words in your dealing with buyers who take a driver approach. Driver buyers may listen to an appeal that uses "we," but they'll tune out of an "I" monologue in a heartbeat. The only exception to this rule: Personal commitments, complete with deadlines!

# "Pass the Nine Iron!": The Driver Approach

**Watch It!**
Don't get too hung up on the idea of "scripting" your interviews with buyers. The other person won't know the script! Your objective is simple, keep your buyer talking about problems that match those of your Template of Ideal Prospects.

**Sales Accelerator**
Any buyer in the network of influence of authority—leaders, directors, influencers, and consumers—can operate under any personal style—analytical, expressive, amiable, or driver. As a practical matter, though, most effective leaders tend to operate from a driver mindset, and the majority of influencers are analytical. Directors and consumers tend to adopt a wider range of styles.

It's going to be very easy for you to figure out when you're dealing with a buyer who takes the driver approach. You'll ask the contact what he or she thinks of X, and you'll get a direct, cut-to-the-chase response. In the blink of an eye, the ball will be back in your court. The buyer will look at you as if to say, "Next!"

Although he or she may not always be easy to deal with, the buyer who adopts the driver style may occupy a significant center of power within your target organization. And, in most cases, you'll know exactly where you stand with these blunt folks.

Keep your questioning approach very direct and to the point. Don't hedge or argue with the driver, or try to bog him or her down with details. It's all right to challenge a driver—but not to argue. Stick to the big picture, and don't be afraid to ask for your contact's opinion!

Words and phrases to use in your questions and preparatory statements for the amiable buyer:

➤ What's your opinion about…

➤ What's the best way for you to…

➤ Which one of these (benefits/results/topics) is of the greatest importance to you during (specific time frame)?

➤ Have I understood you correctly about…

➤ We're sure…

➤ We can…

➤ Isn't it about time to…

Words and phrases to avoid in your questions and preparatory statements for the amiable buyer:

➤ I suggest…

➤ I want to…

➤ In my/our opinion…

➤ You should…

➤ Listen to this…

➤ Do you understand?

➤ Were you aware of…

➤ Did you know…

➤ Let me tell you…

Your questions to the driver buyer should sound something like this:

"Of the three situations you just mentioned, which are you most concerned about during the holiday buying season?" (Rule number one: Drivers get to set their own agenda. Feel free to offer your own list of topics, but don't be surprised when your contact adds to it or shreds it to pieces.)

"What do you see as the biggest challenge in your marketing department—the challenge that, if solved, would result in the overachievement of your goals for the balance of the year?" (Drivers like to win. Focus on not just hitting goals, but beating them.)

"When do you feel X will become a priority for your organization?" (Even a driver who tells you he or she has no interest in what you have to offer will usually give you an honest answer to this question.)

**Bet You Didn't Know**

No matter who your target audience is, you can add drama, decision, and power to any sales question. Here are some examples of "yawn" and "tell me more!" versions of the very same basic questions:

Yawn: Would you be interested in learning about a special sale we're offering next month?

Tell Me More!: If you're shopping for sales next month, ma'am, you may want to consider taking a look at our special offering. Would you like me to put you on our mailing list, or shall I call you before the sale begins?

Yawn: Suppose we could find a way to improve the quality of your widgets. Would you ask us to be your supplier?

Tell Me More!: How would you solve this quality problem to your personal satisfaction?

Yawn: Are you happy with your new appliance?

Tell Me More!: In the last 30 days, what have you found that you would change about your new appliance? What have you found that you really love about it?

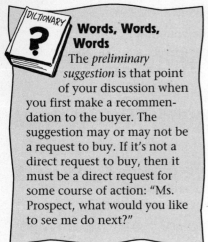

**Words, Words, Words**

The *preliminary suggestion* is that point of your discussion when you first make a recommendation to the buyer. The suggestion may or may not be a request to buy. If it's not a direct request to buy, then it must be a direct request for some course of action: "Ms. Prospect, what would you like to see me do next?"

# The Art of Asking Good Questions

Your aim is to develop a pattern of conversation that makes perfect sense to your buyer, whatever his or her style. Your aim is to speak the buyer's language, to establish a clear progression of questions, a progression that culminates, naturally and logically, in a preliminary suggestion.

You can't issue a successful preliminary suggestion if you don't have a solid grounding in the problems your buyer faces. You can't issue a successful preliminary suggestion if you don't sequence your questions intelligently, in a way that allows the buyer to participate fully in an examination of the issues you raise.

## How Not to Issue a Preliminary Suggestion

Here's an example of a question sequence that yanks the buyer, a leader who operates under a driver mindset, from point to point. It's unlikely, in my opinion, to yield great results for any salesperson who delivers it.

Salesperson: Have you ever seen display cases on the selling floor?

Leader: Nope.

Salesperson: 75 percent of our customers use these kinds of display units with great success. I think they could deliver superior results for you, too. What merchandise would you put in your display cases, if you were going to use this method?

Leader: Hard to say. I'd have to give it some thought. I've never tried anything like that before.

Here comes the preliminary suggestion:

Salesperson: How about this: Why don't you let me set you up with three display cases on your selling floor for the next 90 days and see what happens? (Or: Why don't I come back next week to show you what the display cases would look like?)

## A Better Way

Here's an example of a preliminary with the same buyer that serves as the culmination of a carefully structured sequence of questions. In my opinion, it's far likelier to lead to a partnership.

Salesperson: What's your feeling about display cases on the selling floor? Do you think they work better on the right or on the left?

Leader: I don't believe we've ever used display cases on the floor.

Salesperson: It's interesting, 75 percent of our 200 customers use them on the left side. If we placed display cases on the left-hand side, how do you think your customers would respond?

Leader: Well, I'd imagine it would depend on the merchandise put in the cases.

Here's the preliminary suggestion:

Salesperson: Let's take a sample of all your accessories, and place them in three display cases. I will personally monitor the sales over the next 90 days and report back to you with a summary of what's taken place. Is it worth a try? (Or: I'd like to have the members of my team show you in detail what we can do for you by using samples of all your accessories, and tracking the results for you in a customized report. What would you like for me to do next?)

Remember: Your preliminary suggestions may not be a request that the buyer purchase your product, service, or solution. In many cases—perhaps the majority—you'll close your first meeting with a request for a second meeting, a meeting at which you'll be able to deliver a detailed proposal based on what you've heard from your prospect.

# What If the Prospect Says "No"?

"Tony, it's all very well to ask for action—it's another thing to get the prospect to commit to it? What do I do when somebody throws an objection my way?"

Worry not! In the next chapter you'll learn how to analyze, respond to, and overcome objections—even real toughies.

# The Least You Need to Know

➤ Buyers who stonewall may be able to point you toward other people in the organization, but there's a good chance their organizations do not represent good investments for your time and energy.

➤ Buyers who take the analytical approach need questions that demonstrate your mastery of detail.

➤ Buyers who take the expressive approach need questions that let them expound at length.

➤ Buyers who take the amiable approach need questions that emphasize group acceptance and don't put them on the spot to make a hasty decision.

➤ Buyers who take the driver approach need questions that acknowledge their power and authority.

# Answering Questions, Overcoming Objections

Your initial discussion with the prospect has progressed nicely until—terror of terrors—you come face to face with an objection or a question that leaves you uncertain about how to respond. In this chapter, you learn how to get to the bottom of the responses your conversational partner sends your way and what to say in response that will move the sales process forward.

Most salespeople need no reminding that objections can be presented by suspects, prospects, customers, or even your very best business partner. The tactics you'll learn about in this chapter will work for all four groups.

## Rule Number One: Listen!

I learned the importance of listening early on in my sales career because I started it as a person very nearly deaf. I come from a long line of hard-of-hearing folks; after a stint in the U.S. Navy, I had the choice of wearing bulky hearing aids behind my rather bulky ears, or learning how to read lips to augment my meager auditory abilities. I chose lipreading.

Lipreading is hard work. It takes intense concentration, and you're mentally exhausted at the end of the day. But people can tell you're paying attention, which comes in handy when you're trying to sell people customized computer systems!

Some of my prospects, such as Grady Robertson, president of the Robertson Company in San Diego, came to rely on how closely I had to listen to them. I think Grady knew that I was paying much closer attention to him during my meetings than my competitors were. I hung on Grady's every word—I had to. He knew from the way I sat and watched him like a hawk that I was hooked in, and I think he appreciated it.

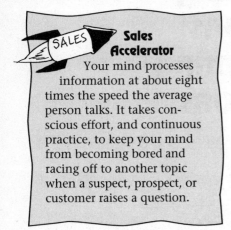

**Sales Accelerator**
Your mind processes information at about eight times the speed the average person talks. It takes conscious effort, and continuous practice, to keep your mind from becoming bored and racing off to another topic when a suspect, prospect, or customer raises a question.

Not long after selling Grady a customized computer system, I took the ample commission check that had come my way as a result and used it to buy a pair of hearing aids. (The industry had finally succeeded in developing a model small enough to fit inside my ears!) Shortly thereafter, I had another meeting with Grady. He was trying to explain a problem his company was having with the installation of his system when he stopped in mid-sentence. I thought the batteries in my new hearing aids had died!

Grady had noticed that my posture was completely different. Instead of leaning forward to catch his every word, I was hunched back in my seat. In fact, I wasn't even looking at Grady as he spoke! I was distracted by the sound of a maintenance man who had brought a ladder into the room to repair some ceiling tiles.

Grady said, "Tony, would you please take your hearing aids out? I need your full and undivided attention right now." Needless to say, I took them out immediately!

The point is *not* that every salesperson needs to wear earplugs and learn to lipread. The point *is* that, in addressing any objection or question from the prospect or customer, you must focus with extreme intensity on what the other person is saying and not on your own agenda!

**Sales Accelerator**
The best way to become an expert listener is to stay in the moment with the person who's doing the talking. Focus intently (but not aggressively) on the other person's every word and physical movement, and constantly ask yourself: "Why is this person telling me this?"

## Why It's So Hard to Listen

Yes, you have to train yourself to listen. This is because it's so easy not to listen. Unfortunately, when salespeople don't listen, simple questions have a way of hardening into extremely difficult objections.

There are many reasons salespeople don't listen effectively when prospects and customers raise questions and objections. Here are eight, in rough order of popularity:

➤ We're too busy thinking about what we're going to say next.

➤ We're too busy thinking about what the suspect, prospect, or customer is going to say next.

➤ We're too busy judging the other person's statement (as opposed to accepting it on its own terms).

➤ We're too busy drawing conclusions based on the other person's physical appearance.

➤ We've been distracted by a single word or phrase that's set off one of our own "hot buttons."

➤ We're thinking about something else.

➤ We don't understand some technical aspect of the topic that's been raised by the other person, and we're too embarrassed to ask for clarification. So we dwell on it.

➤ We assume that a story that's *similar* to one we've heard before is *identical* to one we've heard before. (When you catch yourself thinking "I've heard this before," watch out!)

**Words, Words, Words**

*High-level listening* occurs when words and phrases are heard, and responded to, with genuine emotion. High-level listeners make nonjudgmental associations, offer acceptance and validation, and offer empathetic support. In essence, high-level listening is listening that does not prejudge.

## Take Total Control of Your Mind!

By recognizing and overcoming common listening obstacles, you can make high-level listening more likely in your interactions with buyers.

When the other person asks you a question, you must be prepared to focus your mind so that you'll be in a perfect position to offer an appropriate response. This isn't easy to do, of course. Here are four steps you can take that will help you gain greater control of your mental resources whenever someone raises a question or makes an objection.

➤ Ask yourself: Why is this person telling/asking me this?

➤ Ask yourself: Does this person's body language match this statement/question?

➤ Ask yourself: What are the most important words this person is saying?

➤ Take notes! Use your own personalized system of abbreviations, if necessary, but pull out a pad and pen and start taking down each and every key point while the person is talking.

**Sales Accelerator**

If you can obtain the other person's permission, you may want to record your sales meetings and have them transcribed after the fact. Reviewing these written records can be a real eye-opener, and will help you improve your question—and objection-handling ability. (You'll often stop and ask yourself, "Did I really say that?")

**177**

Remember that this buyer is unique. Even though you may have spoken with lots of other people who had problems similar to this person's, you've never spoken to someone who had this particular problem. You can't predict what the buyer is going to say next, and you certainly can't assume that you know what motivates this person.

# Why Has This Issue Come Up?

"Is that turnaround time set in stone?"

"Who else have you worked with in our industry?"

"What kind of flexibility is there on price?"

You could answer each of these questions—or the hundreds like them—with simple, factual responses. But should you?

"The price is so high."

"You've got no experience in our field."

"The service plan isn't right for us."

You could offer logical responses to each of these statements—or the countless objections like them that your contact may throw up—but should you?

The next sections provide specific strategies and tactics you can use to handle difficult questions and objections.

# Dealing with Questions

**Words, Words, Words**

An *objection* is a stated reason, real or imagined, not to do something, or an expression of unwillingness, reluctance, or hesitation to buy or invest. Objections can, and often do, take the form of questions. Not doing something is often seen as being safer than doing something new, so objections are a part of everyday life for salespeople.

To answer any question in a sales setting, you must first understand why the person you're talking to has raised it. As a general rule, buyers ask questions for one of five reasons:

➤ The buyer genuinely wants additional information, or validation of facts already known.

➤ The buyer either didn't understand, or didn't believe something you or your organization presented.

➤ The buyer has a specific requirement that he or she wants to see addressed.

➤ The buyer is not yet convinced that you fully appreciate the importance of a particular requirement.

➤ The buyer is of the opinion that you haven't put forward an acceptable proposal, and is giving you a chance to revise what you're offering.

With buyers, it's sometimes difficult to tell which of these factors is in play. Fortunately, there's a simple three-step strategy you can use to evaluate questions. By working your way through this three-step system, which never concludes until your buyer acknowledges that you've "got it," you'll be playing it safe. You'll take your best guess about whether or not you should highlight additional information, clarify something, address a new requirement, revise your approach to a previously stated requirement, or highlight a positive outcome that will accompany working with you. Then you'll elicit feedback that will tell you whether or not your assessment was accurate.

When a prospect shares a question with you, you should…

1. Always restate it in your own words.
2. Show social proof to substantiate your answer.
3. Ask whether your answer was sufficient by using a question that influences the direction of the conversation.

## Restating the Question

This is *not* the same thing as repeating the question verbatim! (That's known as "parroting," and it's a very bad idea.) If a buyer asks you, "What kind of warranty comes with the widget?", you'll want to rephrase it to make it clear that you're paying attention, and that you have an idea of the core concern that's guiding the question.

You might say, for instance: "Service is important, isn't it? I can understand why you'd want to get the details on the Model X series warranty." By saying something like this, you'll be likelier to stay on-target with your response, and you'll increase the chance that the buyer will listen closely to your own answer.

Of course, there's no reason to restate questions to the buyer that have obvious or non-essential answers (such as, "Do you enjoy working for ABC Widget?").

## Showing Social Proof

Your presentation of social proof (proof that your product or service will meet the customer's needs) must be totally relevant to the present situation. It must also be easy to understand.

Here's an example of a fairly detailed question from a buyer, followed by an advanced restatement and the presentation of social proof.

> **Words, Words, Words**
> *Social proof* is real-world evidence that your proposed solution works. It may take the form of a testimonial, or it may be a report or summary developed for a current customer.

> Buyer: We've got several executives traveling at the same time to different destinations. Some of the people I track are supposed to reimburse us for some of the expenses they've incurred; others aren't. It can get

pretty confusing. How does your service separate the cost for airfare, limos, hotels, meals, miscellaneous expenses, all that sort of stuff?

You: (Restatement) Ms. Buyer, it's a good thing we use computers, because if a real, live person had to keep track of all those itineraries at the same time, with different locations, budgets, and line-items, it would take forever! (Social proof) Let me show you something I brought along. This is a report for XYZ company, which has a similar accounting requirement for its people. Notice that each person traveling is given a unique accounting code—in this case, the code is different for each category of expense. Your codes would be tailored to each of your executives; you'd assign only the codes that make sense for each person.

**Watch It!**
Asking buyers—particularly leaders and directors—whether they "understand" your response to their objection is a fool's gambit. Avoid it at all costs. (Would you ask your boss if she "understood" the verbal status report you just gave her?) A better course is to ask what else the buyer would like you to review.

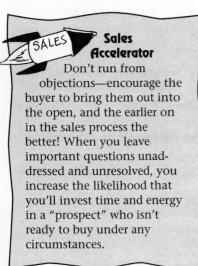

**Sales Accelerator**
Don't run from objections—encourage the buyer to bring them out into the open, and the earlier on in the sales process the better! When you leave important questions unaddressed and unresolved, you increase the likelihood that you'll invest time and energy in a "prospect" who isn't ready to buy under any circumstances.

## Did You Get It Right?

At the conclusion of your response, you're going to request feedback from the buyer, but you're going to do it in a very specific way. You've already taken an educated guess about the nature of the buyer's concern. (In the example I just gave, you guessed that the buyer was trying to highlight a key requirement for the first time.)

When you reach the end of your social proof presentation, you're going to ask for the buyer's input, and give him or her an alternative: "Would what I just outlined work, or would X be better instead?"

Here's what it might sound like:

You: Do you think this approach would give you the specificity you need, or does your office require something that goes into more detail in one of these areas?

If you've missed the boat entirely, the buyer will almost certainly let you know about it here.

## Responding to Objections

Yes, some of the questions you hear during your visit can accurately be described as objections. The advice that follows in this section, which applies to flatly stated objections ("You people are too expensive") can also help you resolve those tricky situations when your response to a buyer's question has led to a greater, rather than a smaller, distance between you.

(To review one extremely effective strategy for dealing with price-based objections, see Chapter 9.)

## Play It Cool

If you're passionate about what you do for a living—and I hope you are—you're going to have to make a determined effort to maintain your composure when a buyer starts launching objections about your product, service, or solution. It's natural, to some degree, to take these remarks personally, but it's also essential to keep your sense of balance and perspective when you're "on the grill" with a buyer.

Don't shoot from the hip. Don't improvise. Don't panic. Follow these simple rules when a prospect tells you your specs aren't right, your price is too high, your reputation isn't good enough, or your quality is suspect:

➤ **Accept the objection at face value.** In other words, don't fight (internally or externally) with the individual who passed along the objection. Don't rebut. Don't get into point-by-point struggles.

➤ **Compare the objection to your own history as a salesperson.** Is this objection something you have historically had no control over? Is it unique to this buyer? Odds are, this objection has something in common with one you've heard before. Ask yourself: "Have I ever sold to someone who told me this?"

➤ **Analyze the objection.** Is it reasonable? Would you make this objection if you were in the other person's shoes?

➤ **Look at the big picture before you respond.** Remember: You don't have to sell every person you come in contact with to be ahead of quota. You just have to sell the right ones!

➤ **Never offer judgments concerning the validity of the objection.** Instead learn how to question the objection!

## Questioning the Objection

After months of (unsuccessful!) struggles with my boss about the objections my prospects were passing along, and after learning to loathe the standard "objection handlers" I found in sales books ("I understand how you feel," and so on), I figured out a way to address the underlying concern that lives at the heart of every objection. I call it questioning the objection.

When you question the objection, you call the buyer's bid and raise him one—tactfully and politely, of course. This approach is dramatic, and it's not what you'll read about in most sales training manuals, but I think you'll find that it delivers some extraordinary results if you try it—and stick with it.

Questioning the objection allows you to get to the bottom of things in a hurry, which is what selling intelligently is all about. After all, if there really is an insurmountable objection, don't you want to find out about it as soon as possible and track down prospects who are likelier to do business with you?

Questioning the objection involves using an "If not, then what?" formula. Here's an example of how questioning the objection works in practice:

> Buyer: "Thanks for showing me the fall line, but your wholesale price is just too high. After we apply our standard markup, the retail price would be too high for the clientele that shop in our stores."
>
> You: "Hmm. If our price were lower—low enough for you to make margin and price it right for your clientele—would you purchase our topcoats for your stores?"
>
> Buyer: (Surprised pause, then) "No—the problem is, the style and material really aren't what I think they ought to be."

Bingo! Price wasn't the insurmountable obstacle you'd been lead to believe. You're perfectly positioned to show off other merchandise to this buyer.

## Bet You Didn't Know

You can use the "If not, then what" technique to question virtually any objection you hear from anyone about anything. ("If the product came with that free two-year service contract you want, would you place an order?") You're not promising to turn the world upside down for your buyer—you're getting a better idea of what's on his or her mind! What this technique really does is force the buyer to look at the objection with new eyes and level with you—and that's an indispensable advantage.

Here's another example that shows you how to put the spotlight on opportunity:

> Buyer: "The price you're charging for your seminar on May 14th is just too high. I can't afford it!"
>
> You: "That's interesting. If the seminar were free, would you want to attend?"
>
> Buyer: (After a long pause.) "Well, to tell you the truth, no, I wouldn't. See, the problem is that I don't really like to be stuffed in some conference room with a bunch of my competitors."
>
> You: "Here—take a look at this. A complete success kit that includes a commemorative audiotape, and book based on the system we'll be discussing. And it's all at a fraction of the price of the seminar."

Or consider the following approach, which can be successful in eliciting new information:

"Ms. Manager, you probably have a good reason for not wanting to [here mention what you're proposing]. Could you share your thoughts with me?"

## Objections That Seem to Leave "No Daylight"

The toughest objections are probably the ones where your contact gives you little or no information to work with. In many cases, of course, you'll be looking at a dead end. But there are ways you can make drama and enthusiasm work for you in these settings. Say you're talking to a manager and he or she says something like this:

"Thanks for your offer, but I simply have no interest whatsoever."

One flamboyant way to get back on the saddle is to pose a "what if" question along the following lines. (Note that the question is keyed to a positive result closely associated with a direct concern of the manager's.)

"Ms. Manager, if the person you trust the most to lower the cost of your long distance bills were to walk into your office with this idea, would you be interested in looking into it further?"

If your contact says "No," say thank you and hang up. File that call under "Hey, it takes some 'No' answers to get to a 'Yes' answer." If, on the other hand, you hear something like "Well, maybe I would give it some thought," you're in business. End the call pleasantly. Check with the reception desk and find out who's in charge of long distance service (or whatever you discussed with the manager). Call that person up and say, "I just hung up with Ms. Manager; she told me that if you were to bring this idea to her attention, she would take a look at it. Here's the idea—tell me what you think."

Another approach might sound like this:

"Mr. Prospect, if one of your salespeople [or: associates] [or: team members] were to hear that objection from one of their best prospects, how would you personally coach them in answering it?"

## Moving Forward

If you remember one principle from this chapter, make it this one: Ask questions that move the sales process forward!

"Does A work for you, or would you rather look more closely at B?" (NOT: "Why doesn't X work for you?")

"If X weren't an issue, would you sign on with us?" (NOT: "I understand how you feel about X; a lot of our customers felt the same way, until they found…")

A question or objection is not a failure unless you accept it as such. By maintaining a positive outlook and always, always, always framing your responses so that they give the buyer an alternative that moves the sales process forward constructively, you can accelerate your average sales cycle and overcome objections that would stop other salespeople cold.

# Winning Commitments

So much for the curveballs the buyer is likely to send your way. If you apply the techniques in this chapter to your first visit, your goal, as you conclude that visit, is going to be to win some form of commitment from your contact. You want to wrap up the meeting in such a way that you know—and your buyer knows—that something specific, something you both agree to, is going to happen next time you get together.

In the following chapter, you'll find out how to make that commitment happen.

# The Least You Need to Know

➤ To answer any question in a sales setting, you must first understand why the person you're talking to has raised it.

➤ When a prospect shares an objection or question with you, you should: Always restate it in your own words; show social proof to substantiate your answer; and ask whether your answer was sufficient by using a question that influences the direction of the conversation.

➤ Don't run from objections—encourage the buyer to bring them out into the open, and the earlier on in the sales process the better!

➤ Impassioned debates over objections lose sales.

➤ Use the "if not, then what" strategy to identify the root causes of objections.

# Getting the Basic Message Across

---

# Chapter 16

## In This Chapter

➤ Personalizing initial encounters with your prospects

➤ Turning a good meeting into a good relationship

➤ What to ask for at the end of the meeting or discussion

---

Some of the most advanced "relationship building" tactics I've ever seen were demonstrated recently during an unexpected weekend seminar with two purposeful, motivated salespeople named Anthony and Nicholas. These are salespeople who truly know how to build relationships with new contacts. These two pros are persuasive, motivated, and relentlessly positive. Like millions of other salespeople in their field, they get up every day and head out the door with a firm sense of the basic message they need to convey to their prospects. And like their millions of colleagues, they don't carry a briefcase, a business card, or any formal presentation materials. They sometimes need help selecting and putting on clothing, though. They're children—Anthony and Nicholas are my nephews—and they are masters at the art of enthusiastic persuasion.

Anthony and Nicholas wanted an hour of uninterrupted play time from me. And they got it.

How, exactly, did they get what they were after? By using two of the "golden rules" of selling you'll find summarized in this chapter. Specifically, they followed rule number one (being honest about the situation, even when it hurts) and they repeatedly embraced rule number two (ignoring the word "no"). They used a personal approach that allowed them to start off their "relationship" with a new "prospect" (read: me) by sending the right initial message. In their case the message was "We're going to have a blast together—you just watch!"

That, it turned out, was the message I needed to hear. It was a significant motivator for me to find a way to "work" with these two seasoned sales pros.

This chapter will show you how to send messages during the initial phase of the sales cycle that are just as personalized, just as compelling...and just as likely to leave the right impression with the person with whom you're beginning a business relationship.

# Is It a Relationship Yet?

When you get right down to it, your basic message to the buyer is quite simple, just as simple, in its way, as the (successful!) preliminary messages about treats and adventures that Nicholas and Anthony sent my way that memorable weekend.

Here's *your* message: "After listening to what you had to say today, I think you should strongly consider doing business with us. What's more, I'm willing to do anything and everything I can to make the experience of doing business with our organization a positive one for you!"

That's the general idea you'll be trying to get across to your contact as the first meeting draws to a close. It's not that you (necessarily) want a purchase commitment from this person. Some selling environments will require you to attempt to win a sale on the first in-person visit; in other cases, perhaps the majority, you'll only be asking your buyer to demonstrate his or her willingness to move the sales cycle forward by scheduling a second appointment with you.

In the final analysis, you're asking your contact to assume equal responsibility for exploring the advantages of a business relationship with you. That means you're asking the buyer to acknowledge openly that he or she has the power, and the duty, to vote "yes" or "no" on the purchase decision, whether that decision will be made now or in the future. You're asking for a commitment for a future decision. (That, by the way, is just what Anthony and Nicholas wanted—and got—from me. They wanted to know whether or not I would spend some time playing with them at some point during my visit. I agreed.)

Here are ten strategies that will help you solidify your relationship with the buyer. By applying the ideas you'll read about here, you'll learn how to develop mutual trust and respect with the contact, and you'll learn how to win commitments that count at the outset of the relationship.

# Strategy 1: Be Honest, Even When It Hurts

Never, ever lie to a buyer. Sell from the heart, no matter what it takes. If you don't believe in what you're selling enough to tell the truth about it at all times, find something else to sell!

Experienced salespeople will tell you that the "problem accounts" are, more often than not, those accounts where a rep overpromised and/or underdelivered. Your goal is always to *underpromise* and *overdeliver*.

You'll be making your appeal for a commitment to the "next step" (whether that's a sale or a future appointment) based on your own personal integrity. To stand any chance whatsoever of turning a suspect into a prospect, a prospect into a customer, and a customer into a business partner, you must—underline must—be ready, willing, and able to stand behind every word that comes out of your mouth. If that means losing a (short-term) customer today, so be it. You can always come back tomorrow. And when you do come back, you will be remembered as a person of integrity.

**Watch It!**
Don't fall into the trap of engaging in deceptive "short-term" selling to buyers who aren't as well informed as you are. Be willing to walk away from a deal and suggest an alternate solution if your initial consultation with the buyer leads you to believe that you cannot deliver a satisfactory solution. Appearances to the contrary, this is a trait of salespeople who routinely exceed quota!

# Strategy 2: Touch People in a Special Way

I'm talking about developing a "signature" gift or strategy that accompanies every first meeting you have with a buyer. At some point in each of my meetings, for instance, I pass along a personalized—that is to say, hand-signed—business card to the buyer I've been speaking with. When dealing with leaders and directors, I always make a point of passing along a gift that highlights my company: a notebook or coffee mug with a double-logo layout that identifies both my company and the target company.

When in doubt, personalize!

The only limit to your "signature" is your own imagination. In the city of Atlanta, there's a shrewd salesperson who knows just how pressed her buyers are for time. She doesn't burden her most promising contacts with requests for in-person lunch meetings. Instead, she takes the time herself—and creates simple, healthy, tasty lunches that she nestles in an instantly recognizable red basket. Twice a week—every Tuesday and Thursday—she makes three baskets and hand-delivers each to people with whom she's called ahead to make a telephone "lunch date." (Would you turn down such an offer? Would you ever forget the person who went to such lengths for you?) She manages to schedule—and conduct—three meetings on these days: 11:45, 12:15, and 12:45!

Talk about a memorable signature! When it comes time to ask her prospects for a business commitment, how do you think they respond? With the same canned, "thanks-but-no-thanks" brushoffs her less imaginative competitors receive? I think not.

---

**Bet You Didn't Know Box**

Developing a straightforward and instantly appealing "signature"—that of being incredibly well informed during all of your conversations with suspects, prospects, customers, and decision makers—may be your best bet for your selling environment.

Some sales reps have concluded that the best way to leave a "personal touch" is simply to do exhaustive library and/or Internet research on each and every target company with which they schedule an appointment. (This strategy is considerably easier these days, now that every other company seems to have a detailed site on the World Wide Web!) You'll know this approach has paid off when your contact says (as many will): "You seem to know an awful lot about our company—did you ever work for us?"

---

## Strategy 3: Simplify, Simplify

**Watch It!**
If the buyer won't make even a tentative commitment to you, or pass along key information, at the conclusion of your first meeting, you may be wasting your time trying to schedule follow-up meetings by phone later on. Think twice before you commit significant time and energy to trying to "turn around" a buyer who won't give you some idea of where you stand at the conclusion of your first in-depth discussion.

Remember: Talk about benefits to leaders; talk about advantages to directors; talk about features to influencers; talk about functions to consumers. Don't lose sight of your audience. Don't explain the solutions to problems your buyer hasn't raised. Put the spotlight on the area of your contact's interest, and then point the discussion toward a commitment.

Too many salespeople dance around the whole subject of "what happens next?" as though buyers had no idea that the goal of your appointment is to establish and solidify a business relationship. Don't beat around the bush! Be direct—but not overbearing—in making it clear that you want to move the relationship forward.

What you say could sound like this:

➤ Does this satisfy your concerns in X area, or do you need to see more from me?

➤ Who else would you want for me to speak with?

➤ Is this program a priority for you this quarter?

If the answers to these vitally important questions aren't worth exploring now, when will you explore them? After you've scheduled, and invested time, effort, and energy, in three or four more appointments?

# Strategy 4: Show Your Feelings

You must have an unshakable enthusiasm about the company you sell for and the product, service, or solution you sell. That means you have to demonstrate pride in what you have to offer!

Enthusiasm is contagious. So is having a great attitude. Most of the buyers you run into each day have to interact with at least one Gloomy Gus. Don't be one of them!

> **Bet You Didn't Know**
>
> Motivational experts have argued that it takes perhaps three times less mental energy to maintain an enthusiastic, positive mental attitude than it does to complain, be angry, or be depressed. If you're skeptical on this point, try this: Schedule "affirmation breaks" once an hour for a full week. Every hour of your work day, take two minutes, nonstop, to repeat some positive message to yourself. ("I can overcome anything!" "Most of the things I worry about turn out fine!" "A higher power watches over me!") See if your energy level—and your attitude—don't perk up!

Your discussions with buyers should include (genuine) statements like:

➤ It's so exciting to meet you!

➤ We've got something very special to talk about today!

➤ This is a real honor for me!

Don't be afraid to use honest-to-goodness exclamation points in your spoken interactions with buyers—most of your competitors will be too timid to do so!

# Strategy 5: Say You're Sorry When You Mess Up

Too many salespeople (heck, too many *people*) seem to assume that it's bad etiquette to admit you've made a mistake. Nothing could be further from the truth!

Taking personal responsibility for your relationship with the buyer means being willing to back up and say those dreaded words "I'm sorry" (or "I apologize" or "That's my fault" or any of their appropriate variations) when something goes wrong. Even if something *doesn't* go wrong, and your contact is simply confused, disoriented, or, yes, even in a bad mood, you should be willing to use the S word, "sorry!"

Guess what? If you really mean it, people tend to get less mean!

# Strategy 6: Look at People When You Talk to Them

It seems like it ought to be second nature, doesn't it? And yet, for most salespeople, it isn't!

Maintaining appropriate (not invasive!) eye contact is like listening, which we discussed in Chapter 15. It takes conscious, unrelenting effort to do it properly! "Eyeballing" your prospect's baby blues for 15 seconds straight is probably pushing it. Maintaining a steady, flexible gaze that alternates focusing on your prospect's eyes, mouth, and chin—and permits eye-to-eye contact whenever your prospect initiates it—is probably a better course.

The right kind of eye contact demonstrates purpose. It's a powerful communication tool. For instance, my nephew Anthony once asked me whether or not I'd play a game of checkers with him—by staring me right in the eye while he made his request. Who could turn down those big brown eyes? I made the commitment—and then thought to myself, as we made our way to the board, "How long could a game of checkers with a five-year-old take?" Two and a half hours later, I was still playing!

I kept my word—just like the majority of your buyers will keep their word with you when they make an "eye-to-eye" commitment that arises out of a question you pose directly and without apology!

# Strategy 7: Get Small Commitments First

Get minor agreements first. Work your way up to the "slam-dunk."

I don't mean that you should invent meaningless questions or statements designed solely to get buyers bobbing their heads up and down like mindless dashboard dolls. (How often does *that* really work, anyway?)

What I'm talking about is a little more subtle. As you complete each topic of discussion, you should reach agreement with your prospect on what's being addressed. If everything's being "put on hold," there's a problem somewhere! What have you and the buyer agreed to? Do you both know what action is going to be taken on each of the topics you've examined? Do you both agree on the issues that need further attention, and do you both understand who's going to be checking up on what?

For every step you take for the buyer, you should, as a matter of professional equity, expect a step in return. This is a relationship, after all, and a relationship is all about the satisfaction of each party's needs! So make it clear that you expect closure and cooperation on key issues from your contact before you make a raft of commitment of your own. That way, when the time comes for your contact to address the "buy/don't buy" decision, it won't come as a surprise!

190

# Strategy 8: Ask, and You Shall Receive

Whenever you ask, you will receive something. You may not get what you ask for, but you will get something!

I do believe that the more you ask, the more you sell. But *what* do you ask? An effective proactive salesperson might revise the famous quote from the Bible as follows: "Ask in the appropriate way, and at the appropriate time, and thou shalt receive what thou art after." Here's a short list of topics you should make a habit of asking about. If you keep on "checking in" in these key areas, the odds will increase that you'll eventually work your way through to a position where you can ask the appropriate question at the appropriate time—and win what you're after.

➤ **Ask about opinions and impressions.** "What are your thoughts so far?" "Does this look like something that would work for you?"

➤ **Ask about ideas for improvement.** "What would you improve?" "If you could change one characteristic of our product, what would it be?"

➤ **Ask about other members of the team.** "Who else will be taking a look at this?" "Who else, besides yourself, will want to take a look at my suggestions?"

**Watch It!**
Never ask a buyer "Do you have any questions?" It's too easy for the person to simply answer "No"! Instead, ask "What questions do you have?"

# Strategy 9: Don't Take No for an Answer

I have an iron-clad policy about the word "no"—I never accept, at face value, any interruption that contains the word! You shouldn't either. Instead, you should ask yourself, "Exactly what is this person saying 'no' to?"

Consider the following "no" interruption and the response that follows:

> Buyer: "No, Ellen. We are not going to refinance our home to fund the room addition." (Or, "Nope. We've made our decision. We're not refinancing.")

> You: "You know what? That's a smart decision. There are three alternate ways you can get the funds necessary to make your home more comfortable for you and your family. They are..."

Isolate *what* the person said "no" to—and work from there.

Lots of salespeople are scared stiff by the word "no." That's silly. If you doubt that making a commitment to work your way around the word "no" is an effective philosophy for sustained sales success, listen in on the tactics employed by the average four-year-old in

191

the backseat of the average minivan someday! As any parent or uncle can attest, these "salespeople"—who have a funny way of getting what they're after—have absolutely no fear of the word "no." Why should you?

# Strategy 10: Issue a Call to Action

**Sales Accelerator**
Make your last impression as impressive as your first. Send your contact a personalized thank-you letter after your first meeting. Be sure to mail it no later than the day after you sat down with the buyer.

**Sales Accelerator**
Do everything within your power to wrap your in-person meeting up on time or ahead of schedule. Many buyers start to get antsy when meetings with salespeople stretch beyond their allotted time, and antsy buyers have a way of tuning out of your discussions.

This is the part of the meeting where the rubber really hits the road. This is where you ask, in no uncertain terms, for a commitment.

Some salespeople take a laid-back approach when it comes to specifying commitments. As you've no doubt gathered by now, that's not my style. By the same token, any number of salespeople think that they have to come on like John Wayne, and start ordering people around, in order to win a commitment from a prospect. That's exactly the opposite of the approach you'll be taking when you deliver your call to action. Take a look at these examples and you'll see what I mean.

➤ "Ms. Prospect, what do you need to see between now and the time you make your decision that would help position our widget/widget cleaning service/whatever as your first choice?"

➤ "Mr. Prospect, may I ask your opinion? If you were me, what next step would you suggest that we take between now and the end of this (week/month/quarter/year)?"

➤ "Ms. Prospect, taking into consideration what you've already seen, what, if anything, do you need to (hear/see/feel) to gain a greater feeling of ownership of our (widget/widget cleaning service)?"

As you gain experience in your own sales work, you'll develop additional call-to-action statements that are perfectly suited to your selling environment.

*Do not*, conclude the meeting without issuing a call to action!

# The Presentation

In many cases, your call to action will result in an appointment, the purpose of which is to allow you to make a customized presentation based on the information you've gathered so far. In the next chapter of the book, you'll learn how to make that presentation powerful, persuasive, and on target.

# The Least You Need to Know

➤ There are ten vital strategies you can use to solidify your relationship with the buyer and clarify your basic message during the initial meeting—learn them!

➤ Among the most important of these strategies are showing enthusiasm, getting small commitments first, and (eventually) issuing the call to action, which typically serves as the ending-point of the first face-to-face meeting with the prospect.

➤ The call to action is where you ask, in no uncertain terms, for a commitment.

➤ Even if you're not in a position to ask for the sale, you should prepare a call to action that moves the sale forward.

➤ You should never conclude the first meeting without issuing a call to action!

# Chapter 17

# Creating Your Presentation

**In This Chapter**

➤ What you need to know before you plan

➤ The basic sequence of your presentation

➤ What to say to whom

In this chapter, you learn how to plan a formal presentation that leaves your prospect(s) saying, "Wow!" (In Chapter 18, you'll learn how to execute your plan.)

You noticed, I hope, how far along in this book this chapter comes. There's a reason for that: Far too many salespeople rush the presentation process. I don't want you to be one of them!

## Fool's Gold

"I had a great phone call—I'm going to close this sale on the first visit!"

"I've already got the contract for the one department—next week, once I make my presentation, all the branch offices will sign on."

"They've worked with us before—the new vice president will be easy to close."

Some salespeople make the mistake of leaping ahead to presentation mode before they do much of anything else. They start presenting before they know anything of consequence about the target company's mission, before they identify who the most appropriate contact is, before they know what the current problems are, and before they even know whether or not the person they're speaking with is interested in looking at a solution. None of that matters. These salespeople are out to give "their" presentation—the same presentation the last 16 target companies heard. That's a great way to lose time, energy, and momentum!

If you've got one "boilerplate" presentation you give again and again to your prospects without any variation, or a presentation that contains only minimal customization or research based on the particular organization you'll be talking to, then you're not going to reach your maximum potential as a salesperson. That's a guarantee.

Should you "know your stuff" well enough to be able to improvise your way through an emergency? Absolutely! Just about every salesperson has a story to share in this area. I'll never forget the time I had to develop customized material for a new seminar in the warp-speed time of nine hours! There had been a communications mixup; I thought I was speaking to a group of all-new salespeople at Company X, where I had spoken the previous year, but I was in fact scheduled to speak to the same exact human beings who'd taken in my program beforehand! Fortunately, my all-new program came out sounding good enough to win me a standing ovation!

> **Sales Accelerator**
>
> Some (but not all!) of the material you use will stay the same from presentation to presentation. Descriptive material about your company's history, its ranking in the industry, its mission, and its financial position can usually be incorporated to new presentations with little or no alteration. Similarly, introductions of your team and its local resources, as well as overviews of your service policies and guarantees, can usually be imported "as is."

There's a difference, though, between being comfortable enough with your "core material" to summon a little creativity during a crisis like that, and relying on the same stock phrases and timeworn suggestions over and over again in your presentations. You've put too much energy into the sale to bore the prospect (or yourself) with a rote presentation that doesn't take into account the unique situation you've identified.

During my seminars, I often run into salespeople who ask me whether or not it's "really necessary" to do customized research for each and every new presentation. I always tell them that they have a choice between *winging* the presentation and *winning* the presentation. I prefer the latter, and I hope you do, too!

# Who's Out There?

Whether you'll be talking to one person or several people, your presentation will be much better received if you take a few moments to figure out exactly who your audience is. It's true that you don't ever know for certain who will be in attendance during your presentation, because there's always the possibility that unexpected guests will show up at the last minute. (You'll learn how to handle this eventuality in the next chapter.) But you should, by this point, have some basic idea of who'll be evaluating what you have to say during the presentation. That means you need to have an initial understanding for each member of the target organization.

If you can't answer "yes" to each of the following questions, you're not ready to start working on your presentation.

➤ Have you met, or at least spoken by telephone, with each person you know will be in attendance at your presentation? Who likes surprises? Call ahead and introduce yourself to Ms. Bigg, or leave a message on her voice mail if you can't track her down.

➤ Do you know the correct spelling and pronunciation of each person's name? Double-check this information, because a mistake here can be both quiet and disastrous!

➤ Do you know each person's title? Get these right the first time, too!

➤ Have you developed a reliable working hypothesis as to each person's style? You remember: analytical, expressive, amiable, driver.

➤ Have you developed a working hypothesis as to each person's role in the network of influence and authority? You remember: leader, director, influencer, consumer.

➤ Do you know why each person is attending? Does he or she want to? Does he or she have to?

➤ Do you know what the objective of your presentation is? Is it to be placed on a pre-ferred supplier list? Receive a purchase order? Selected as a smaller group of suppliers being given a chance to advance to the next level of competition? Figure out what you want from this meeting—and adapt your closing call to action accordingly.

➤ Do you know which members of the group are likely to be advocates for your cause—and which may be adversaries? If you know in your bones that the person with whom you've spent most of your time thus far is likely to be hostile to your cause, you should ask yourself why you're working on this presentation.

> **Bet You Didn't Know**
>
> Your presentation may include elements that are delivered by someone else in your organization—such as your sales manager, a technical specialist, or your credit manager. If other people are going to be involved in your presentation, make sure they have all the information you need. Go over your plan of attack, let them know the *exact* topics they will be asked to cover, and pass along any concerns or questions you feel your audience may have with regard to these topics. Clarify exactly how much time is available, both for your associate's portion of the meeting and for your presentation as a whole.
>
> Rehearse your own part of the presentation. Then, if at all possible, watch as your associate rehearses his or her part of the presentation.

# How Do You Start?

You start your presentation by offering appropriate information about your company, its goals, its products, and its history. Don't expect to spend all afternoon talking about how wonderful you are! This is a "get-acquainted" period that may last, say, three to five minutes. Be prepared to move directly to the next step.

# The Heart of Your Presentation

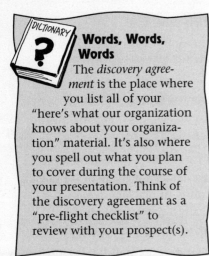

**Words, Words, Words**

The *discovery agreement* is the place where you list all of your "here's what our organization knows about your organization" material. It's also where you spell out what you plan to cover during the course of your presentation. Think of the discovery agreement as a "pre-flight checklist" to review with your prospect(s).

**Watch It!**

The elements of your discovery agreement must not be too detailed. If you include encyclopedia-length descriptions of each aspect of your presentation, your prospect(s) will, quite naturally, want to respond to the points you raise. Save the in-depth descriptions for the presentation itself. Shoot for one brief sentence per agenda item.

The people you're meeting with are special, and so is the organization they work for. This is a group with unique problems and opportunities. You've worked hard to learn all you can about it, and that hard work is going to be evident in the customized portions of your presentation, which will form the heart of your presentation outline.

These customized portions will include, at a minimum:

➤ A discovery agreement.

➤ Discussion, display, or demonstration of functions, features, advantages, and/or benefits, depending on who is in attendance, interspersed at appropriate points with...

➤ Responses to prior specifications you've been asked to meet.

➤ Responses to specific questions that arose during your earlier meetings with your prospect(s).

➤ Responses to specific questions that arise during the presentation itself.

➤ A logical summary of key points and conclusion, complete with your proposed "next step" action.

That first element—the discovery agreement—is worth reviewing in detail. It's basically a proposed agenda for your presentation.

You must review the discovery agreement with your prospect(s) before addressing the other customized elements of your presentation. By doing this, you're giving the other side the opportunity to make any last-minute changes or additions to the agenda *before* you start talking about what you have to offer. Offer *concise* summaries of each key point you plan to cover during your presentation. Review each point in chronological order.

If you don't have consent, you can't present!

Here's an example of what a discovery agreement might look like. Note that the document below does *not* reference products, services, or solutions, nor does it make any claims about what's right or wrong. It is simply an accurate, detailed list of what you, the salesperson, found out—discovered—during interviews, sales calls, and other pre-sales activities.

**Words, Words, Words**

*Consent* is what happens when you've communicated to your audience what you know so far…and they've given you a "thumbs up" or "we're on the same wavelength" message when you offer them the opportunity to correct your summary of the situation before you.

---

DISCOVERY AGREEMENT FOR ABC CORPORATION

World's largest widget reconditioning organization

Persons interviewed: James Collins, Data Management Supervisor; Brenda Smith, VP/Operations

Topics discovered:

➤ Accounting department is currently experiencing payroll errors of 24%

➤ Accounting department has an accounts payable backlog of six weeks

➤ Accounting department has an accounts receivable backlog of 12 weeks

➤ Human resource department's files detailing retirement fund availability is out of date

➤ Human resource department's implementation of 401-K plan is now on hold

➤ Human resource department's benefits program is in place, but is in need of review

➤ Human resource department's state forms for government contractors need to be filed

Discovery:

Everyone at ABC Inc. who was interviewed is in favor of outsourcing the accounting and human resource functions stated above. ABC wants to maintain direct control and therefore will only entertain on-site services. ABC also has a need for temporary services in the manufacturing and process areas, but these are a lower priority. ABC is looking for a single source for all outsourcing needs, however.

# "Sounds Great!"

You review the agenda. You ask the members of the audience for feedback, and make appropriate revisions and additions. Actually, this revision-and-addition phase generally won't (or at least shouldn't) be too extensive. Usually, your discovery agreement will touch on the most important issues that were raised in your previous meeting, and those same issues will be at the top of the list this time around. You'll hear something like, "Sounds great! Let's get going!"

After winning consent of your discovery agreement, you'll move ahead to the all-important "discussion, display, and demonstration" phase. The order in which you address the points in this section can make all the difference.

I hope it will come as no surprise to you to read that the various audience members you'll be addressing are all members of the target organization's network of influence and authority, and that each constituency wants to learn more about a particular aspect of your product, service, or solution. You remember:

> Leaders want to learn about benefits.
>
> Directors want to learn about advantages.
>
> Influencers want to learn about features.
>
> Consumers want to learn about functions.

Is that breakdown becoming familiar—or perhaps even more than familiar—to you now? Good! Because that analysis of the buyer(s) you'll be facing, an analysis you should be able to recite in your sleep, will provide you with everything you need to develop your outline for this presentation. Just move down the list, from leaders to directors:

➤ If there are leaders present, be prepared to address their concerns first. Highlight and discuss the benefits of what you have to offer. It could sound like this: "As soon as you begin using our service, you'll notice that you have an additional $5,387.00 each year—15 percent of your long-distance bill—to spend as you see fit. As a bonus, you'll be able to communicate with each of your key executives whenever you want, no matter where there are." Take a break for questions and answers.

➤ If there are directors present, be prepared to address their concerns next. Highlight and discuss the advantages of what you have to offer. It could sound like this: "What you'll find interesting is that your departmental changes will only reflect the actual communications initiated by your department. When it comes to budget forecasting, you'll love the accuracy, and the clean look, of the reports you'll be receiving. Here are some samples. Would anyone else care to take a closer look?" Take a break for questions and answers. Then...

➤ If there are influencers present, be prepared to address their concerns next. Highlight and discuss the features of what you have to offer. It could sound like this: "Every time a call is placed, it's marked by your digital packaging algorithm; when it's terminated, you're charged with two-second rounding. Here's a location map for our cellular sites, and a rundown of our fiber-optic configurations. I'll let you review that for a moment while we take a break." At an appropriate point, take a break for questions and answers.

➤ If there are consumers present, be prepared to address their concerns, too. Highlight and discuss the functions of what you have to offer. It could sound like this: "Each time you want to connect more than one person, you just call 1-888-555-8586 and our operators will help you through the entire procedure. Here—let's give it a try. Does anyone want to suggest a group we could call right now?" At an appropriate point, take a break for questions and answers.

Plan to address each constituency in turn, and work your way through the group. Mind you, we're talking about a rough outline here, not a script that must be adhered to at all costs. If the president of the company wants you to focus on a function for the benefit of a consumer who's present, follow the president's lead!

# To Demonstrate or Not to Demonstrate?

If you sell a product, service, or solution that lends itself easily to an in-person demonstration, you may want to consider conducting one during your presentation. Be aware, however, that there are both pluses and minuses to demonstrations in this setting.

Here are some of the most important advantages:

➤ Demonstrations let your prospects actually see, hear, or feel what you're selling.

➤ Demonstrations leave lasting impressions; they're rooted in direct experience.

➤ Demonstrations may get prospects talking about what would (or will) happen after a purchase takes place.

➤ Demonstrations give prospects something "concrete" to talk about after they return to their facility or workgroup.

➤ Demonstrations have the potential to give you an insurmountable edge over the competition (especially if your competition does not give a demonstration, or attempts to give one and executes it poorly).

Here's the flip side—the potential disadvantages of an in-person demonstration:

➤ Demonstrations can go wrong, perhaps disastrously wrong. You'll run into some sales reps who take the view that nothing that's plugged into an AC outlet while a prospect is watching can be counted on to function properly.

**201**

➤ Demonstrations whose execution you delegate to a colleague may, if things go haywire, cause that colleague to lose composure and say something everyone regrets.

➤ Demonstrations may not engage the prospect as much as you think they will.

➤ Demonstrations may engage the prospect too much—and leave you unable to comply with some variation of the request, "Can I see (it all/some more/a full-scale example) before I make my decision?"

The bottom line? If you're really, really confident in your ability to execute the demonstration crisply, professionally, and proficiently, it may just be worth the risk. Two words of advice, however, are in order. First, develop a backup strategy—something you can do or say just in case the widgets don't rotate or synchronize in quite the way you've promised. (That strategy should *not* include the words "This has never happened before.") Second, make sure you (or whoever is conducting the demonstration) get plenty of rehearsal time before your presentation.

# Responses

You'll want to build plenty of time into your proposal to address the technical and practical questions that have arisen earlier in your interviews. And, as I noted above, you'll want to give your audience the chance to pose any relevant (or, for that matter, irrelevant!) questions about each component of your discussion/display/demonstration phase.

# Wrapping Up

Your conclusion will summarize key points and revolve around a new call to action, one that takes your objective into account and moves the sales process forward.

As you no doubt recall, examples of effective calls to action appear in Chapter 16 of this book. You'll see exactly what an effective conclusion to your presentation sounds like in Chapter 18.

So, that's the basic outline! Now it's time to take a look at some additional advice that will help you prepare for a successful presentation.

# Equipment and Materials

Two words of advice here: Plan ahead! Make sure that whatever you decide to bring along to your presentation is a) actually packed in your case before you leave for the site, and b) fully functional. I once saw an auditorium full of cheering people reduced to complete silence while the star performer—one of the nation's most respected business experts—

stood helplessly onstage in front of an empty black-board. He was waiting for a maintenance man to bring him a piece of chalk.

The moral here: Missing or defective presentation equipment kills momentum and deadens interest. Make your list and check it twice before you head out the door.

## Pros and Cons

There are lots of tools you can use during your presentation to add drama, variation, and visual interest to what you have to say during the presentation. Take a look at Table 17.1 before you make any decision about what you'll be bringing along to add punch to your presentation.

**Sales Accelerator**
All the technical whizbang in the world won't help you if the prospect doesn't understand what you're saying during the presentation. Make sure you're speaking directly to the concerns of your prospect(s), and explain (or avoid altogether) technical terminology that may be confusing.

**Table 17.1   The Pros and Cons of Various Presentation Materials**

| Method | Pros | Cons |
|---|---|---|
| Three-ring presentation binder | 1. Portable<br>2. No electrical power required<br>3. Can be modified easily<br>4. Color can be easily used<br>5. Easy to use | 1. Low-tech image (this may sometimes be a pro if your audience is high-tech adverse)<br>2. Good for only a small audience size of one to two individuals<br>3. Shows wear and tear easily and must be maintained |
| Flip charts | 1. Great for small-to medium-sized audiences of 5 to 15 people<br>2. No electrical power required<br>3. Versatile, high visual impact because of its size<br>4. Can be interactive, you and your audience can write on it during your presentation | 1. You must have excellent hand-writing or hire someone who does<br>2. Because of their size, they are difficult to transport; they damage easily<br>3. Their life-span is relatively short<br>4. Writing legibly takes time and can be distracting |
| Overhead projectors | 1. Easy to use<br>2. Bright, clear image<br>3. Great for medium to large audience size of 15 and higher | 1. Usually requires a screen<br>2. It's electrical, so it can break down<br>3. Usually requires that the room lights be dimmed for best viewing |

*continues*

**Table 17.1  Continued**

| Method | Pros | Cons |
| --- | --- | --- |
| | 4. Very interactive —you can write upon the transparencies as you conduct your presentation<br>5. Audiences can follow along with identical handout material<br>6. You can easily jump forward or backward to facilitate answering questions | 4. "Low-tech" image |
| Laptop, computer-controlled presentations | 1. High-tech, animation, entertaining to watch and participate in<br>2. Highly customizable to your audience<br>3. Existing video, graphs, and slides can be incorporated | 1. Highest investment of all methods<br>2. Learning curve may be substantial, software and hardware knowledge mandatory<br>3. It's electrical, so it can break down<br>4. Relatively fragile<br>5. Requires an expensive projector for audience sizes of two or more |

# The Ten Commandments of Successful Presentation Planning

Here are ten guidelines that will help you prepare a top-notch presentation.

1. When in doubt, thou shalt over-research those of thy buyers that fit the Template of Ideal Prospects (see Chapter 6).

2. Thou shalt tailor thy presentation topics to thy audience.

3. Thou shalt build in a slot for thy audience to grant approval to thy agenda before starting in earnest.

4. Thou shalt memorize names, the better to use them when addressing thy prospects directly.

5. Thou shalt give thy audience the opportunity to ask questions.

6. Thou shalt select presentation material that suits thy setting, audience, and budget.

7. Thou shalt know thy objective, and prepare a call to action that reflects it.

8. Thou shalt always strive to move thy sale forward.

9. Thou shalt rehearse ahead of time—several times—and look closely at that which does not yet flow smoothly.

10. Thou shalt time thy rehearsals, and edit out that which makes them run beyond thy allotted time; for behold, the dissipation of time is an abomination unto thy prospects.

If you follow these ten steps—and adhere to the other advice I've laid out in this chapter—you should have a flexible, adaptable outline that clarifies all the bases your presentation will have to cover. In the next chapter, you'll take a look at the challenges you can expect during the real-world execution of that presentation!

# The Least You Need to Know

➤ Follow the overall presentation outline detailed in this chapter.

➤ Write an accurate, objective discovery agreement (which serves as the agenda for the presentation meeting), and build in time for your audience to consent to it—that is, agree with it and make additions.

➤ Develop material for, and plan to examine, the concerns of leaders, directors, influencers, and consumers, in that order.

➤ Choose your presentation materials carefully.

➤ Follow the Ten Commandments of Successful Presentation Planning.

# Chapter 18

# Delivering Your Presentation

## In This Chapter

➤ Treating your prospect's space with respect

➤ What you can expect during the presentation

➤ What to do at the conclusion of your presentation

In the last chapter, you learned how to develop the rough outline that will guide your presentation. In this chapter, you learn how to make the presentation work in person. We'll examine room set-up, seating, and precisely where you'll be positioned for the maximum positive impact. If you try the advice that follows, you'll be sure that each and every one of your presentations is a memorable one.

## The Best Seat In the House: Yours

Have you ever noticed how little fun it is to have to jockey for position when you queue into your local crowded multiplex cinema for "open seating?" That's really something of a misnomer, because the seating arrangement doesn't leave you feeling very open at all. If you're like most of us, you feel a certain degree of anxiety or discomfort in these settings, a feeling of being "hemmed in" from all sides. Usually, the sensation doesn't last more than the few minutes it takes to snag a seat for the next special-effects epic, but most of us are glad when the "filing in" portion of the evening is over. For some people, though, these social situations cause serious anxiety that lasts for quite some time—even panic attacks!

What's happening in those situations is called "incursion on one's territorial zone." When the physical space around our bodies is violated by other individuals, it causes stress. Honoring another person's personal space, on the other hand, can help to build mutual good feeling and cooperation. Both of these principles hold true not only at the movie theater, but in other settings as well—like your presentation! It's time now to learn how you can avoid any type of stress or keep it from taking place during your presentation to your prospect as a result of "space invasion."

**Sales Accelerator**

Offer to let your prospect(s) see, touch, and evaluate any relevant product samples. Make sure it's immaculate; bring a clean handkerchief to remove fingerprints and the like. Ask about reactions to certain aspects of the product. If at all possible, leave the product sample with the prospect for day or two—but no longer! You want the newness of the experience to help move your sale forward.

**Words, Words, Words**

The *confidential zone* (0 to 18 inches) is the "frontier" of your person. Other zones, extending outward in concentric circles and reserved for social exchanges of lesser and lesser degrees of intimacy, are known as the *individual, sociable,* and *common zones.*

# In the Zone

Imagine there's an invisible 18-inch barrier surrounding your body. Actually, you probably don't have to imagine too hard, because there almost certainly *is* an invisible 18-inch barrier around your body. This is your "confidential" zone. Here in the United States, this is the area most people hold as essentially private, a space only to be occupied by one's spouse, one's significant other, one's close relatives (children, for instance), and one's domestic pets (pythons excluded). Barrelling thoughtlessly into another's personal zone is generally tantamount to a physical challenge!

There are three other zones you should be aware of. The zone between 18 and 32 inches from your body is known as the "individual" zone, the region where most Americans are comfortable with social or business interaction that involves people they know. The zone between 32 and 44 inches represents, for Americans, the "sociable" zone. It's about the distance between you, when you're sitting at your desk, and a visitor who's sitting at a chair placed in front of your desk. In this zone, most of us are comfortable interacting with people we do not yet know well in social and business situations. Finally, there's the region outside these three zones. It's known as the "common" zone, and it's the area where we Americans are comfortable with (or at least occasionally prepared to accept) announcements of unexpected entrances from others.

# "Permission to Come Aboard?"

Let's assume, for now, that you're making a presentation at the prospect's office. You're dealing with only one person.

You must always ask for the prospect's permission before you make the transition from the common zone (that is, upon entering the prospect's room or area) to the sociable zone. Say "May I come in?" or something that's darn close. After a period of "getting acquainted," you must ask for permission before you place any material on the prospect's desk. Putting a binder, brochure, sample, or anything else on the prospect's desk or equivalent area means you're entering the individual zone, and you can't do that until you've been granted permission!

You must—I repeat must—enter the zones one at a time. That means standing until you receive an invitation to sit! (It also means asking, "Is this seat okay?"). Do not take up residence in the sociable zone without permission. I've watched many a well-researched presentation collapse because the salesperson:

➤ Took a seat without being invited to do so, and/or

➤ Treated the prospect's desk as though it were his or her own desk, and/or

➤ "Hemmed in" the prospect by consistently operating in his or her personal space.

These three classic presentation mistakes—which only seem minor in nature to the chronic underperformer—represent violations of the sociable, individual, and confidential zones, respectively. If you don't think the heedless act of ignoring these invisible "borders" can affect your commission check, you're sadly mistaken. Play it safe. Don't act like you own the place! Gain permission at each appropriate zone's border before proceeding.

If you find it's necessary to stand while making your presentation—for example, if you must use a dry-erase board or chalkboard—ask the prospect to join you at the board. Give the prospect a marker or piece of chalk; this brief point of contact within the person's confidential zone will help to encourage him or her

**Sales Accelerator**
Conducting a one-on-one presentation? Gain explicit permission to move into the sociable and individual zones, and never set up shop within the prospect's confidential, or private zone. Your best strategy is to begin your presentation in earnest once you've been granted access to the sociable zone, then win entry into the individual zone (where you'll be doing most of your presenting work). You may choose to make *brief, occasional* stops in the confidential zone while you hand over samples, materials, presentation tools, or papers. This can reinforce positive feelings in your prospect—as long as you don't overdo it!

**Watch It!**
At times, your prospect will feel so good about what you're saying or demonstrating that he or she will sit on the same side of the desk or table you're sitting on. That's a sign of acceptance. Don't fight it!

to become engaged in the chalk-talk. With a little luck, your prospect will move up next to you and occupy the sociable or (even better!) individual zone as you outline your points on the board.

# All Together Now

The same basic principle concerning personal space incursion applies to presentations you give to groups (with the notable exception that you may not want to single one member of the group out by asking him or her to stand up, join you at the blackboard, and present, as it were, before the class). Always ask, in some way, for permission before you plant yourself in the sociable and individual zones of any person present, and don't take over the person's confidential space under any circumstances.

It would be nice if those were the only ideas you had to keep in mind while delivering a presentation to a group (which, to my way of thinking, is any gathering of people larger than one). Alas, you're going to have to think about some other things, too.

**Sales Accelerator**

Reviewing your discovery agreement before moving on to the specifics of your presentation is always essential. If you've just been introduced to brand new contacts, people whose role in the organization or personal style is unfamiliar to you, you'll want to be doubly sure that you confirm all the key information with all present, and win assent, before proceeding.

Making a presentation in your prospect's meeting or conference room can be quite tricky. Why? There are two main reasons:

➤ Despite your best efforts at researching all the angles ahead of time (see the previous chapter), the conference-room presentation may come as a complete surprise to you. Your prospect may suddenly say, "Why don't we go to the conference room—let me go get Jeff and Sally." Perhaps you've never met, or even heard of, Jeff or Sally! You're going to have to size them up on the spot.

➤ Your opportunities to rearrange the room for a proper setup may be severely limited. This doesn't mean you shouldn't try to set it up to your best advantage—but it does mean that, in some cases, you're going to have to make do with what's there.

Setting up the prospect's conference room on the fly can present some real challenges. The best room configuration for a group presentation of more than five is the classical "U" shaped configuration, which you can arrange using three tables. If you have less than five people attending, then it's best to use a standard rectangular conference table.

Whenever you're making your presentation from a "U" table configuration, be sure you begin your presentation while standing in the front, at the very top of the "U." Within the first third of your presentation, you should begin to walk inside the "U" as you make your point or speak directly to someone. Never, under any circumstances, should you go "outside" the "U" (that is, behind someone).

Whenever you're using a standard conference table, make sure that you're seated in the exact position shown in the following illustration. That's the only position you'll be able to use to make easy visual contact with everyone and exercise influence on the agenda.

*Where you should sit when you give a presentation at a rectangular conference table.*

One final word of advice on dealing with group presentations: Create extra sets of handouts or product samples, if you are using these. Rest assured that someone will drop in unexpectedly, or an opportunity for your prospect to pass the material along to someone else will arise.

## Welcome to Our Humble Home

The prospect is coming by your place of business for a presentation. You've got much more control over the surroundings! That's the good news. The bad news is that, for some reason, it's incredibly easy to procrastinate when it comes to setting up for these meetings.

And don't they always seem to be scheduled for 8:45 in the morning, or some other impossible hour? Rather than show up at your office at the crack of dawn to track down everything you need and review your presentation materials, do the work ahead of time (no later than the day before). You may not *think* that preparing your facility for a meeting with a prospect is likely to be much more challenging than preparing for a flight across the country. Trust me. It is.

Room set-up has an extraordinary effect on human behavior, and that means it has an extraordinary effect on the way your prospects perceive your presentation. Now that you've got control over the environment, and a little bit of lead time to work with, put those elements to work for you!

**Sales Accelerator**

Use people's names when you talk to them during your presentation!

**Watch It!**
The proper environment really can win over customers who are "on the fence"—so don't underestimate the importance of setting up your facility when a prospect is getting ready to visit! Some salespeople think to themselves, "What's the big deal about setting up a room? Get a few chairs, a coffeepot, cups, a flip chart or two—and bingo, you're done!" Take that approach, and you'll lose sales you ought to win.

Before you even start thinking about where to put the tables and chairs, you should work your way through the following Meeting Prep checklist.

---

### Meeting Prep Checklist

❑ **Make sure the room is well lighted.** A dingy, poorly lit room will affect the internal clock of your prospect(s), and perhaps even cause them to tune out what you're saying. Virtually all human beings start to lose their mental edge when they're kept confined inside a poorly lit room. Brighten your presentation room up as much as you can—but keep the curtains or blinds drawn if you can. You don't wan't people daydreaming and staring out the window.

❑ **Find a way to keep noise to an absolute minimum.** Unplug all phones; turn off any speakers, beepers, and pagers; let your neighboring officemates know that you've got an important meeting between the hours of X and Y. If possible, select a room with virtually no "noise leakage" problem.

❑ **Remove clutter ruthlessly.** The presentation room is no place for stray computers that have nothing to do with your meeting, or boxes full of old files, or any other extraneous objects. When your contacts walk through the door, they should see a room that's completely clean and absolutely free of unsightly clutter.

❑ **Arrange for refreshments.** When your guests finally walk in the door, they should have access to coffee (both high-test and decaf), tea, juice, soda, and water. This is a wonderful way to show your audience that you're truly grateful for the presence of your guests. If possible, offer coffee and tea mugs with your company logo on them.

---

Once you've attended to these matters, you'll be able to arrange the tables and chairs for maximum advantage. As I've said, I favor a "U"-shaped setup for groups of five or more, and a standard rectangular table for smaller groups. If you're addressing more than 15 people at any time, you may need to adopt some seating arrangement that incorporates aisles that allow you easy access to the people who ask you questions.

**Watch It!**
Don't make your guests squint. Be sure the table and chair settings don't leave any of your prospects facing directly into the shafts of sunlight that can peek between blinds and around curtains.

## What It's Going to Sound Like

After everyone's in place, you'll stride to the front of the room and issue an initial pleasantry. I strongly recommend the following, which has worked for me on hundreds of occasions:

> "Hi there! I'm (name). During my presentation this morning, we're all going to have jobs to do. Mine is to talk, and yours is to listen. Please let me know if you get done before I do."

You may choose to make a few *brief* introductory remarks here; a few sentences about your company, an introduction of a team member. Keep it very short. From there, the presentation will follow the rough outline that you read about in Chapter 16. Take a look at it again now, step by step.

# Your Discovery Agreement

I prefer to commit this to writing and pass it out to each and every member of the group, then summarize it verbally. It's also a good idea to develop a visual aid that's big enough for everyone to see and features the same information.

Please remember that the discovery agreement provides an overview of what you know about this organization's goals, plans, objectives, and challenges. It also summarizes what you've established or accomplished to date by working with particular team members.

*Important reminder:* The discovery agreement is not an outline of what you can do to help this prospect's situation, nor is it a detailed outline of the presentation to follow!

After your review, you'll take the time to gain acceptance or agreement from everyone in your audience before you proceed to the other items on your agenda. What you say could sound something like this:

> "Ladies and gentlemen, do you feel that I've accurately described the current challenges in your shipping and receiving department, or would you like to make any modifications before we begin?"

No matter what your audience says in response, you win. With a question like that, you'll either gain immediate acknowledgment and acceptance of your assessment, or you'll find out exactly how much you've missed the mark by. That's certainly good to know, right?

Sometimes, your audience will want to tinker with the wording of your discovery agreement. When this happens, be sure the suggestion is in the best interests of the group you're addressing. "Is everyone in agreement that we should look further into Jake's suggestion for an automated taping machine for the department?" If the answer is yes, then add that subject to your discovery agreement and—if at all possible—your agenda.

In the vast majority of cases, though, you'll simply get the green light to proceed to your agenda. I'd suggest summarizing the outline of your presentation for everyone's benefit and then hanging an oversized written version of the agenda in the back of the room. When you complete an item on your agenda, you should ask:

> "Ladies and gentlemen, have we covered this item to your satisfaction?"

When you get a "yes" answer that is shared by everyone in the room, head to the oversized agenda with your marker in hand and cross that item off the list.

## Contents and Question-and-Answer Sessions

Your sales presentation will have one opening (which will always feature a discovery agreement) and one closing (which will always feature a call to action), but it may have several contents and question and answer periods, each devoted to a particular element of your presentation. As you saw in the last chapter, these questions can come in several categories.

**Sales Accelerator**

Be prepared to offer "typical" questions of your own—questions other prospects have put to you—if your audience has no questions about a portion of your presentation. This will usually stimulate a dialogue.

This is the "meat and potatoes" of your presentation. You must, without fail, address every issue of importance to your audience, and you must tailor benefits to leaders, advantages to directors, features to influencers, and functions to buyers, in that order. (You saw some examples of these appeals and summaries in the previous chapter.)

One of the best ways to begin the content portion of your presentation is to make a statement like this:

"Ladies and gentlemen, that's our agenda. In the next hour, you will learn how Widgetco will be able to make your team's task of (insert overriding goal of your prospect here) within the next (insert time period it will take you to order, deliver, and install whatever you sell). If for any reason you decide not to use widgets, you will be able to take what you learn here this (morning/afternoon) and enhance the specifications for your final selection in this area."

Talk about an attention-grabber! This is a statement that sounds risky, but really isn't. If they don't decide to buy from you, what are you going to do—repossess all the materials you passed along?

The more questions the members of your audience ask you about the particular elements of your presentation, the better. Follow all the guidelines you read about in Chapter 14 for answering questions, and be prepared to open up the discussion with phrases like "Would anyone else like to make any additional comments?"

If time gets tight because of lots and lots of questions from your prospects (a good sign!), you may want to make a proposal along the following lines:

"In the interest of keeping on schedule, shall we hold questions until we reach the end of the agenda?"

## The Call to Action

We've already examined the form of the call to action as it applied to your earlier appointments with prospects. Only a few more observations are appropriate here as you consider the call to action you should issue at the end of your presentation.

There's a time to ask for a "yes"—and a time to simply set up a mutually agreed-upon next step. I'd argue that the formal presentation (especially one you deliver before a group) falls into the latter category. People will almost certainly need time to digest and discuss all the information you've given them.

Suppose you'd been listening to a presentation for the past hour. Which type of call to action would you be most likely to respond favorably to?

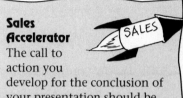

**Sales Accelerator**
The call to action you develop for the conclusion of your presentation should be realistic, within the power of your audience, and in the best interests of the prospect(s). It should also seek to move the sale forward.

➤ So, ladies and gentlemen, you've seen what we have to offer. What do you think? Shall we get the service started on the 17th of this month? (Or, if you're a fan of the "presumptive close:" "Would you rather start on the 17th, or the 21st?")

➤ "So, ladies and gentlemen, that's what we have to offer. You've been very generous with your time and attention, and I appreciate that. You'll need some time to think over everything you've seen and learned today. Shall we set a time on next Thursday to find out what you want to do next?"

For me, it's an easy call. The first response leaves you open to something along the lines of, "You know, you've done an excellent job today, but we're just not ready to make a decision like that right now." (If you're presenting to a group, how can you expect to get any *other* response to your question?) After that, you'll probably hear the same old line salespeople always hear: "Let me get back to you sometime next week."

The second approach, though, which is respectful of everyone's time—and of the peculiarities of group dynamics—is likely to result in a more direct response: "Sure. What time on Thursday is good for you?"

## Once You're Rolling

There are certain important guidelines you'll want to bear in mind as your presentation moves forward.

During your presentation, you *should*...

➤ Set clear starting and ending times, and try like the dickens to stick to your schedule.

➤ Use index cards as prompts for topics.

➤ Consider using a flip-chart or overhead transparency system that establishes the outline of your talk.

➤ Consider using at least two different types of visual media during your presentation.

➤ Gain visual contact with every single member of your audience.

➤ Learn to "scan" the room—that is, keep your eyes on the people in the audience at almost all times.

➤ Keep a pitcher of water and a glass handy. You'll probably get thirsty.

➤ Count to ten after you ask any question. Wait out those silences by adopting a silent, nonconfrontational "What do you think?" expression.

➤ Take a drink of water while you're waiting for answers from your prospects.

During your presentation, you *shouldn't*...

➤ Read statements verbatim from a piece of paper.

➤ Talk while you are facing any other direction than toward the audience.

➤ Interrupt any member of the audience.

➤ Continue to hold a pointer or marker after you've used it. The risk that you'll engage in some distracting nervous tic is just too high!

➤ Carry change (which is noisy!) in your pockets or hands.

➤ Exceed 60 minutes without a break for your prospect(s). In some settings, 45 will be pushing it.

# The Least You Need to Know

➤ Learn how to respect the personal space of the people in attendance.

➤ Set up the room so that it works to your advantage.

➤ Prominently feature your agenda, and return to it often to mark as "complete" those items you've covered to everyone's satisfaction.

➤ Issue a call to action at the close of the meeting—but don't push for an instant up-or-down decision.

# Part 5
# Building (and Maintaining) Alliances

*So, you've built up geniune interest in your product, service, or solution...and now it's time to formalize things. In this part of the book, you learn the very best ways to get commitments from prospective buyers. Surprise, surprise, your strategies here will have a whole lot less to do with "closing" the other side than they will with "opening" yourself up to delivering tangible results.*

*You'll also learn how to use your existing contact base to secure invaluable referrals for new business!*

# Making Guarantees, Meeting Expectations

In the preceding chapters of this book, you learned what goes into a winning presentation. Now it's time to examine what goes into developing honest-to-goodness business commitments; commitments that make sense for both your company and the representatives of the target organization. In this chapter, you'll learn about the perils and opportunities related to making guarantees to your prospects and customers, how to operate ethically (and, in all likelihood, stay on the right side of the law), and how to make long-term credibility a reality in your sales career. In this chapter, you'll learn about the tools you'll be able to use to great benefit as the sales cycle nears its completion for the first time with a given contact—or as you formalize new commitments with current customers.

In the next chapter, you'll look at the portion of the sales process where you negotiate the deal, and in the chapter following that, you'll find out exactly what it takes to finalize the relationship.

# Why Do Salespeople Love to Make Guarantees?

Salespeople love to make guarantees because they can provide a competitive edge—the kind of edge that often moves prospects from the "I don't know" category to the "Okay, let's give it a try" category. Lots of salespeople tell themselves that guarantees work because they highlight positive aspects of the product or service under discussion. Actually, they work because they tend to make it appear to the buyer that there's no risk involved in making the decision.

Sometimes guarantees deliver great results for your company's bottom line and your commission check. Sometimes they backfire. If your organization has authorized you to make guarantees to buyers, there's somebody who should make a habit of reading the fine print backwards and forwards, and it's not your prospect. It's you!

There's a wrong way, and a right way, to tell people about your organization's guarantee. Consider this example:

> "Our widgets are guaranteed. If you don't like what you see when they're installed on your line, you'll get your entire investment back."

**Watch It!**
Among the many potential problem areas connected to "blanket" guarantees: delivery and availability claims; data sheets listing specs that can change without notice for reasons beyond your control; and service response times. (That promise to offer support "any time" the customer needs it can come back to haunt you.) Be realistic about what your company can deliver—and be honest.

It sounds great, but is it accurate? You'd better find out! Will your organization *really* refund all monies if the customer doesn't like the way a single widget looks? And that phrase "entire investment" is a disaster waiting to happen. What if your customer had to modify the ventilation systems in six manufacturing facilities in order to accommodate your product? Would you be willing to bet that a hungry attorney wouldn't be able to convince someone, somewhere, that this expense should be included in the customer's "entire investment?"

The odds are that your company has spent a good deal of time and legal brainpower developing the language of your guarantee. Read it! And when you talk about the guarantee to buyers, avoid sweeping statements you can't back up. Stick with something like this:

"Our widgets are guaranteed. Let me go over our policy with you when we're finished here, and then I'll give you a copy of your own so you can review it."

# When Not to Say the "G" Word

You should never begin a sales relationship by appealing to a guarantee. Period.

That means you should not attempt to work the guarantee into your opening statement, either on the phone or in person. Appealing to a guarantee at this phase of the relationship is a sign of weakness, not a sign of strength. What, your prospect may ask, is that guarantee meant to compensate for?

If your suspect or prospect asks about a guarantee, by all means, give him or her all the details. Other than that, though, save references to your guarantee for the final stages of the sales process, when you're talking specifics about the money your buyer will be spending. (An obvious exception: If your contact asks about a guarantee, you should responsibly summarize all the details.)

# The Right Side of the Law

I'm not a lawyer, and I don't know about the specifics of your selling environment, so I'm not going to pretend to be able to pass along advice about the legal ins and outs of your business. What I'm going to pass along is even better.

Below, from the home office in Julian, California, you'll find my personal Top Ten List on the subject of avoiding legal problems, with apologies to David what's-his-name. If you follow the advice I've laid out below, you'll help your organization—and yourself—avoid lawyer's offices and the courtroom. We've been talking about guarantees in this chapter, and I assume you already know that no one can guarantee you that you'll never run into problems with lawsuits. I can promise you one thing: If you *don't* adhere to all the steps in the following list, you'll end up regretting it someday!

> **Sales Accelerator**
>
> A complaint is *not* a personal attack. It's:
>
> ➤ An opportunity to show how good you really are.
> ➤ Valid until proven otherwise.
> ➤ A way for you to learn how to perform better.
> ➤ A way to gain ideas on how to make your products, services, and solutions.
> ➤ A way to make your business relationships even stronger.
>
> When someone takes the time to complain, they're saying they're interested in making the business relationship work.

---

**Parinello's Top Ten Ways to Stay Out of Legal Trouble on the Sales Front Line**

(We hear a drum roll, accompanied at points by the sound of breaking glass...)

NUMBER TEN: When asked to sign something, explain that you don't have signature authority. Hey, you're a salesperson. Sales managers and senior executives deal with this kind of stuff.

NUMBER NINE: When asked to speak to lawyers, politely decline the invitation. News flash: Lawyers live to start trouble. That's their version of prospecting.

NUMBER EIGHT: Follow the rules your company has established for handling escalating customer complaints. In other words, don't improvise, and don't promise to put anyone in touch with the president of the organization on your own authority.

*continues*

---

*continued*

NUMBER SEVEN: Never make claims beyond the limits of your sales role. Translation: Don't pretend to know something you don't, no matter how tempted you may be to assume the mantle of the expert.

NUMBER SIX: Be familiar with any and all regulatory issues that affect your industry and the products, services, and solutions you sell. Talk to a veteran sales rep of integrity or check out back issues of your industry trade magazine if you're having trouble isolating the specifics.

NUMBER FIVE: Know what your organization's policies are. Ask your sales manager for all the relevant details that affect you.

NUMBER FOUR: Don't try to rewrite your organization's policies. They're there for a reason, so don't pretend you've got the authority to summon a one-person emergency meeting of the board of directors. Warning: Violating this rule means you can get both your boss *and* the law mad at you, which is not a pleasant situation!

NUMBER THREE: Put customers first when they're right, but let them know, tactfully, when they're wrong. People who tell you earnestly that the customer is "always right" should also have to be held accountable for commitments customers hear—or think they hear—as the result of such a philosophy.

NUMBER TWO: Do what you say you're going to do. There's no substitute for follow-through! It builds goodwill and keeps people out of court. If you can't do it, don't say you can.

NUMBER ONE: Tell the truth. Honesty and integrity, as the old saying has it, have a distinct advantage over falsehood. The truth is always easier to remember!

# Three Keys to Credibility

What the list you just read really boils down to is this: Don't make basic procedural mistakes, and make every effort to boost your own real-world credibility.

The rest of this section covers three simple steps you can take that will help you present, not just the image of credibility, but the experience of credibility, to your suspects, prospects, customers, and business partners.

## Stay Away from the Words "I Think"

The two simple-sounding words "I think" can leave prospects swearing you've told them something you haven't really told them. They slip unnoticed into the buyer's consciousness, after undergoing an instantaneous—and inaccurate—internal translation. When a salesperson says "I think X is the case," a strange thing happens. A fair number of prospects (those who haven't been badly burned by such doubletalk) will interpret the salesperson as saying "I am virtually certain X is the case, and I'll get back to you if I'm wrong about that, so you can assume, unless you hear otherwise, that X really is the case." Usually, of course this is not at all what you mean—so don't say "I think"!

Consider the following exchange, which illustrates the kind of careless "I think" statement some salespeople make to their prospects day after day:

> Prospect: Does your service plan cover my town?
>
> Salesperson: Our contract provides for comprehensive service coverage in major metropolitan areas all over our sales region. I think it covers your area. According to *Widgets Monthly*, we've got the best service ratings in the industry.

**Words, Words, Words**

Your *credibility* is the degree to which people find it easy and worthwhile to believe you. True credibility isn't a short-term display of veracity meant to help you "close the sale"—it's a pattern of believability that holds up over the long haul. If you've only got credibility for the duration of a single meeting or phone call, you don't really have credibility!

If it turns out that the coverage is *not* offered in this prospect's area, this salesperson's credibility goes out the window, and it's going to be very difficult to win back! Here's a better approach.

> Prospect: Does your service plan cover my town?
>
> Salesperson: Our contract provides for comprehensive service coverage in major metropolitan areas all over our sales region. However, I don't know if it specifically covers your area. I can tell you that, according to *Widgets Monthly*, we've got the best service ratings in the industry. Let me make a phone call at the end of our meeting to get the answer for you. (Jot the note down so your contact can see that the query will not be forgotten.)

# Highlight (Real!) Service-Based Commitments

Speaking of service—that's a great way to establish, and reinforce, your credibility with the prospect. Prove your commitment! Go to the correct person within your organization and get all the specifics about the after-sale service commitments you offer. Do whatever you can to get your sales manager (or other figure in authority) to spell this out for you in black and white. It's worth agitating for because it helps you establish a serious competitive edge.

Once you get the specifics of your "lockout" service commitments in writing, *make sure the customer gets a good look at exactly what you offer!*

**Words, Words, Words**

A *lockout* is something you can offer your suspects and prospects that no one else can. Free follow-up service that your organization is willing to confirm in writing is a lockout commitment—if none of your competitors offers the same service. By highlighting that which you offer, and are willing to commit to, you "lock out" the competition.

You say your competition offers a similar policy to yours? Similar is not identical! Unless your competition offers an identical service policy, you can almost certainly highlight *something* of value to your prospect that represents a lockout. Remember: Many buyers are extremely sensitive to service issues! Clarify exactly what your service plan offers, and try to establish a (credible and verifiable) dollar-value for it. Get your management's authorization to put it all into writing, pass it on to the prospect, and see what happens.

## Broadcast the Value You Deliver for Current and Past Customers

This can be a truly invaluable tool for building your credibility among suspects and prospects.

Broadcasting means telling people about verifiable success stories. When you broadcast specific positive outcomes from a current customer, you're not just telling the customer that "Our widgets worked for Joe Smith over at ABC Company." You're telling him or her, "We were able to help Joe Smith reduce his overhead costs by 12 percent last quarter while increasing overall effectiveness." The implication, of course, is that your prospect should feel free to contact Joe Smith and confirm the success story.

If you're going to use this dramatic approach to build your credibility—and I urge you to—you have to be willing to take the following steps.

**Sales Accelerator**

You'll get a better response by broadcasting positive results within your current customer's industry or business niche than you will by highlighting sales to people unfamiliar with the industry in question. (Make sure your current customer knows, and is comforatable with, the target audience with which you plan to share your quantifiable successes!)

1. Work with current customers to establish exactly how well (or how poorly!) your product, service, or solution is actually working. Yes, that means taking a good, long look at something that isn't performing the way it should, and agitating with top management to develop and implement the solution. File it under "doing the Lord's work."

2. Once you isolate the (no doubt innumerable!) customers who are thrilled with what your organization has accomplished for them, you have to quantify the level of the success. That means someone has to be able to put a real, verifiable number on what you've done for your customer. If your customer is willing to do the number-crunching for you, that's great! In many instances, though, you'll need to ask for raw data from the customer, analyze it yourself, and submit it to your customer for

approval. Yes, it takes some time—but probably not as much time as you think. The truth is that this is work you should be done anyway for all your current customers! When the budget-crunching campaign starts in at your customer's headquarters, don't you want to be able to demonstrate, in no uncertain terms, the value you add?

3. Finally, you must let your contact know that you plan to use the information you've developed and confirmed in your attempts to reach out to other customers. Don't worry—if you're delivering on your promises, the vast majority of your contacts won't mind at all.

It's true: Broadcasting the results you've delivered for real, breathing, current customers isn't for everyone. Salespeople who think the job of selling stops once a purchase order is issued have a hard time with this one. Then again, salespeople who think the job of selling stops once a purchase order is issued don't make very much money!

Make the commitment. Make the calls. Do the digging. Make quantifying your results for current customers a part of your regular account reviews. Then use the most compelling of those hard-number results to demonstrate to suspects and prospects just how special—and how reliable—you and your organization really are.

Once your prospect understands that, it's a pretty good bet you'll be in a position to start talking about the specifics of doing business together. In the next chapter, you'll find out everything you need to know about the preliminary to the sale commitment—the negotiation phase.

# The Least You Need to Know

➤ Use your organization's guarantee language carefully, and only after having reviewed its written specifics.

➤ Stay on the right side of the law; follow the ten rules for avoiding ethical and legal wrangles.

➤ Stay away from the words "I think"—they're prone to misinterpretation that can come back to haunt you later on.

➤ Highlight service-based commitments—being able to spell these out in black and white can be a major competitive advantage.

➤ Broadcast value you've delivered to satisfied customers—demonstrate how remarkable (and quantifiable) the solutions you've delivered really are.

# Negotiating

If you've followed the contact and presentation approach I've outlined thus far—if you've encouraged the prospect to raise objections early, and if you've consistently elicited meaningful feedback and "buy-in" at key points in your presentation—nice things will start happening hereabouts. You'll start getting serious with some of the prospects you've been talking to. Current customers will begin to think seriously about the benefits of doing even more business with you.

Any number of sales trainers would suggest that you bring your "closing skills" into play at this point. As you'll learn in the next chapter, I'm not big on the whole philosophy of "closing" sales. I prefer to think in terms of formalization of relationships, of new beginnings, and of openings. Before you get to that formalization stage, however, there may be a preliminary hurdle: establishing terms that make sense to your organization, terms that your prospect can work with.

In many selling environments, good negotiation skills represent the difference between the superstars and the mid-level performers. So take advantage of the strategies in this chapter—and learn how to ensure a positive outcome when your prospect starts asking you how much "flexibility" your organization can show in any given area.

# Who Negotiates?

Often, the negotiation phase begins when your prospect asks you to engage in preliminary discussions with people you haven't had much contact with up to this point: buyers, purchasing agents, or people who work in the contracts department. Other parties whose presence indicates that you may have entered the "things-are-getting-serious" zone include consultants and attorneys sent in to talk about terms and conditions.

In other cases, you'll be negotiating directly with the prospect(s) you've been working with all along: Mom and Dad return to your showroom with some "questions about pricing" on that car their daughter took out for a spin yesterday.

# What Happens?

What does the word "negotiation" mean to you?

If you're in sales, there's going to come a time when you're going to be called on to negotiate at some level. For many novice salespeople, the word "negotiation" summons up images of high-level adversarial meetings between well-dressed representatives of corporate titans, with all parties wearing dark glasses and grim looks, and with each camp waiting for the other side to blink. This sort of scene certainly takes place, but it's not the norm in day-to-day sales work!

For the average salesperson, negotiation is likely to involve many situations and many conversations, not just one intense meeting. And the discussions we hold with our prospects (if we're doing our jobs correctly, at any rate) are likely to be low-key, or sometimes even casual—anything but adversarial. That doesn't mean that good salespeople define negotiation as "giving the store away." It means that they handle matters of give-and-take, of compromise, of establishing the correct fit, a little bit at a time, and usually without getting their prospects too agitated. If you ask me, that's the way it should be.

> ### Bet You Didn't Know
>
> The "I have to take it to my boss" or "I have to sell it to the higher-ups" approach is an old, outdated, and time-consuming negotiating tactic that can frustrate your prospect and lose sales for you. Avoid it if you can—but be prepared to respond (pleasantly!) with dictates from bigger, more terrifying committees in your own organization when prospects try to use this ploy on you. ("I've never seen anything like this; I'll have to take it to our warrantee and service departments. That may take up to a week—would you like to provide me with a letter of credit so I can hold your order?")

Engaging in negotiation means understanding that you have something that you are willing to give up, something that your prospect believes he or she ought to have. By the same token, your prospect must have something that you are willing to trade for. For the professional salesperson, that's really what negotiation boils down to. The trick is to do so without giving away revenue your organization can't afford to part with!

> **Words, Words, Words**
> *Negotiation* is the act of formalizing the terms of any aspect of a business agreement.

## Ten Areas for "Give and Take"

There are, broadly speaking, ten areas where you can expect your prospects to ask for concessions from your organization. No matter what your superiors say (or imply!), you won't be weakening the foundations of the republic if you ask an appropriate person within your organization exactly how much "give" there is in each of these areas during the negotiation phase. If the answer is "none whatsoever" in all ten areas, your organization isn't giving you enough negotiating support!

Make no mistake. There's going to be more wiggle room in some of these areas than there will be in others. The point is, you should know where the wiggle room is! The more you know about your organization's "dealbreaker" positions in each of these areas, the better a negotiator you'll be.

Expect prospects to ask for concessions on these 10 items:

1. Price. Expect a request to lower your prices—and don't cave in too early! Price is rarely the main reason an interested prospect decides not to buy.

2. Delivery/availability. Set the right expectations; don't promise what you can't deliver.

3. Payment terms. If you can, you should defer financial issues such as this one to a higher authority.

4. Interest rates. Ditto!

5. Down payments. Ditto!

6. Performance specifications. Stick to what's on your spec sheets and hard data; don't speculate about what future releases or programs will be able to do. (If you do, you'll run the risk of stalling your sale until the new stuff is available.)

7. Repair or replacement of items. You'll be safest when you simply refer the prospect to your organization's contract or written agreement. If pressed, explain that you need to talk to higher-ups.

8. Return policy or warranty conditions. Ditto!

9. Service policies and conditions. Ditto!

10. Penalties/consequence for late or poor performance on your organization's part. Performance guarantees say a lot about your organization's commitment to success.

# Negotiating by Operating Style

You'll remember that, in chapter 14 of this book, you learned about four different styles of social interaction that related to your questioning strategy: driver, expressive, analytical, and amiable. The vast majority of the representatives of your target organization will pursue one of these operating styles during the negotiating phase, as well.

I strongly recommend that you review the questioning techniques outlined in Chapter 14 before you enter into negotiations with your prospects, and that you consider the following additional notes on the negotiating habits of each of the four groups.

## The Analytical Approach

Remember these folks? They live to pick things apart, find flaws, and request new data. When negotiating with someone who adopts an analytical style, bear these points in mind.

LIKELY OBJECTIVE: This buyer wants a black-and white resolution to each and every point he or she raises. The resolution should be both timely (being on time counts for a great deal with these folks!) and thorough. So stick to the facts, don't skip any steps, and shine a spotlight on your in-depth research!

LIKELY TACTICS: Expect an all-consuming focus on facts and figures. Expect a rigid, formal discussion and decision-making process (akin to Robert's Rules of Order).

POSSIBLE ACHILLES HEEL: Rigid, unemotional decision-making style may lead this buyer to rely too heavily on logic. May cling to procedural points at the expense of other, more important questions. Likely to be uncomfortable with, and perhaps ill-informed about, issues that can't be quantified.

YOUR APPROACH: Show proof for every statement you make. Use data, studies, or contracts from past experiences. Substantiate your case; supply as much written material as possible. Keep in mind that, unlike the amiable or expressive buyer, the analytical buyer is unlikely to show outward emotion.

## The Expressive Approach

These are the buyers who love to talk, talk, talk, preferably about themselves. When negotiating with someone who adopts an expressive style, bear these points in mind.

LIKELY OBJECTIVE: This buyer typically seeks proof of his or her own influence, connections, and persuasive ability. This buyer is likely to want to find a way for everyone to win (and have a party, with this buyer occupying the center of attention, afterwards). So let this buyer know how much you respect his or her pronouncements!

LIKELY TACTICS: Expect this buyer to be animated, disorganized, and highly opinionated. He or she may try to gain points from you by saying, "Let me play the devil's advocate…"

POSSIBLE ACHILLES HEEL: Susceptible to flattery. May be self-centered and a poor listener. Sometimes has great difficulty seeing anyone else's point of view; you'll gain influence if you accept his or her outlook as more or less divinely inspired.

YOUR APPROACH: Give in on selected issues. Expressives love to win, especially while everyone is watching. Try to find a way to let the buyer "win" something he or she wants. Where you can honestly and credibly do so, be prepared to use language like "We don't normally do this" or "I've never seen my company make an offer quite like this."

## The Amiable Approach

These people avoid conflict and dissension; they want to keep everyone happy. When negotiating with someone who adopts an amiable style, bear these points in mind.

LIKELY OBJECTIVE: As a general rule, this buyer wants to do what's right for everyone, and would prefer it if negotiations were unnecessary because everyone already agreed on everything. So help this buyer make the negotiating process simple, painless, and relatively quick. Keep things simple, and emphasize how happy what you're doing together will make everyone in the organization.

LIKELY TACTICS: There may be no "tactics" as such. The truth is, amiable buyers often are very poor negotiators. They may simply focus on the solution that ruffles the fewest feathers.

ACHILLES HEEL: These buyers are easily convinced and can (at least initially) be swayed to the

**Sales Accelerator**
Learn to act profoundly surprised when a prospect asks for a concession. This serves as a reality check! Make a hyper-specific (and thus honest) statement like, "Gee—nobody's ever asked for free alterations on a Brooks Brothers suit that's already sale priced before." Then stop talking and see what happens. Many prospects will withdraw their request on the spot. Those who don't will often reduce the requested concession.

**Sales Accelerator**
A "qualified no" is not the same as "no!" Ask questions or offer alternatives when your prospect says something like "I just can't afford the suit and the alterations."

➤ "You know, there's an alterations shop down the street that does excellent work at very reasonable prices."

➤ "Maybe I can get you a 10 percent discount coupon toward alterations, since you're a first-time customer. Would that make sense?"

➤ "What's your total budget?"

thinking of others. Warning: If you push these buyers too hard, they'll call off all discussions and buy nothing.

YOUR APPROACH: Keep it low key! Any negotiations must sound more like friendly conversations. Forget about high-pressure tactics. They simply will not work. Treat this person as though he or she was a family member by making credible, honest appeals: "I care about this project, and I want you to know I'll be looking out for your interests as it goes forward."

## The Driver Approach

Stand back! Prospects who adopt a driver style, you'll remember, are the ones who get right to the point. When negotiating with someone who adopts a driver style, bear these points in mind.

> **Sales Accelerator**
>
> People love to say things like "You can do better than that" during negotiations. Don't get tricked into negotiating against yourself. Always make a serious attempt to get the other person to state his or her negotiating position before you start making concessions: "What kind of (terms/discount/price) did you have in mind?" Remember that the answer you receive is a position, not Holy Writ.

LIKELY OBJECTIVE: One word: Victory! Forget anything you may have read about "win-win" outcomes. In this person's world, only one person gets to win. Guess who it's going to be?

LIKELY TACTICS: Intimidation, intense focus, and an overbearing attitude. Don't be surprised (or lose your composure) if this buyer issues mild, or veiled, threats.

ACHILLES HEEL: That hardheaded attitude may cost them—these buyers have been known to dig in on a single issue and lose sight of just about everything else. The "all-or-nothing" approach has its limitations!

YOUR APPROACH: Hold on to your wallet and be prepared to take the heat! "Acceleration" is the word to remember here. You may be surprised at how quickly this buyer gets to his or her bottom line position.

## It's Your Reality, Too!

All too often, we salespeople take what our prospects say at face value. For instance: Does your heart sink and your pulse start to race when a prospect assails your price as too high? Do you, at some level, think to yourself, "My goodness, she's right! The cat's out of the bag! Our prices *are* too high!"? In short, are you letting this prospect define reality for you? That's a serious negotiating handicap!

When you hear blanket statements like "Your delivery date is totally unworkable" or "Your price is too high," ask yourself:

➤ How well do I know this individual or organization? How well do I know this individual's style (analytical, amiable, expressive, driver)? Is it too early in the conversation for me to be addressing this particular topic with this person? Is it possible the issue that's been raised is a "smokescreen" hiding some other topic?

➤ What is the organization's focus? Is there a good reason for the pronouncement you just heard? In the case of a price objection, is the organization in an aggressive cost-cutting mode?

➤ What is this person's perspective? For instance: Note that "too expensive" means very different things to different groups of people!

➤ Is this person serious—or is he or she engaging in the ritualistic posturing many superiors require of those who conduct negotiations?

Assuming the prospect is always right can be hazardous to your career! Prospects love to say things like, "We're committed to one-hundred-and-twenty-day repayment terms. We simply have to have them." Most of these statements are driven by a familiar principle: Ask for the moon and you might get it. Instead of conducting the discussion along the lines that such pronouncements would seem to require, *ask questions* that (tactfully) challenge that assumption.

### Bet You Didn't Know

Suppose the prospect tells you, "The discount you're offering on your widgets is totally unacceptable." How should you respond?

WRONG: "We can increase the discount to 2 percent, but that's the furthest we've ever gone with this line of widgets."

RIGHT: "What are you paying now for your widget service—and what does that service include?"

The second approach will give you valuable information. Perhaps the prospect really is paying less now, but the current price doesn't include, for instance, a warranty, a liberal return policy, on-site training, or some other aspect of your package to which you can assign a (specific or approximate) dollar value.

# Deadlock!

It's easy to misjudge deadlocks. Your sales manager won't appreciate it if you come pleading for special terms because you "think" that problematic delivery date is the only thing standing between you and closing the deal. You have to know that this issue, and only this issue, is going to scuttle your sale.

Say the prospect tells you something like this:

> "If we're going to do business with your organization, you simply have to relax your payment terms. We have to get 90 days before we can discuss any further concessions or business opportunities."

This sure *sounds* like a deadlock. But is it? Maybe—and maybe not. If you've never relaxed your terms for any customer, and your sales manager refuses to discuss the matter, your best course of action may simply be to walk away. Before you do, though, say something like this:

> "Just for the moment, let's put the question of our payment terms aside. What other changes in our position do you feel would be necessary for us to have a workable relationship?"

Maybe your prospect will hold to the earlier pronouncment and refuse to discuss any other issues. Congratulations! You've reached true deadlock. You must now decide whether to appeal to the Pope for special dispensation, or walk away from the sale.

**Words, Words, Words**

A *deadlock* is a complete standstill or lack of progress in the negotiating process.

In some cases, though, your prospect's negotiation ploy will be revealed as such. The other side will raise three or four issues that "might be worth talking about." Leave the contentious terms issue to last, and address all the other issues with your prospect, from easiest to most difficult. After working through all the other issues on the table, what appeared to be a dealbreaker will, in most cases, be resolvable, thanks to the cooperative effort and attitude you've developed.

# Nipping "Buyer's Remorse" in the Bud

There are steps you can take during the negotiation phase of the sale that will help to minimize the number of people who turn around and try to reverse their purchase decision. To turn "buyer remorse" into "buyer acceptance," you should...

> ➤ Be wary of any negotiation session in which the other side raises few (or no) points, or asks few (or no) questions. You may think you've done a great job of working out the terms, but it's possible you've simply overwhelmed the prospect into giving

verbal "agreement" to points he or she will never commit to in writing. Don't leave important questions unexamined and unanswered!

➤ If at all possible, put your contact in touch directly with satisfied customers.

➤ Call your customer-to-be. If you've set up an appointment for the contract to be signed, don't hesitate to call the day before to be sure everything is still "on."

➤ Follow through! Lots of salespeople start to "slack off" when prospects seem to be heading in the right direction. Don't make that mistake! Pay as much, or more, attention to your prospect as you ever did. If your sale requires credit applications or other documentation, stay on top of things.

## The Least You Need to Know

➤ Ask your superiors where you can grant concessions and where you can't.

➤ Review the four operating styles (analytical, expressive, amiable, and driver) and plan your negotiating strategy accordingly.

➤ Don't assume everything the other side says is right.

➤ Ask questions when confronted with a deadlock.

➤ Use the negotiation phase as an opportunity to prevent "buyer's remorse" later on.

# No Such Thing as "Closing"

**In This Chapter**

➤ Avoiding "close-itis"

➤ Learning to "open" business

➤ Drawbacks of common "closing techniques"

At last—the moment is here! In this chapter, you learn what it takes to finalize the commitment with your prospect. It's time to get the business—or, as some sales professionals put it, "go for the close."

I'm not fond of the word "closing." If you're like me, when you hear that word, you start thinking of endings. The point at which your prospect turns into a customer isn't the ending of anything. It's the beginning of a new relationship for which you, the salesperson, bear a large (perhaps the largest!) measure of responsibility. Winning the business means accepting that responsibility without reservation—not playing head games.

## Hurry Up and Get the Signature!

We salespeople are not known for our patience. I think that's because our income is directly related to our own day-to-day activities. Nothing can happen too fast for our sales process; we want accelerators, "tricks," keys, strategies, the stuff that will get the signature on the bottom of the piece of paper as soon as possible. We want to cross the finish line in a hurry—and we tell ourselves that there will be time to worry about the details later. We suffer from what I call "close-itis."

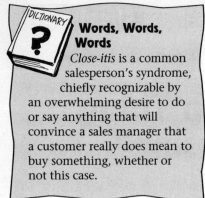

**Words, Words, Words**

*Close-itis* is a common salesperson's syndrome, chiefly recognizable by an overwhelming desire to do or say anything that will convince a sales manager that a customer really does mean to buy something, whether or not this case.

Early on in my sales career, I let a detail slip past me. Although I'd been pursuing the lead in question for nearly two years, I'd been fixated on "getting the business," and not on building a relationship with my contact. I focused on the things I thought were important, but I didn't spend much time asking my prospect what *he* thought was important. In a number of situations, I'd been able to get by with this approach. This time, I couldn't.

There we were, my sales manager and I, in the office of the president of the company. He was reviewing the contract with the director of procurement. My sales manager and I were operating under the assumption that this was the final stage, the payoff for all my hard work—a formality. Page by page they flipped and looked, flipped and looked. On the sixth flip of that seven-page contract, when I thought we were home free, the president looked up and said, "We've got a problem here."

The president needed five years of spare parts support. The contract specified three. I simply hadn't looked closely enough at the specifications my prospect had passed my way. I did a lot of stammering about typos and oversights and division approval. Then my sales manager and I left the facility, promising to find a way to turn the three into a five. We never did. I lost the sale.

What a nightmare! I had been so fixated on "getting the business" that I'd neglected to explore the service question as fully as I should have. Hey, wasn't service something you worry about after the sale? If I hadn't been so focused on the close, I might, at some point in out discussions, have been able to get my contact to find some room to change that five-year requirement, or trade something that made it easier for the target organization to accept some compromise. But not now.

# Blown Closings Are Rooted in Blown Openings

The final commitment to do business together isn't the end; it's a beginning. Instead of focusing on "closing" (even though your sales manager, like mine of many years ago, may insist on using the word), you must make a commitment to opening relationships.

There are as many ways to open a sale as there are steps in the sales process. Remember: The act of opening up your relationship with the prospect isn't something that gets pasted on at the end of the exchange! Everything you've done up to this point will affect the prospect's final decision. It's absurd to pretend otherwise.

There are no "magic tricks" you can use to convince the prospect that he suddenly wants to do business with you. There's only good, sensible sales work—the kind outlined in the previous chapters of this book—and a compelling "call to action" meant to help your prospect focus on the most important issues—and take action.

> **Bet You Didn't Know**
>
> One great way to open a relationship, and take out some insurance against last-minute finalization crises, involves an early contract meeting. This allows you to establish direct contact with the decision maker (that is, the individual we've referred to as the leader or authority decision maker in this book) as soon as you've established interest and fit for the target organization. Ask this person to grant you the privilege of an in-person meeting, *whether or not* this person is acting as your contact on this sale.
>
> Say wonderful things about the other person/people you're meeting with—and pass along a copy of your standard contract. You're not asking for a signature! Say something like, "Whether or not you end up doing business with our firm, I wanted to meet with you to show you what our standard business agreement looks like. I've used a yellow highlighter to show you those clauses our organization has never changed—I'm sure your company has such terms. If you see something here that you couldn't live with, please call me. There may come a time in the not-too-distant future when you decide you want to become one of our customers, and I wouldn't want anything to slow that down." You can also ask for another meeting with this person at the critical point when the decision finally comes down about your product or service.

## Four Closes That Don't Work

The only close that works consistently is the "open." It's the "close" that starts from the moment you begin talking about a new idea with your contact (whether that's a new prospect or a current customer). This the close that allows you to address critical issues, terms, and conditions while there's plenty of time to explore alternatives. It's the "close" that's built into everything you do with your prospect, the one that allows you to suggest formalization *naturally and comfortably* as part of the opening of the relationship, without high-pressure tricks or "we'll-worry-about-that-later" doubletalk.

That's the only "close" you should count on is one that I'll show you how to make a reality a little later in this chapter. Unfortunately, the "open" is not the only "close" you'll hear about from sales managers and sales

> **Sales Accelerator**
> If you make *early* contact with the leader (also known as the authority decision maker), who has ultimate authority over purchasing what you have to offer, you'll be in a good position to appeal to this person if it looks like a competitor is about to steal your sale away. If the sale goes through, you'll still want to keep in touch with this person over time, simply to solidify the business relationship for the long term.

trainers. There are four popular "closing strategies" that show up in virtually every industry and selling environment. Each of them is fatally flawed. Take a look, and you'll see what I mean.

## The "Cutting the Price" Close

"If you make your investment today, I can save you 5 percent of the retail price!"

Usually, the prospect beats the salesperson to the punch by asking for a steep discount before those "magic words" reach the air. Or perhaps the prospect, fully aware that a company that volunteers to cut its price is likely offering a "discount" that's illusory at best, presses for steeper cuts than the ones you've outlined. In either case, the salesperson runs (heck, sprints) to the sales manager and says, "They're tough, boss—the only way to get this sale is to lower the price." This little drama has shown up at every company I've ever worked for.

The price-cutting tactic has some serious drawbacks. For one thing, it becomes habit-forming for salespeople, to the notable detriment of the company's profit margin. For another thing, the prospect usually comes away feeling that he or she could have gotten a better price if only the "holdout" had been longer or more insistent.

Break the discount addiction right now! Here's how:

➤ Add value in the form of optional services or add-on items, rather than lowering your price.

➤ If you're going to offer lower-than-list prices, do it up front, and make it clear that that's what you're doing. You'll be in a better position to refuse later requests for discounts ('We're already below our list!") and you'll be able to identify price-conscious buyers earlier.

## The "No Risk" Close

This is where the salesperson offers to allow the prospect to "try the system out for a few days." This offer is usually accompanied by those irresistible words: "If you don't like it, we'll take it back."

Drawbacks? Oh, there are a few. "No risk" means, for lots of prospects, "no commitment." You often end up putting a whole lot of product out on loan. Your storeroom shelves may get filled up with expensive—and used—capital investment. And there may come a time when you have to sell off that beat-up inventory at reduced commission rates. That eats away at your organization's profits. Another problem is that you'll spend a lot of your time showing uninterested, unqualified prospects how to use your product, service, or solution.

Here's a better way to use your capital resources and your selling time:

➤ Schedule product presentation and demonstration days. These are regularly scheduled events that allow prospects to come on-site and use what you sell. This way,
any prospect you talk to is going to have already
taken the time to come to you, and demonstrated
interested in spending time with your
organization's stuff.

➤ If you insist (or your sales manager insists) on
some variation of the "no-risk" close, make it
necessary for the prospects in question to attend
a short training period (say, two hours at your
facility) before you pass along the loaner. Once
again, this acts as a qualifier.

> **Watch It!**
> Trial periods and loaners can serve as power-ful selling tools, but they're better at helping you to qualify a particular prospect than they are at helping you finalize the sale.

## The "Show Special" Close

"Stop by our booth and take advantage of our convention special!"

This is really a "special event" close; it applies to any and all special promotions that run
"for a limited time only."

I agree that the words "sale," "liquidation," or "estate auction"—and their hundreds of
cousins—are attention getters. The words "all sales final," which are frequently part of the
message customers receive as part of special promotions, are also pretty noticeable. The
truth is, these promotions generally deliver one-time customers, rather than long-term
relationships.

Some salespeople swear by the "special event" technique. To my way of thinking, this
type of selling incorporates two very serious drawbacks. First, your organization may get
an undesirable reputation, that of the company that's running its yearly "going out of
business" sale. (Honestly, how many times can a company go out of business?) Second,
your sales style runs the risk of reminding prospects more of the local swap meet than of
a true sales professional.

If I had my way, special promotions would be extended to existing customers only.
Prospects would learn about the added value you deliver to your customers—and they'd
want to *become* customers as a result! Save the bigger and better specials for your biggest
and best customers; if you're really set on impressing a prospect with a special offer, make
it retroactive. Once a customer reaches a certain level of loyalty, they're entitled to X.

## The "Make a Choice" Close

**Watch It!**
With the exception of some selling that takes place via direct mail, there is almost always more than the dual "this-or-that" purchase choice outlined in the "make a choice" close. Beyond being ethically suspect, this close, when used to pressure contacts into spending more money than they anticipated, may actually cross the line into "bait-and-switch" territory. Stay out of legal trouble; stay away from heavy-handed "make a choice" maneuvers.

"Will it be the model with the wire wheels, or will the hubcaps do?"

Do you want delivery Friday or Monday? Will you be paying by credit card or check? You can probably see this one coming a mile away when salespeople try to get you to commit to a purchase. How do you imagine your own prospects feel when they hear it from you? These days, buyers are well informed. They may see this technique as an insult—especially if it's applied too early in the relationship.

I've listed this strategy as a technique that doesn't work, because I don't think it does. (At the very least, it's not a great way to build the foundation for long-term relationships.) The truth is, though, that the "make a choice" maneuver been around for as long as salespeople can remember, and it will probably still be around long after you and I have departed for our eternal reward. I like to stay away from it. Your sales manager may not let you. If you have to find a way to breathe some life into this "old-timer" close, you should make sure your question accepts and respects the prospect's current state of knowledge.

## Using the Open to Win Business

When you've invested significant amounts of your time, your organization's money, and your own expertise and the expertise of others into a detailed analysis of the ways you can solve your prospects' problems, you're entitled to ask a direct question. So that's what you're going to do.

**Sales Accelerator**
The best way to formalize a new business relationship is to encourage the prospect to tell you what to do next. Accordingly, some variation on the question "What do you want me to do?" is worth considering closely.

Here are three examples of questions that open up the business relationship and formalize commitments. Ask them with confidence. Notice that the accent throughout is on what *you* can do for the prospect—not on what you want the prospect to do next. At the same time, you're going to want to make it clear that you're approaching the other person, not as a supplicant, but as a true business partner. You're not asking for business because you need business— you're asking for business because you believe both sides will benefit from the relationship!

➤ "Mr. Prospect, now that you've had a chance to talk to your team about the recommendations you heard in the presentation last week, what do you think? How do you want me to proceed from here?"

➤ "Ms. Prospect, how does what we outlined in our presentation sound to you? Do you want us to move forward with paperwork and delivery on the widgets we discusses?"

➤ "Mr. Prospect, I've had the honor of learning an awful lot about your organization over the past X weeks. This program we've been discussing seems to represent something that could really help you. Do you want us to get it started for you?"

**Sales Accelerator**
Never forget: You have equal business stature with everyone at the target organization—up to and including the president of that organization!

➤ "Ms. Prospect, from what you've told me so far, it seems that we've got a very good match here between what you need done and what we offer. Shall we set up a date for you?"

It should come as no surprise to you to learn that any attempt to "close" the sale with these questions by posing them to prospects who still have major unresolved questions will fail spectacularly! If it does, you've got more selling—more intelligent asking and listening—to do. If it doesn't, you've got yourself a new customer.

## "So, I've Got a Customer!"

That's great! But remember—selling means more than getting a signature on a piece of paper. All the same, it is *nice* to get the signature on the piece of paper (or watch the customer pass along his or her charge card.) And it's even *nicer* when one customer who signs on with you leads you to *another* customer who signs on with you. In the next chapter, you'll get the lowdown on getting referrals and testimonials from your current customer base.

## The Least You Need to Know

➤ Although sales managers may insist on using the word, there really is no such thing as closing, because…

➤ The final commitment to do business together isn't the end; it's a beginning.

➤ There are lots of popular, but counterproductive, strategies for formalizing business (such as the "make a choice" close).

➤ Formalize commitments by asking direct, but not abusive or overbearing, questions.

➤ You're not asking for business because you need business—you're asking for business because you believe both sides will benefit from the relationship!

# Referrals and Testimonials

**In This Chapter**

➤ When to ask for referrals

➤ How to formalize praise

➤ Using small gifts to good effect

This chapter is about the neglected art of turning praise into dollars. In it, you'll learn how to secure powerful referrals and endorsements from current customers. You'll be learning about tools that will help you expand your business at all levels, increase your personal income, and shorten your selling cycle—so take advantage of what follows!

## Two Guiding Principles

I've mentioned at several points in this book that the referrals, and enthusiastic testimonials, of current customers can serve to move your selling career forward in a dramatic and exciting way. The habit of asking for praise and support is such an important (and, for most salespeople, unfamiliar) one that I want to devote a significant amount of time and attention to it here. The first things I want to draw your attention to are two basic rules concerning testimonials and referrals. They're so simple, and such apparent matters of common sense, that they're easily overlooked and easily forgotten. If you're smart, you'll post them somewhere you can see them every day.

## Rule Number One: Quality In Equals Quality Out

Any attempt to "exploit" a relationship to which you have not added measurable value will backfire. Count on it! What we're talking about here is the law of reciprocity. If you take the first step and do something that benefits another individual, that person will, as a general rule, be favorably disposed to do something that benefits you when the opportunity arises. It is true, however, that salespeople sometimes have to find ways to make it easy for people to follow their instincts on this score.

## Rule Number Two: You Can't "Make" People Do Anything

You can *ask* anybody for anything. But don't expect someone who doesn't believe you deserve what you're asking for to help you out. This goes for testimonials, referrals, and, come to think of it, just about everything else in life.

## Praise = Sales

**Watch It!**
Shyness, or "not wanting to push too hard," is no defense when it comes to approaching satisfied customers about referrals and testimonials. The most impressive referrals and testimonials arise from situations where the customer *voluntarily* offers heartfelt praise for you and your organization. The question is: How do you respond to that praise?

"You've really saved the day for us!"

If you're like most salespeople, you get quite a lot of praise over the course of a given month. Most of it probably makes you smile, feel good for a moment, and remind yourself that you really are in the right job after all, despite what your Uncle Vito said all those years ago. Those are all great reactions to praise—but they're not all you should be doing! When people say things like "you've really saved the day," what they're passing along is not just emotion and attention, but also cold, hard cash—presuming, that is, that you know how to translate that praise into new professional alliances.

Recognizing praise—and figuring out how to build bridges when you hear it—is a skill you can, and must, master. Whenever you receive praise during your sales work with prospects, new customers, and current accounts, a flashing red light needs to go off somewhere, and you need to start using the strategies outlined in this chapter to ask for referrals and testimonials.

## Four Types of Praise

There are four different areas of praise:

➤ Praise for your products or services

➤ Praise for your organization

➤ Praise for your selling style and/or approach

➤ Praise for you as an individual.

Each can serve as an excellent foundation for referral and testimonial requests.

## Praise for Your Organization

"That's a quality organization you work for. You should be very proud."

Whenever someone has something good to say about your company, that person is complimenting your organization's culture, image, policies, industry position, or leadership. This is praise that's focused on the way your outfit operates, or is perceived as operating.

## Praise for Your Products or Services

"We've looked high and low for a supplier who could deliver quality like you do. I can't tell you how glad we are you got in touch with us last quarter."

When someone has something good to say about what you offer your customer, they're focusing on your technology, performance, innovations, quality, service, or reliability.

During a recent seminar, someone asked a question about this list: "Aren't the first and second items the same?" They're not! Praise for your products and services is worth understanding on its own terms. You can have superb service and a flawless product that makes BigCo, International one of your very best customers. Until, that is, your company's CEO makes a careless remark about BigCo's industry that winds up on the front page of the *Wall Street Journal*. At that point, it doesn't matter how great your product or service is. Your top person has ticked off the customer's top person. You're probably going to lose this account—not because of the way the customer perceives your product, but because of the way he or she perceives your organization!

Your business criteria are *not* identical to your technical criteria. In fact, for some organizations, it's very difficult to leave customers completely satisfied on both fronts.

## Praise for Your Selling Style

"Miss Salesperson, I like your style! You really know how to take charge."

This is the kind of praise that confirms that your outlook, your way of interacting with suspects, prospects, and customers, has hit the mark with your contact. This person respects your operating methods (as a direct result, no doubt, of your decision to adhere to the methods described in this book!).

Contrary to what many novice salespeople fear, prospects appreciate and respect salespeople who show confidence, persistence, and determination.

**Watch It!**
When asking for referrals, remember that people are most comfortable associating themselves with others of a similar social or economic status, and guard these relationships carefully. Don't push people to exceed their boundaries in these areas. If the person providing you with the referral doesn't know you very well, be prepared to get a referral of equal or lesser business or economic stature. If the person in question does know you well, be prepared to get a referral of equal or greater business or economic stature.

## Praise for You as an Individual

"Ellen, you're the type of person it's a real pleasure doing business with."

The prospect or customer trusts you implicitly and has nothing but the highest regard for your character. This is the kind of praise you love to tell your friends, family, and sales managers about—the praise that, when combined with stellar sales performance, will lead to awards and commendations.

What do you have to do to win this kind of praise?

➤ Be a true team player.

➤ Be considerate for others.

➤ Have respect for the jobs everyone in the organization does.

➤ Say "please" and "thank you"—and mean it.

➤ Make a commitment to add value to the other person's day.

➤ Make an effort to take on important tasks that "aren't really your responsibility."

# Whenever You Hear Praise from a Happy Customer...

When a good customer says something wonderful about you, your style, your organization, or your solutions, you should write the remark down on your handy-dandy legal pad and say something like this:

> "Mr. Smith, you just said (repeat or summarize what the person just said, as reflected in your notes.) Would you mind personalizing it for me?"

Extend your note—and indicate where you want the person to sign.

I'd estimate that, one out of ten of the people you talk to will say "Sure; I'll even go one step further—I'll put it on my letterhead for you."

Another five or six out of ten people will say, "That depends—what do you want to use it for?" Reach into your briefcase and pull out one of the targeted prospecting letters you learned how to write earlier in the book—the ones with the big headline at the top. Say, "Mr. Customer, I'd like to put what you just said at the top of this letter and send it out to 100 of my best prospects. Is that okay with you?" Most of the people who hear this question from you will say "yes" and be happy to do so.

Three or four of every ten people you talk to about signing off on their praise will say "Gee, I'd really rather not." Say, "Hey, that's no problem—I understand what it's like to have to get clearance for something."

# Referrals

The best time to ask for a referral is immediately after you've received praise in one or more of these four areas.

You may have gathered, from earlier passages in this book, that I'm a big fan of "starting at the top" when contacting suspects. I love calling CEOs, presidents, executive directors, and other important types—people who make things happen. One of the most important reasons for this habit of mine is that the potential for referrals to *other* important types is so much greater when you start at the top!

But there's certainly no *law* stating that you should only ask for referrals from leaders. You can ask anyone in the influence and authority network. The language you use will be essentially the same, although you may wish to tailor some of your requests to specific elements of the contact's personality or experience.

The rest of this section gives some advice on what you should say to suspects, prospects, customers, and business partners (in that order).

**Sales Accelerator**
When asking for referrals, always consider the position the person occupies in the network of influence and authority—and expect "parallel" referrals. Leaders can be counted on to refer you to other leaders. Directors will put you in touch with other directors. Influencers will connect you to other influencers. Consumers will introduce you to other consumers.

## Getting Referrals from Suspects

You're working in your territory, try to hook up with companies that are willing to move forward with you in the sales process. If you do this regularly (and, if you follow the advice in this book, you will), you'll eventually run into people who will sing the praises of you, your selling style, your organization, or your products—perhaps as a strategy for getting you off the phone or out the door! When you hear the prospect say something nice to you, seize the opportunity! Ask for a referral.

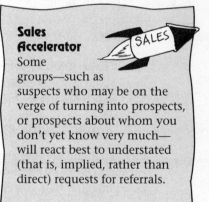

**Sales Accelerator**
Some groups—such as suspects who may be on the verge of turning into prospects, or prospects about whom you don't yet know very much—will react best to understated (that is, implied, rather than direct) requests for referrals.

Here's a model for what you should say to prospects who offer praise, but have no real interest in your offering:

> "Ms. Suspect, thanks for your nice words about our custom-built decks and spas. It sounds as though you've already done an outstanding job at fitting your backyard to your lifestyle and liking. Is there anyone else you'd like to introduce me to in (your town/your street/your neighborhood), or perhaps someone in your family (or some other group) who would enjoy a spa in the backyard?"

And here's a model you can use with those who offer praise and *do* have a real interest in your offering:

> "Mr.Prospect, it's so nice of you to express an interest in our life insurance program. As you begin to take a look at what we have to offer, please keep in mind that we have other programs designed specifically people who are the age of, say, parents or aunts or uncles. Is this a good time to talk about who falls into that category?"

# Getting Referrals from Prospects

Here are two examples of referral requests you can use with prospects. One takes the direct approach; the other is a little more circumspect. Choose the one that seems to you to be most appropriate to the situation.

**Watch It!** Don't ask prospects for referrals until they've had the chance to see your offering or sit through your sales presentation.

➤ **"Full Speed Ahead" approach:** "Ms. Prospect, it's great to hear you say that about my presentation. My entire team—including a couple of members of my family—helped me out with it. Our next logical step would be for you to visit one of our customer sites. (Assume the prospect agrees with this.) Would it be at all possible for you to invite Mr. Marketing Expert to come along with us?" (This assumes that there is another department—in this case, the marketing department—that could benefit from what you have to offer.)"

➤ **"Take It Slow" approach:** "Mr. Prospect, thank you for your positive comments about my presentation. As you move forward in your evaluation, would you mind doing me a favor? (Assume the prospect says yes.) Would you give some thought to who you know in your industry whom you might want to introduce me to that I might be able to present this offering to?"

Please remember—the above models are presented for your consideration in dealing with prospects who, on their own initiative, take the opportunity to praise you to the heavens. *Don't* imagine that you can ask any and every prospect for a referral like this, or that prospects who smile and say "That sounds very interesting" are ready to give you a referral.

**Bet You Didn't Know**

The sample prospecting letter that appears in Chapter 11 can carry even more impact when you target it toward a referral from a current customer. Change the headline to a written testimonial, one you've received explicit approval from the customer to use. Expand the P.S. so that it reads, "Mr. Customer suggested that I contact you; I'll call you on (date) at (specific time). If this is an inconvenient time, please leave word as to when I should make the call." In addition, write the following sentence along the bottom of the envelope: "Mr. Customer suggested I send you the enclosed information." (See Appendix B for more information on formulating successful sales letters.)

## Getting Referrals from Customers and Business Partners

There's no question about it. Your current customers are your very best source of referrals. As a group, they're an even better source than your business partners—there are so many more of them!

As a practical matter, the techniques for eliciting referrals from your best customers is the same as the one you'll use for business partners.

Make a list of your very best customers and business partners, complete with the name of the most highly placed contact you've ever met with during your relationship with this customer. You want to focus only on those who have received truly outstanding value from you. Be ruthlessly honest on this point! Let's say, for the sake of argument, that you have ten such accounts. You're going to focus only on your highest-ranking contact within each of those accounts.

Get ten coffee mugs with your company logo on it, and matching brass and leather coasters. (These can be ordered from many sources.) Then customize each cup—apply a tag specifying the *specific*, quantifiable results you've delivered on one side of the tag, and the *intangible*, but nevertheless important, solutions you've delivered on the other side of the tag. The tag should look like one of those "clearance price" tags you can find in appliance stores. One side might say "$2,400 in shipping department savings each year!" The other side might say, "Consistent on-time delivery of your customer orders."

Now comes the fun part. Collect the business cards from all the individuals in your organization who have helped you serve and support the customer in question. Ask each person to sign the card and include a message of thanks. Now personalize each mug a little more by popping in a trinket related to a hobby or interest of your prospect's (golf, say, or gardening). Finally, gift wrap each mug.

**Watch It!**
Some organizations (notably, those with ties to or relationships with the government) may have policies banning employees from accepting any gifts at all. Make sure you are not violating your customer's gift policy! When in doubt—ask.

Hand-deliver each package to your contacts (and make sure the right cup goes to the right contact, or all your work will be in vain)! Say, "Ms. Customer, this is a personal gift from my team to you." Explain the information on the tags—and get ready for the compliments.

Reserve the "coffee cup" approach I just described—or any variation on it involving, for instance, customized pen sets, crystal bowls, vases, or other snazzy-looking nonconsumable items—for the top 10 percent of your current customer base.

Take my word for it: This is going to be a great meeting.

On your way out the door—or at another point that seems appropriate to you—make your request for a referral. "Ms. Customer, is there anyone you know here in (geographic area) whom you might be able to introduce me to, someone to whom we might be able to deliver the same or even better results?" My experience is that waiting until the "thanks-for-coming-by" portion of this meeting will virtually always result in at least one or two highly promising referrals. I call these "golden referrals"—they lead to a more loyal customer base, a shorter sales cycle, and, yes, even greater amounts of add-on business from the person who *gives* you the referral.

This strategy, as I've outlined it, is a proven winner. Wouldn't *you*, at the very least, offer a name or two to a salesperson who delivered honest-to-goodness results—and then went to all that trouble to tell you about it?

Actually, the reason this technique works so well is that it dramatically demonstrates, for your very best customers, precisely what you've done for them. In the next chapter, you'll learn how to make sure the same basic message gets out to *all* your customers, and you'll get some important advice on repairing relationships with customers who didn't get your best.

# The Least You Need to Know

➤ Any attempt to exploit a relationship to which you have not added measurable value will backfire.

➤ Wait until your contact offers genuine praise before you ask for referrals.

➤ Don't ask for testimonials until you've delivered significant value to the organization.

➤ Strongly consider using the "coffee-cup approach"—that is, customize a small, dramatic gift for key contacts within the top 10 percent of your customer base.

# Part 6
# The Long Term

*Lots of salespeople (and sales managers) seem to think that selling starts with your first contact with the prospective buyer...and ends when you receive a signature on a purchase order. In this part of the book, you learn how to build loyalty by demonstrating and quantifying the value you've delivered, how to develop strong muliti-contact support groups within your current customer organizations, and how to win add-on business from current accounts. In addition, you'll learn how to overcome the most common obstacles to success in sales...and you'll find out about what it takes to turn your sales job into a sales career that keeps you personally and professionally satisfied in the long term.*

# Adding Value Over Time

Customers are the reason you show up for work every morning, the reason your company exists. As important as it is to persuade prospects to turn into new customers, it's also important to be sure that the solutions you deliver are being used, and are of benefit to, the people who are *already* your customers.

In this chapter, you'll learn how to quantify and demonstrate the value that you deliver to your customers, improve your existing relationships, and increase the likelihood that you can develop new sources of revenue from existing customers.

## Looking at Your Customer

Can you picture your customer sitting on a three-legged stool?

That stool works just fine as long as there really *are* three legs. The minute one of the legs gives way, though, the whole thing comes tumbling down, and your customer is sprawled all over the floor. Customers who have the supports kicked out from beneath them don't usually come back for more.

There are three vitally important "legs"—supports—to your relationship with the customer.

➤ Trust

➤ Expectations

➤ Investments

Take a look at each right now.

# Trust

When you tell your customer something, is it the truth—the whole truth and nothing but the truth? Do you keep your word, no matter what—and let your customer know ahead of time on those rare occasions when a projection suddenly looks unrealistic? Do you always, without fail, try to determine what is in your customer's best interests—and then act in accordance with those interests?

Trust is absolutely essential in any meaningful business relationship—whether you're selling computers, designer clothing, cosmetics, chemicals, or accounting services. What makes trust happen? The authority of your word, for one thing. If you state something definitively, and then make a habit of coming back and overruling yourself because of the people "back at headquarters," your trust is going to take a hit, no matter how earnest or innocent your initial statements were.

So think before you speak! Never give any customer reason to doubt the authority of your word. When a customer asks something about which you may not yet have all the facts, say so! Keep the customer's trust. Say something like this:

> "This is such an important issue that I want to do a little research for you and get it right. I'll get the answer from the person who's directly in charge of this area and report back to you no later than Thursday by phone."

Then (you guessed it) keep your word!

# Expectations

Many salespeople—I'd venture to guess that it's a solid majority—work a lot harder at setting up customer expectations than they do at fulfilling them. Don't make that mistake! If you promise a result to your customer—put it in writing and make it clear, *after* the sale, that you intend to do anything and everything necessary to turn it into a reality. I recommend monthly or quarterly progress reports, delivered in person and on paper.

Sometimes customers develop unrealistic expectations because salespeople make completely unintentional—and usually, pretty vague—statements that customers choose to interpret in ways that are convenient to them. Although this type of miscommunication isn't exactly dishonest, it can result in outcomes that are just as catastrophic as situations where salespeople lie through their teeth.

Here again, the answer is to *put things in writing*. When a requirement comes up that's outside of your normal operating procedures, develop a written summary. Let the appropriate people in your own organization take a look at your written summary of the specifications, plans, or procedures your prospect wants. Once everyone on your side has had the chance to review, revise, and restate, you can then deliver the final written summary to your customer. No surprises. No breaches of trust. No unrealistic expectations based on in-person exchanges you can point in one direction, and the customer can point in another.

# Investments

Your customers will expect a return on every investment they make by working with you. If they don't get a return, then what they thought was an investment turns into a loss.

Here's the latest news update: Relationships that your customers associate with financial losses don't fall into the "mutually beneficial" category.

You and your organization must prove—not just once, not just twice, not just this quarter, but continually—that a return on investment is taking place. And if a return on investment *isn't* taking place, then you have to take personal responsibility for changing what needs to be changed until one does take place.

In just a moment, you'll be taking a close look at some strategies you can use to determine—and publicize—the value you deliver to customers. For now, remember that the only way to turn customers into business partners is to consistently deliver value that's both measurable (real, live, dollars and cents) and intangible. Delivering intangible returns on investment—greater exposure, increased goodwill among potential donors, better relations with the surrounding community, increased prestige, whatever—is good. But it's not enough. You must be able to show *why doing business with your organization is a sound financial decision.* (And in these days of lean budgets and instant reorganizations, you'd better be able to show that in short order!)

## Bet You Didn't Know

Business partners expect more—sometimes a lot more.

Your customers should receive periodic demonstrations of the quantifiable and intangible value you're adding to the organization, and your business partners—those customers who have, over time, become more closely allied to your organization in several strategic business areas—should receive even more attention. Fortunately, they'll usually give you more in return for your efforts, too. Not only can business partners be counted on to pass along significant amounts of hard-earned capital, they'll also help you develop new products, services, and solutions, and develop collaborative marketing strategies with you.

In many situations, accounts with business partners are maintained by highly skilled senior salespeople who act as parts of large "account teams" that include members of almost every functional department of your organization. These teams usually report to an upper-level manager or executive-level person.

# What Your Customers and Business Partners Want

Salespeople who find themselves wondering "What are they after?" haven't done enough work to identify what their customers and business partners really want.

Any relationship with a customer or business partner must be guided by an understanding of precisely what the other side wants out of the relationship. The list below—and the comments that follow—will give you an idea of the general requirements customers and business partners always make of a salesperson. The specific expressions of each of these requirements in your own situation will, of course, require some more digging on your part.

**Sales Accelerator**

Take the time to find out exactly what each individual customer requires from your relationship by conducting formal or informal polling.

Customers and business partners want salespeople who...

➤ Understand them on a personal level.

➤ Understand the products, services, and solutions they sell.

➤ Show up on time for meetings.

➤ Show up prepared to address the topics on the agenda.

➤ Drop in without an appointment rarely, and only when there is something of significant value to discuss.

➤ Return phone calls promptly.

Take a look at each of these requirements in detail—so you can track down the specifics that will inform your relationship with each particular customer and business partner.

## The Relationship Matters!

Understanding your contact on a personal level is absolutely essential.

What drives your contact? Makes him or her happy? Gets him or her riled up? Makes him or her cackle with glee?

Each and every person on the face of this earth is unique and distinct in the sight of the Creator—but salespeople have a disturbing habit of treating Contact A, who faces business problems similar to those of Contact B, as though he or she *were* Contact B.

The French have a saying: *Vive la difference!* Find out what special, distinctive, personal approaches your contact takes to business and to life in general. How does this person make decisions? Express opinions? Measure success? Set goals? What hobbies, sports, and avocations make this person's life more interesting?

The more you know, the better positioned you'll be to develop a truly meaningful relationship with each and every one of your Contacts and business partners.

## The Organization Matters!

Understanding the goals of your customer's organization is just as important as understanding her or his personal goals. Here are some ideas on how you can make this understanding happen.

➤ Make yourself available to attend any and all of your customer's meetings that involve discussions of what you've sold.

➤ Make every attempt to invite key players within your own organization to visit with your customers, so that they, too, can get an insight into your customer's world.

➤ Meet as many different directors within the organization as you possibly can—and be sure you get at least a handshake from the leader/authority decision maker who presides over the area that uses what you sell.

➤ Read and frequently review the organization's mission statement. (I've known some people who've gone so far as to memorize—and quote—the mission statement of a customer!)

## Showing Up on Time Matters!

"Tony, isn't this one pretty obvious? Isn't itsecond nature not to keep a customer waiting?"

Yep. It's obvious. And maybe it *should* be second nature. But plenty of salespeople still let this one slide. Why? It's easy to get busy—darn busy—in this crazy business world of ours.

**Watch It!**
Beware! At some companies, promptness is an essential, and explicitly stated, component of the corporate culture. Showing up late for a meeting is tantamount to insulting the CEO's sainted, grey-haired grandmother. If you know you're going to be delayed because of some unavoidable occurrence (say, an epidemic or a nuclear attack), then by all means telephone your contact—or perhaps ask your manager to attend the meeting for you.

**Sales Accelerator**
Some customers will be more than happy to make you "feel at home" during your visits to the company site(s). They may go so far as to turn you into a "virtual employee" by listing your name in the company directory, accepting articles for the company newsletter, and even allocating temporary office and file storage facilities. This is a privilege—don't abuse it! Respect your contact's time (and all confidential information and facilities).

All the same, there's very little that gets your customers and business partners more irritated than having to cool their heels while they wait for you. So this point is worth emphasizing—and re-emphasizing—on a daily (or hourly!) basis.

I once sold a million-dollar computer system to a certain company. Things got hectic one morning, and I didn't allot enough travel time for a scheduled "how's-it-all-working-out" meeting with my contact. Now, that sort of traffic dealy didn't happen very often to me, so I convinced myself, during my drive to the facility, that it wasn't that big a deal. The system was up and running. The traffic was worse than I'd anticipated. I was human, like everyone else on the highway. What was the big deal?

As it happened, the president of this firm decided, at the last minute, to sit in on my meeting. Would you like to know how long I kept the president of that company waiting? Well, I'm not going to tell you, because it still makes my stomach churn. I will tell you this much. That was the last time I ever saw that top executive—and it was the last time I ever showed up late for any meeting with a customer.

## The Agenda Matters

If your customer expects you to be in attendance at a meeting, it behooves you to find out what it's about ahead of time. Don't waste everyone's time, effort, and energy by staring around the table blank-eyed and repeating the mantra of the unprepared: "Let me look into that for you."

The more you can look into *before* the meeting, the more answers you'll be able to provide. The more answers you provide, the happier your customer will be.

## Appointments Matter!

Yes! There are some situations where dropping in without an appointment makes sense as part of your initial contact method. But we're not talking about getting a share of the contact's attention now—we're talking about managing a relationship over the long term, and that means respecting your customer's time.

Never "drop by for a chat" because you happen to be in a customer's area. Use the means of contact for which your customer expresses a personal preference. When in doubt, set up an appointment ahead of time.

## Returning Phone Calls Matters

"I can't possibly return all these calls by the end of the day!"

You're right. You probably can't. Let's face it: A typical sales day will include more action items than you actually have time to complete. That means you'll need to prioritize your activities. Some of the messages you receive from customers will fall into the "call me when you can" category; others will fall into the "emergency!" category. Make sure you're not putting off returning calls in the latter category.

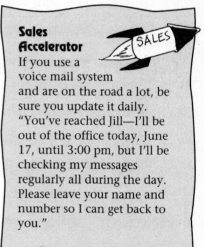

**Sales Accelerator**

If you use a voice mail system and are on the road a lot, be sure you update it daily. "You've reached Jill—I'll be out of the office today, June 17, until 3:00 pm, but I'll be checking my messages regularly all during the day. Please leave your name and number so I can get back to you."

I use the following categories to classify incoming messages:

Urgent (must be returned within two hours)

Critical (must be returned the same working day)

Important (must be returned by the next working day)

Casual (should be returned as soon as a slot arises)

Customers count on you to be there to talk to when things get weird, and if you don't come through for them, they won't come through for you. Remember: It's their checks that keep the lights in your office on!

# "Sole" Music

It's music to any salesperson's ears to learn that his or her company is the sole supplier of widgets to a particular customer or group of customers. The question is, how do you get that music to play? The answer is deceptively simple-sounding; be willing to perform, and measure that performance, for each of your customers.

During your in-person meetings with customers, I strongly suggest that you ask your contact some variation on the following question:

"Ms. Customer, what will it take for you to give our company all of your widget business?"

The answers you get may be expressed in a thousand different ways, but I'll bet you a nickel that you'll be able to file whatever you hear under one of the following headings:

"Give us the proper return on our investment!" (That is, "Make it so clear that this was a great idea that, if I had it to do over again, I wouldn't hesitate for a second, or even change a thing about the way this was implemented.")

"Give us an appreciating asset!" (That is, "Make other areas of our business more efficient and profitable—deliver significant benefits beyond the initial area in which your product, service, or solution operates.")

Take a close look now at each of these demands. If you learn about them and develop strategies for making them happen, you'll be on your way toward being able to demonstrate exactly what you've done for your contact. Once you've done THAT, you'll stand a very good chance of becoming the sole supplier for your customer.

# Let Them Eat R.O.I.!

*R.O.I.* is short for "return on investment." It's what the customer gets in return for investing in your organization, above and beyond the investment itself. If your product, service, or solution causes more problems than it solves, or delivers results that do not defray the costs associated with working with you, then it has not delivered any return on investment.

As a salesperson, you're going to have to make a commitment to helping your customers realize, measure, and appreciate a business-related or personal return on investment after their purchase.

There are three categories of R.O.I.:

➤ **Hard value/tangible R.O.I.:** After a little research, this is easy to see and easy to measure. This is the direct, quantifiable impact your solution has had on the organization in your area of activity. Examples of hard-value R.O.I. would include increases in revenue, earnings, income, margin, or market share that can be directly traced to (for instance) the sales training you offer; or decreases in taxes, expenses, staffing expenses, or overdue debt that can be directly traced to (for instance) the accounting services you offer. Hard value R.O.I. is generally measured and expressed in numbers and percentages: "Revenue is up 12 percent and expenses are down since your sales reps were trained in our program!"

➤ **Soft value/intangible R.O.I.:** This is harder to see and measure, but nevertheless represents significant advances in areas of direct relevance to your customer and his or her organization. Examples of soft-value R.O.I. would include improvements in customer relations, market exposure, or image management—or a decrease in worries, problems, or risk in some other area of your customer's business or personal life. Soft-value R.O.I. is usually measured and expressed by using descriptive words and phrases: "The possibility of negative media coverage on X issue has now been substantially eliminated, thanks to the strategies we've put into place."

➤ **Emotional R.O.I.:** This is easy to observe, but hard to measure. Emotional R.O.I. is sometimes referred to as the "emotional paycheck" accompanying a particular course of action. Usually, emotional R.O.I. takes the form of internal feelings of pride, recognition, prestige, social status, or increased self-esteem: "You've done the right thing by investing in this activity center; an industry leader like your company needs to be able to maintain strong community relations with the city in which it operates."

There are only three ways to measure the R.O.I. of what you're selling. They are, in order of preference:

➤ You work with your customers and get a commitment from them to collect the information, assess it, and generate a (formal or informal) report. Despite what you might be thinking now, many of your customers will be highly motivated to take this step, because they, too, will want to know how well your product, service, or solution is working.

➤ You take the initiative and (perhaps while at the customer's facility) personally collect all the information, assess it, and generate a report of your own that your customer either revises or signs off on. This approach will help you handle those customers who simply don't have the time or resources to track down the information you need to determine your R.O.I.

➤ You make a responsible estimate of what the R.O.I. is without collecting hard data, an estimate based on substantial industry experience or trend analysis, then get your customer to either revise it or sign off on it. This approach will allow you to handle customers who are uncomfortable with either of the above techniques.

**Sales Accelerator**

The best place to collect hard data for your R.O.I. analysis is by interviewing consumers (front-line people) in your customer's organization, or by talking to the people responsible for managing those workers.

---

**Example of Return on Investment (R.O.I.) Calculation**

Product: Radio advertising

Customer: Vito's Italian Restaurant

Scenario: You sold your radio spots to Vito Benefito, the owner of the restaurant. Vito's ad featured a half-price meal deal to patrons who mentioned the radio ad. The ad has been running for two months, and now Vito is considering cancellation. Your aim is to prove the worth of your product by means of an R.O.I. presentation. You meet with Rosa, the head accountant, and you establish the following numbers:

Price of airing one month of radio spots: $2,700 per month.

Production time for one month's radio spots: $300

*continues*

*continued*

Total cost of one month's ads: $3,000

Number of meal deals: 100 per month.

Average amount of meal deal checks: $40.00

Total gross revenue from ad: 100 x $40.00 = $4,000

Return on investment (Total gross revenue/total cost of ads): 133%

*Advertisements achieve payback (that is, deliver revenue equal to 100% of expenses) in 22 days!*

# Deliver R.O.I. Plus!

Can there be anything better than R.O.I.? You bet there can. It's called the "appreciating asset," a phrase that describes a product, service, or solution that not only delivers tangible value in one particular functional area, but also helps the organization stay ahead of the game in at least one other field.

Let me give you an example of what I mean. Suppose your customer buys lubricating oil from you, and suppose that the oil you sell is one of the best brands available. Using your oil cuts down on equipment wear and tear—as we'd expect—and thus increases the average lifespan of the equipment in question by, let's say, 15%. When you can measure and demonstrate that, you've shone a spotlight on your R.O.I.

> **Words, Words, Words**
>
> Your *product or service* represents an appreciating asset when your customer can offset costs that go up (such as labor expenses or replacement parts purchases) by means of using something that you sell—something that either stays the same, or increases in cost more slowly, than the cost being offset.

But is that the ONLY way using this oil benefits your customer's business? No! Because there are fewer breakdowns, the manufacturing process is interrupted less frequently, and that means that overall efficiency improves in a measurable way! Not only are you helping your customer replace equipment at greater intervals—you're helping him or her to get more product out the door and keeping labor costs down by reducing down time!

Use the same research techniques you learned about for developing R.O.I. assessments to find out whether or not your product represents an appreciating investment for the customer you serve.

# If It Ain't Working Better Than They Expect—Fix It!

Any attempt to quantify the R.O.I. you deliver to your customer—any attempt to determine whether or not what you're offering represents an appreciating asset for your customer—carries with it the responsibility to change anything that doesn't deliver superior results. If you don't take responsibility for the outcomes your customer experiences, you will not get sole supplier status!

You say you want to win sole supplier status? Then your goal is to *exceed* the customer's expectations, and to do this on a regular basis. It's not as hard to pull off as you might think, but you have to set up some ground rules at the outset of the relationship—ground rules that will usually help you measure everything that needs to get measured.

First, get buy-in from your contact. Establish a mutually acceptable goal—say, a 10 percent reduction in down time over the next two quarters. Then say, "If we can exceed your expectations, and reduce down-time by 15 percent or more during the next two quarters, will you give us sole-source status for the balance of the year?" When you ask this question of the right person—typically, the highest-level person you know in the network of influence and authority who has direct authority over decision making in your area—your contact will start getting very specific about how your outcomes are going to be measured! Most leaders and directors will give you the commitment you ask for...if you make a persuasive case that you can deliver on your promise!

This is an excellent time to lay the groundwork on the help you'll need for implementation and review. Say, "Mr. Leader, in order to deliver results like that—results that the rest of the industry will envy—I'm going to need some help from some of the people who work in the assembly department. Specifically, I'm going to need assistance from Joan Director and Stanley Consumer, so we can get the training right, monitor your assembly processes, and deliver the superior results we're both after. Can you help me set up contacts with those people?"

**Watch It!**
You can't secure sole-supplier status if your goal is to walk away from the sale once the purchase order is issued. You must make a personal commitment to oversee and implement, on the shop floor or in the cubicles of end-users, the solutions you've proposed.

When the leader says "Yes," you're ready to rock and roll—and ready to start helping to implement, in a hands-on way, the solutions you've been speaking so highly of all through the sales process.

## Once You Pull It Off

Will it take time, effort, dedication, and a certain level of diplomatic skill to deliver the above-average results you've promised your contact? You bet it will. And that's the same time, effort, dedication, and diplomacy that will make it easier for you to sell to subsidiaries, sister divisions, and parent companies and further distance yourself from the competition!

Once you walk on water for the contact with whom you made your original "if-we-exceed-this-target" agreement, you'll want to ask about the possibility of repeating your miracle for other parts of the organization. You should:

➤ Ask your current contact to endorse your existing performance for the head of the division (or the CEO of the company) and request a meeting where all three of you can talk about how to duplicate the results elsewhere within the organization. If that doesn't work, you should…

➤ Ask your current contact to endorse your existing performance for the person to whom he or she reports, and request a meeting where all three of you can talk about how to duplicate the results elsewhere within the organization. If that doesn't work, you should…

➤ Ask your current contact to "author" or "co-author" an article in the company newsletter about the results you've been able to deliver. (I put the words "author" and "co-author" in quotes because, in most cases, people on your side will be doing most or all of the writing, at the customer's request. Let him or her take as much of a role in the development of this article as seems appropriate; let him or her take all the credit for the article if this is desired.) If that doesn't work, you should…

➤ Ask your current contact to supply a dramatic testimonial for use as the headline in a prospecting letter targeted toward sister operations and subsidiaries. If that doesn't work, you should…

➤ Approach the subsidiary outfits yourself on the phone, drop a couple of strategic (and appropriate!) names and talk about the possibility that you can repeat your success.

# Making It Happen

There's an old saying about opportunity coming along disguised as hard work. It's certainly relevant to the strategies you've just reviewed on keeping customers happy.

Will implementing the ideas outlined in this chapter always be easy? Absolutely not. Will they take time, dedication, elbow grease, and commitment? You bet they will. Are they likely to leave you feeling a little stressed out at the end of the day? Well…it's a possibility. But as long as you stay focused on the basics—delivering and demonstrating value—you'll be ready to move forward, even though keeping everything in perspective will probably be a bit of a challenge from time to time.

In any successful sales career, there have always been "bumps in the road." In the next chapter, you find out what the most common ones facing salespeople are—and how to handle them before they start affecting your most important asset: you!

# The Least You Need to Know

➤ There are three vitally important "legs"—supports—to your relationship with the customer: trust, expectations, and investments.

➤ Each of the legs must support your relationship with the customer; the lack of any one will cause a collapse!

➤ Measure everything that needs to be measured for your customer (and be prepared to display some initiative in doing so).

➤ Commit yourself personally to fixing what doesn't work.

➤ Find out what it will take to become the sole supplier.

➤ Once you've delivered measurable value, work to develop business with subsidiaries and sister companies.

# Dealing with Career Obstacles

It's time to take a look at the common hurdles and potentially devastating misconceptions that can overtake your career. In this chapter, you learn how to recognize, and respond appropriately to, the career obstacles that can stop even experienced salespeople in their tracks.

## Classic Misconceptions

There are a number of potentially dangerous misconceptions floating around about the sales profession. I've managed to dispel all of them over the past quarter-century or so, but it's important to understand that I didn't do this by launching a public awareness campaign whose aim was to straighten out what everyone in the country thinks about salespeople. I did it by focusing on the two groups that mattered:

➤ Me, and

➤ My suspects, prospects, customers, and business partners.

Those are the only two groups of people whose opinion really matters when it comes to dispelling negative sales myths: Your own sweet self, and the buyers you come in contact with every day. If *you* believe the stuff some people say, you can sabotage your career. If you fail to dispel the myths (typically by means of setting a good example in person), the people who buy from you, or think about buying from you, may lose faith in what you have to say. So get things straight in your own mind first!

Enough preparatory talk. What are the most damaging myths people associate with sales work—and how should you counteract them?

# Myth #1: Only Someone Who Talks a Good Game Can Sell

Actually, fast-talkers who do nothing else don't do really well in the world of sales. Occasional talk, peppered by lots of intent listening, is the way to go. And a good listener will outperform a good talker every time.

When I'm not learning about the individuals and companies I'm talking to, I'm not getting any closer to my goal of learning enough to be able to satisfy their needs, and I'm certainly not getting any closer to the goal of closing any individual sale.

# Myth #2: Sales Is a Numbers Game

Actually, sales *is* a numbers game—the further ahead of quota you get, the more money you make!

Lots of sales trainers get all worked up about prospecting ratios and "closing" percentages. Certainly, you should make an effort to establish, in general terms, your own activity bar—the levels of prospecting that make your goals possible. Your sales manager will probably have important input on this score. But the profession of sales not dependent (as some would have you believe) on dialing wildly, or cold-calling without direction or purpose. Sales work is about people, not numbers. It's a lot more like brain surgery than bingo. It should be carefully planned, carefully executed, and rigorously monitored at all key points.

# Myth #3: To Be Successful in Sales, You Have to Have Thick Skin

Some real attitude problems have arisen in sales because of this myth. In the name of developing a "thick skin," lots of salespeople have adopted a persona that is, in a word, insufferable.

Do you need to call on internal reservoirs of strength do deal with the inevitable setbacks that come your way as a professional salesperson? Absolutely. But that's not the same thing as developing an outer persona that turns others off. Always remember: The aim is to build bridges, not to force ourselves on unsuspecting buyers, engaging in some sort of mental game whose unspoken rules are "I succeed, you fail, hasta la vista, baby!"

## Myth #4: Sales Has Its Unavoidable Ups and Downs

Sales only becomes a rollercoaster ride if you let the process drive you. It only has ups and downs if you don't have goals. It only becomes a maze of "hot periods" and "cold periods" if you mismanage your time during those seasonal shifts that may be inherent to your business. It only has lulls if you practice the "ready, fire, aim" school of sales planning.

"Everyone's on vacation—it's a bad time to sell." Baloney! Don't say it; don't even think it. (By the way, have you noticed that salespeople who whine a lot about this "bad time to sell" problem are running into managers, and whole organizations, who simply won't accept the excuses anymore?)

**Sales Accelerator**
Remember: You must work the middle of your funnel with strict dedication! Every single day of your sales week, you should ask yourself, "What can I do to move someone to the next level of commitment?"

**Bet You Didn't Know**

No matter what you hear anyone else say, there really is no "bad" season, month, week, or time of day to sell. There is always opportunity for salespeople who are committed enough to find it.

You can put that fact to your advantage. Picture this scenario; While your competitors have given up on July ("Everyone's on vacation!"), you take advantage of the "lull." You target people who are less likely to be away on holiday—and you get through to them more easily, because there are fewer gatekeepers to contend with!

## Myth #5: You Have to Be Good at Handling Rejection in Sales

I refuse to acknowledge that rejection has taken place until I've made a conscious choice not to learn anything from any given situation I've encountered. You should do the same.

There are fourteen million sales professionals in the United States. Each and every one of them, I'll warrant, has heard the word "no thanks" more often than the average individual. The fact that they must deal with this message as part of their work does not mean they're substandard human beings!

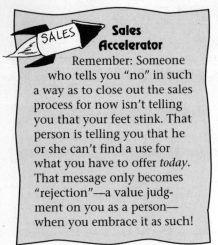

**Sales Accelerator**

Remember: Someone who tells you "no" in such a way as to close out the sales process for now isn't telling you that your feet stink. That person is telling you that he or she can't find a use for what you have to offer *today*. That message only becomes "rejection"—a value judgment on you as a person—when you embrace it as such!

# Myth #6: Sales Is a Dead-End Career with Little Promotional Opportunity

Would it interest you to learn that 85 percent of the company leaders in America today were once salespeople? They carried sample cases just like the rest of us do. They made cold calls. They dialed for dollars. They made product presentations. They handled objections. They did it all.

Today, they're the overwhelming majority of corporate presidents, CEOs, and the like. Yep, sales is a dead-end job, all right—especially when you consider that the end of the road is the place where "the buck stops," the very top of the organization.

# Common Pitfalls

What can go wrong on the way to sales superstardom? Plenty. Here's a look at how to deal with some of the obstacles that can make your journey to success longer and more difficult than it has to be.

## "Me? Make Telephone Calls?"

After you've had your sales job for a while, and managed the territory that came with it, you may reach a point where you say to yourself, "Self, I've worked long and hard developing this territory. I think it's about time this territory started working for me!"

After you make this observation, you may stop, or slow down dramatically on, the number of proactive sales activities (like cold calls) that used to be part of your day. Even if you think you're immune to this syndrome, you're not. Prospecting for new business is one of the hardest activities any salesperson must perform. It has a way of slipping off the "to-do" list even when we don't mean for it to. Underneath, you may be thinking, "Hey, I'm ahead of quota. I'm a star! And stars don't make calls; stars take calls!" Actually, I've run into a couple of salespeople who adopted that attitude openly, as their guiding philosophy. Perhaps you have, too. Don't use these people as role models!

What to do? One good strategy is to save your cold calls for right after you make a presentation. At that time, you're on a high. You just got done being the center of attention. You're pumped! Put that energy to good use. Make a proactive cold call or two...or three...or five. Another great time to make a few cold calls is *immediately* after you've done something nice to reward yourself for having just closed a sale.

The basic principle is clear: To the degree that you can, *make cold calls while you're still feeling unstoppable!*

# "Revenge Is Mine!"

"How could they be so blind? Why are they so afraid of change? Why aren't they return-ing my calls? What's taking them so long to make a decision? *I'll show them!*"

This type of negative, career-limiting talk points outward, but it's really self-destructive. Where does it take you? Toward unhealthy, energy-consuming emotions: Anger, retribu-tion, and revenge. Will those emotions change the fact that the other person has differerent priorities? Or will they only serve to exhaust you and damage the relation-ship?

Imagining potential customers as enemies will cost you sales!

There are two ways to overcome this problem. First, change your approach. If focusing on what the pros-pect stands to gain by using your product, service or solution hasn't worked, try focusing on what he or she stands to *lose* by failing to take action. How many customers is he or she losing? What's the dollar value of each of those customers? How much is his or her organization losing every day?

> **Watch It!**
> Keep your cool and focus on the other person's needs. When salespeople put their own interests first, they always come in last.

Second, *change your state of mind*! It's time for you to take responsibility for actions that are influencing the reactions of the buyers you're talking to! Do something that radically changes your state—and preferably leaves you feeling better and more enthusiastic—before you keep doing what isn't working at the moment. I've found a way to change my state of mind that involves taking time out to focus on something I absolutely love doing—surfing—when things seem to be going wrong. You should develop a "feel-good" exercise like this, too. It's the ultimate antidote for the "revenge is mine" syndrome.

# "Backup? What Backup?"

One of the most common—and most easily avoidable—sales obstacles is known as "failing to fail-safe." When you *don't* fail to fail-safe, you leave yourself plenty of options, plenty of backups, plenty of strategies that are all ready to use when Plan A doesn't work out exactly as you'd hoped. When you *do* fail to fail-safe, you focus only on what's in front of you at the moment—and pray like the dickens that nothing goes wrong with it. Some people say this way of working is inspiring, or that it leaves them feeling energized. I say it's a good way to go broke when a big account evaporates without warning.

Remember the line from *Apollo 13*? "Failure is not an option!" There may be no way to *completely* control the outcomes of your sales work, but there's nothing that says you can't develop enough backup plans to make failure an extremely *unrealistic* option.

Ask yourself: What's the worst case scenario—and how can you plan an alternative? What would you do if everything fell apart on the XYZ account tomorrow morning? How many prospects are in your funnel to replace that income? What can you do right now to make that number higher? Which prospects are the most valuable? What can you change in your approach that will give them these people the time and attention they deserve?

## Internal and External Competition

We humans like to make life as complicated as possible, so we find ways to make the fact of competition something to beat ourselves up over. We tend to look at competition as a win-lose scenario, when the truth is a little more complex. (Think about it: Is it ever possible for a given prospect to purchase from more than one supplier in order to resolve a specific problem.)

**Watch It!** Never use the words "competitor" or "competition" with your contacts—and try to avoid naming competitors during meetings with buyers. Instead, talk about "alternative solutions."

Handling external competition means dealing sensibly with competitors in the marketplace. If you ever lose a sale to a competitor, you should feel free to ask your prospect what the primary reasons were, from their perspective, of the decision that came down. Learn from the experience. Always ask your prospects, *early on*, whether they'll be looking at any alternative products, services, or solutions.

And when you know a competitor is calling on your prospect, but you haven't lost any business yet, accelerate! Look for ways to pick up the pace—and get your prospect what he or she needs posthaste (without, of course, making him or her feel rushed).

How about internal competition? I file this topic under "Learning not to beat yourself up." There's nothing wrong with wanting to be the best you can be. But don't try do so at the expense of your own self-esteem. Find goals that inspire and encourage, and reinforce them with positive affirmations. Using your work as an excuse to raise your own blood pressure is a losing proposition that can shorten your sales career—and your life!

So knock off the negative self-talk. Revisit your short- and long-term goals; read and update them frequently. Find someone you can talk to, someone who will help you get your feelings out in the open, someone who will share in your successes and help you put your failures into perspective.

And if you're bound and determined to kick yourself around the block for a presentation that went awry, get it out of the way and move on. If that's a hard principle for you to turn into reality, it's possible that you're suffering from...

## The Big One: Burnout

You're most susceptible to burnout when you're at the top of your game—and when you're struggling for air. Salespeople who manage to make ends meet every month are usually too preoccupied to burn out. Those who are operating at the high and low ends, on the other hand, are often vulnerable to big problems. That's my experience, at any rate.

Burnout is nature's way of telling you to start moving again. As I mentioned earlier in this book, I learned a lot from the times I experienced serious burnout problems. Each time I encountered major burnout problems, of the "what-on-earth-am-I-DOING-here" variety, I tried to ask myself some important questions—and gave myself a day or so to review them in depth, on my own, and with the benefit of a pad of paper and a pen. Those questions included the following:

➤ Do I really want to keep this job?

➤ If so, what's my goal now?

➤ Why is that goal important to me?

➤ How is what I'm doing bringing me closer to that goal?

➤ What can I learn from the situations I've just encountered?

➤ How can I change what I'm doing now, so that it's easier for me to get closer to my goal?

➤ What would it take for me to say "I love what I do for a living"?

➤ How can I change my setting, at least in the short term, in a way that will improve my outlook?

That last question turned out to be particularly important. I suggest you explore it in depth if you're facing serious burnout problems. There's a saying in the sales world: A change of scenery is as good as a vacation!

# Your Success in the Long Term

If you've gotten this far in the book, you've either gained a lot of knowledge that will help you make some serious progress in improving your sales performance—or you're an avid recreational reader!

Your personal career path in sales can take many directions. That's what's both good and bad about selling for a living: It's good because it gives us choices that no other profession can, and it's bad because those choices often lead to some less-than-enjoyable detours. In the next chapter, you'll learn about how to chart a course for yourself—a course that will help you reach your goal of long-term career and financial satisfaction.

# The Least You Need to Know

➤ Overcoming the common stereotypes about salespeople means making sure that YOU know those stereotypes don't reflect reality.

➤ Overcoming the common stereotypes about salespeople also means making sure that *your suspects, prospects, customers, and business partners* know those stereotypes don't reflect reality.

➤ With just a little foresight and planning, you can avoid common pitfalls that short-circuit sales careers.

➤ You're most susceptible to burnout when you're at the top of your game—and when you're struggling for air.

➤ Beat burnout by changing your setting, changing your state, and asking pertinent questions.

# The Road from Here

This is the last chapter of the book—and the beginning of your personal encounter with high achievement in the world of sales. In this chapter, you learn about some important ideas that will help you point your career in the right direction—and *keep* you moving, over the long term, in a direction that makes sense to you and leaves you feeling satisfied with what you do for a living.

What we're really talking about, of course, is figuring out what true success in the world of sales—your success, not anyone else's—will feel like. We're talking about how you can make success a meaningful personal reality, how you can keep it alive in your career and in your life.

# Success

The word "success" is used a lot in the sales world; it seems to mean different things to different people. Your sales manager may define success as you hitting your quota—but as we've seen in this book, you stand to gain a great deal by shooting somewhat higher than that. Many of today's most acclaimed motivators and success trainers will tell you that success means "doing the very best you can do." But what happens if you do your best—give everything you've got to your sales work—and you don't get the results you want? What happens if you don't hit your goals, and you need some strategies for making up lost ground...and the sooner the better? What happens, for that matter, if you *do* hit your goals, but you find that they don't leave you feeling satisfied or fulfilled, as you'd assumed they would? Does that really count as "success"?

I define success as accomplishing what you set out to do as long as it inspires you—and then repeating that which works, so that it leaves you feeling even more satisfied.

The kind of success I'm talking about falls into that "you-know-it-when-you-see-it" category. It's the kind of success that energizes you, makes you want to "do it again," in a bigger, better, and more comprehensive way. You can probably think of at least four or five incidents from your own career right now that fall into this category. When did you sell something and think to yourself, "This is the job for me!"

That kind of success can actually reinforce itself. If you consistently and intelligently follow your natural instinct to deliver a "repeat performance," that kind of success will let you deliver results that are even more impressive that the last time.

## Beyond Fake Success

In the final analysis, you'll want to take a look at whether your sales efforts, whatever form they take, are leading you toward the type of success I've just outlined. I'm not talking about "success" that's measured in goals established by other people, or by abusive, exploitative, or ineffective contacts with buyers, but success that leaves you feeling better about yourself. This is real success, and in my experience, it always leaves four tell-tale signs.

## Real Success Makes You Smarter

I'm not talking about I.Q. levels or performance on some scholastic exam. I'm talking about getting to know the essentials better—developing a stronger sense of who your customers are, what they need, and how what you have to offer solves their problems. Real success gives you a firm grasp of the basic principles of your industry or field of operation in a way that short-term, hit-and-run, get-the-signature-and-get-out-of-town selling never can.

## Real Success Gives You Courage

When you set up a solution that actually works for someone, don't you feel like you're on top of the world? I certainly do. Real sales success makes you a player; it gives you the ability to take chances (because sales means risk!) on a consistent, day-in, day-out basis. There's no room for "playing it safe" or "standing pat" when you experience real sales success—you want to use what you've learned to get in front of more people and find a way to deliver more solutions!

## Real Success Makes You Want to Take Action

You know the feeling: You're on a mission! Once your courage points you toward a plan, you won't need anybody to talk you into taking action. You'll already feel that "fire in the belly," and you'll want to find a way to make something happen—so you'll do more of what worked before, or try variations that seem likely to deliver the results you're committed to achieving. And speaking of results...

## Real Success Makes You Want to Find Out What's Working

Real success motivates you to find out: "Is what I just tried working as well as what worked last time?" If you feel uneasy about learning the results of a new approach, you can rest assured that you're *not* being driven by a burning desire to recreate satisfying past successes!

When you're inspired by real success, you want to know whether or not what you just did is likely to make it happen again. After every step you take, you'll want to find out: "Did the result of my last effort take me closer to my goal, or move me further from it?"

## And About That Goal...

You probably remember this from earlier on in the book, but it's worth repeating here: You and I must have both short- and long-term goals to guide our life's work.

**Sales Accelerator**
Experiment with success! Remember: A slight variation on something that's already working can work the sales equivalent of a miracle. I'll never forget the year I decided to send Thanksgiving cards, instead of December holiday cards, to all my suspects, prospects, customers, and business partners. What a response! I beat everyone else in the country to the punch by a month!

**Words, Words, Words**
*Convictions* are strong, unshakable beliefs (like, "What I do benefits each and every one of my organizations customers and prospective customers"). Ask yourself: Am I convinced that I'm working for the right company? That I'm selling the right products? That I'm pursuing the right career? That I can achieve the goals I've set for myself? If the answer to any of these questions is "no," there's a problem with personal convictions that will affect your success level!

Remember, your goals should be:

➤ Attainable

➤ Easy for you to understand

➤ Totally in line with your personal convictions and your organization's mission statement

Make sure your short-term sales goals support your long-term sales goals!

> **Bet You Didn't Know**
>
> Goals that don't fire you up are goals that are screaming to be reassessed! Long-term and short-term goals should compel you to take action. If your goals have a way of making you feel uncertain, hesitant, or lethargic, you need to take another look at the goals you set in Chapter 7!
>
> Examples of short-term goals that have motivated the salespeople I've trained include:
>
> I will hit 125 percent of my sales quota this month!
>
> I will land 16 new accounts this quarter!
>
> I will make 50 cold calls every week!
>
> Examples of long-term goals that galvanize salespeople include:
>
> I will make at least $100,000 in total income this year!
>
> I will land 75 new accounts this year!
>
> I will win my division's MVP award this year!

# Continuous Personal and Professional Development

My assessment is that you must be serious about personal and professional development, or else you wouldn't be reading the final chapter of this book! Beyond hanging on to this book, and reviewing pertinent chapters from time to time, however, you may be wondering: What's your best strategy for keeping that winning edge a month, a year, or ten years from now?

Ready for a surprise? The key to making sure you're committed to continuous personal and professional development as a salesperson is to *have fun*. Over the past decade, I've worked with close to one million salespeople. (I know; it's a ridiculously big number, and it gives me pause even to write it down, but it's the truth!) The most successful of them, I found, took remarkably similar approaches to the task of making sure that sales work stayed a blast—and didn't turn into a bust.

The rest of this section reviews what the top performers have in common in this area.

## Superstars Learn to Radiate Unshakable Confidence

Confidence—or faith, if you prefer—is the opposite of fear. Confidence is how superstars respond to the inevitable challenges that come their way. Confidence is a way of thinking. Confidence is probably the single best way to re-insert *fun* into the sales process—even (especially!) when you're up against a real challenge.

A good friend of mine, Brandon Toropov, told me about Kenneth Branagh's film of Shakespeare's play *HENRY V*, one of the great cinematic object lessons in the development of charismatic personal confidence. This movie is about the kind of confidence that rubs off on other people (like battle-weary English soldiers and, yes, skeptical prospects). Throughout the film, Shakespeare's unforgettable hero says things like "All things are ready if our minds be so"—despite the fact that he's up against some pretty stiff odds from time to time during the play. And Henry wins, largely because of the way he thinks about himself and his mission. If you're ever in need of a personal confidence boost, check out the video of Branagh's superior film and watch it from beginning to end.

Another good way to build the kind of unshakable confidence that leads to *fun* is to hook up with other confident people. For you, this may mean joining the local chapter of Toastmasters (a marvelous organization I've discussed elsewhere in this book), enrolling in a local community college course on a topic of interest to you, listening to an audiotape series, or even attending a seminar conducted by a confident motivational speaker—like, say, me! (For more information on my seminars and audiotapes, you can call 1-800-777-8486.)

When you do what you enjoy, you trust yourself more! In the end, though, all you really need to get a feeling of confidence, pleasure and satisfaction from your sales work is *you*. To a large degree, this is a matter of

**Words, Words, Words**

*Unshakable confidence* is complete trust in someone or something. Confidence in one's own ability to pick up the phone, ask the right question when you hear a prospect's objection, ask for a referral, or interact with a gatekeeper is a universal trait of salespeople who routinely exceed quota.

**Sales Accelerator**

To boost your own confidence on the job, purchase a journal and track your own progress, on a daily or weekly basis, as you pursue the steps laid out in Chapters 2, 3, 7, and 8 of this book. The more frequent and detailed your notes, the better your progress will be—and the more confident you'll feel about your sales work!

personal desire. Desire, like willpower, comes from within. You have to make a commitment to point your desire toward your work in such a way that everyone around you knows instantly that you're doing exactly what gives you pleasure, right now. (Shakespeare makes the disguised King Henry V tell one of his skittish soldiers, "I think [the king] would not wish himself any where but where he is.")

### Bet You Didn't Know

Passion destroys fear. Passion also gives rise to confidence. That's a guarantee!

To build confidence, ask yourself every month: What, specifically, do I have an overwhelming passion for? What gives me joy and pleasure? Write the answers down! Then find a way to take what you love and put it into your sales work. I've performed this exercise many times; once, I listed the fact that I love anything to do with the ocean. Within six months I was the international sales rep for the largest supplier of oceanographic equipment in the world! A similar exercise led me to launch a (highly lucrative!) career as a public speaker—a decision that certainly didn't hurt my yearly sales totals.

## Superstars Learn to Build Synergy with Other Team Members

Isn't it interesting how most of the pointless bickering and internal gamesmanship in any given sales department can usually be traced to the mediocre (or below-mediocre) performers? You know why that is?

### Sales Accelerator

Celebrate your every victory with the team that helped you to create it! If you ever win an award (not an unlikely scenario, I note with all modesty, for readers who follow the advice in this book), don't hog the spotlight. Take the award to a trophy shop and have the names of key fellow team members etched on next to yours. Then place it in an area where everyone can see it!

Superstars only have time for great relationships with their fellow team members! They haven't got room in the schedule for aggravation and rumor-spreading...so they don't waste their energy in these areas.

Don't look for trouble. Have fun with your team!

Today's workplace focus is on team-building. So support your team. Your manager, the members of your organization's administrative and clerical staff, your organization's shipping and receiving workers, the people in the parts and service department—all these folks are part of your selling team. Treat them with respect. Introduce them to the suspects, prospects, customers, and business partners you interact with every day. Get appropriate team members (such as credit managers or people in the order processing department) involved in important calls.

Whatever you do, don't take a bad day or a bad call or a bad presentation out on the members of your own team! That's an error you may regret for months or years to come.

## Superstars Learn to Build Rapport

If you want to be a top salesperson, you're going to have to become experienced at developing business and personal rapport—being likeable, someone others genuinely enjoy interacting with. This too is (stop the presses!) fun! But that doesn't mean it's easy. Building rapport is an acquired skill, one you must develop over time. If I had to boil the art of rapport-building into a single phrase, that phrase would probably be "equal business stature."

Establishing equal business stature (a concept we examined briefly a little earlier in the book) means approaching situations with your buyer as a partner, not a supplicant, no matter what his or her rank. Salespeople who establish equal business stature with their suspects, prospects, customers, and business partners learn to understand the problems these people face, and learn to present their own ideas *in a way that the other person can understand.*

Establishing equal business stature is essentially the same thing as banishing fear from your relationship with the buyer. It means understanding, and responding empathetically and tactfully to, the preconceptions people have about salespeople. Let's face it: Buyers (and particularly very highly placed buyers, those whom we've identified as leaders/authority decision makers) are scared of you. They're afraid you're going to either:

➤ Waste their precious time

or

➤ Talk about something with which they're not familiar

The best way to overcome these fears from the other side is to *calm down* and develop a superlative opening statement (see Chapter 12). An opening statement that proves your value and makes a point that's of importance to the buyer will go a long way toward allowing you to build rapport—and take part in a mutually enjoyable discussion between equals.

## Superstars Use Rituals to Increase Energy

Sales superstars have a ball...by giving their job their all.

Even if you've been in sales for a while, the ideas you've learned about in this book will require time, attention, and energy if you're going to turn them to your benefit. The top salespeople I've worked with know when, and how, to turn up the juice—and take full advantage of new ideas—by using little rituals that hardly anyone else notices.

One of the ways superstar performers turn up their mental and physical energy is to visualize their future actions successfully and, in so doing, establish rituals that condition them for high performance. For instance, before a prospecting call, a top sales performer might close his or her eyes for a few seconds—and "see" the prospect sitting at a desk, "hear" the prospect asking a question, and silently respond with an appropriate, persuasive, confident answer. Such near-instantaneous conditioning can deliver stellar results.

> **Sales Accelerator**
>
> Sending positive signals to your brain is a sure-fire way to make what seems to be impossible very doable—one realistic step at a time. Your brain is loyal to the messages you send it. SEE yourself doing something and think, "I can do that!" Your brain will accept the message as reality ... and start supplying scenarios that will help you attain the goal you're focusing on.

Here's another great ritual related to prospecting work on the phone. After every call you make, *write down* at least one part of the exchange that went well, as well as one part that you'd like to improve the next time around. Don't beat yourself up: Visualize positive change—and you'll usually find you have the energy to make it a reality!

The act of visualizing positive change, constantly, throughout the day, is a consistent habit of superior salespeople. Give it a try...and you'll soon see that the seemingly "impossible" goals you set for yourself suddenly don't look quite so impossible!

# Welcome to Your World

I hope you got as much pleasure and inspiration out of this book as I got out of writing it. Working on this volume has been a wonderful experience, because I've been able to share my experiences and insights with you in a way that can help you grow and improve in your sales career. That makes me feel great! My challenge to you as I close this book is twofold: take what you've learned within these covers, and turn the ideas into reality for yourself—and then pass the good stuff along by helping someone else, someone who's ready to follow in the path you've blazed toward success.

Be yourself—and sell with passion!

# The Least You Need to Know

➤ Real success makes you smarter, gives you courage, makes you want to take action, and encourages you to monitor your results.

➤ Surprise, surprise: The key to making sure you're committed to continuous personal and professional development as a salesperson is to HAVE FUN.

➤ To build confidence, ask yourself every month: What, specifically, do I have an overwhelming passion for?

➤ The act of visualizing positive change, constantly, throughout the day, is a consistent habit of superior salespeople.

➤ Share what you've learned in this book with others!

# Words, Words, Words Glossary

**Advantages** The ways in which a product, service, or solution, will be tailored, modified, customized, or otherwise changed to fit the precise need or needs of an individual or organization, or the ways in which something you offer will be superior to what a competitor has to offer.

**Amiable style** The buyer who takes an amiable approach is agreeable, devoted, responsible, warmharted, considerate, caring, practical, patient, and (usually) pretty indecisive. This person doesn't like "upsetting the apple cart."

**Analytical style** The buyer who takes an analytical approach is factual, serious, steadfast, hard-working, exacting, systematic, and critical. He or she can be an extremely valuable ally as the sales process moves forward. The analytical buyer lives for details, details, details!

**Authority decision maker(s)** An individual or group of individuals who will actually make the final decision to purchase (or not to purchase) whatever it is you're selling. Also known as leaders.

**Benefits** The good things happen when someone uses a product, service, or solution.

**Business partners** The people and organizations in this category not only have bought from you; they've come to depend on you. Business partners depend on your company's resources to grow and prosper.

**Buyers** The people who could conceivably buy from you or are buying from you know. When you make a cold call to a referral you've never met before, you're interacting with a buyer. When you sit down for a meeting with your organization's biggest customer, you're interacting with a buyer.

**Call to action**   The act of asking, in no uncertain terms, for a commitment, though not necessarily for a purchase commitment. (Other types of commitments might be for a future meeting, or a promise to explore an issue with another person within the target organization.)

**Close-itis**   A common salesperson's syndrome, chiefly recognizable by an overwhelming desire to do or say anything that will convince a sales manager that a customer really does mean to buy something, whether or not this case.

**Commodity sales**   The sale of something that is typically bought in bulk and consumed continuously. Products such as industrial solvents, oil and gas, and certain paper goods are generally considered commodities.

**Common zone**   The next zone beyond the sociable zone. See also *confidential zone*.

**Complex Sales Model**   Associated with the sale of products, services, and solutions to organizations; may require group decisions and long time-frames.

**Confidential zone**   An invisible area approximately 18 inches outward in all directions from your body. Other zones, extending outward in larger concentric circles and reserved for social exchanges of lesser and lesser degrees of intimacy, are known as the individual, sociable, and common zones.

**Consultative selling**   Taking on the responsibility for a full, thorough, and all-encompassing professional diagnosis of the problem—with no preconception as to the outcome.

**Consumers**   Occupants of the largest (and, technically, lowest) level of the company, that of the people who actually use products and services.

**Convictions**   Strong, unshakeable beliefs (like, "What I do benefits each and every one of my organization's customers and prospective customers").

**Credibility**   The degree to which people find it easy and worthwhile to believe you. True credibility isn't a short-term display of veracity meant to help you "close the sale"—it's a pattern of believability that holds up over the long haul. If you've only got credibility for the duration of a single meeting or phone call, you don't really have credibility!

**Customer**   An individual or organization with a need that you can satisfy—a person or group of people who trusts in your abilities and talents to exceed their expectations. A customer invests time, money, and energy to buy from you in order to get problems solved.

**Direct selling style**   That selling style best suited to relatively simple sales environments, where one person is likely to give you a "thumbs-up" or "thumbs-down" decision in a relatively short period of time. Direct selling means solving a single pressing problem, typically in a short-term setting, and not digging too deeply beneath that problem.

**Directors**   Individuals who are held responsible for the timely completion of the goals, plans, and objectives of the leader.

**Discovery agreement**   The point in your presentation where you list all of your "here's what our organization knows about your organization" material. It's also where you spell out what you plan to cover during the course of your presentation. Think of the discovery agreement as a "pre-flight checklist" to review with your prospect(s).

**Driver style**   Buyers who take a driver approach are determined, tough, efficient, assertive, dominating, decisive, direct, and, not infrequently, hungry for power and authority. Driver buyers have a way of delivering "yes" and "no" answers crisply and quickly—and sticking to their guns.

**Ending question**   Thought-provoking query that comes at the conclusion of an opening statement; it gets your contact thinking about what you've said, and encourages him or her to make a comment.

**End-user selling**   Selling directly to the person or organization using the product.

**Expressive style**   Buyers who take an expressive approach are a little like that fellow in the old joke who, when asked what time it was, started giving an explanation about how he chose the watch he wears. These buyers are friendly, enthusiastic, spontaneous, talkative, self-promoting, independent, commanding, and creative. They love to be the center of attention, and they can sometimes be a bit manipulative.

**F.F.A.B.**   Functions, Features, Advantages, Benefits. (See separate listings for each.)

**Farmer**   *See Hunter/Farmer model.*

**Features**   The components, pieces, and parts of your product.

**Functions**   The ways someone uses—or operates by means of—a product, service, or solution.

**High-level listening**   This occurs when words and phrases are heard, and responded to, with genuine emotion. High-level listeners make nonjudgmental associations, offer acceptance and validation, and offer empathetic support. In essence, high-level listening is listening that does not prejudge.

**Hunter/Farmer model**   Hunter salespeople and farmer salespeople have different overall goals in their sales work. All sales organizations need a healthy mix of new market share (obtained by "hunting" for new customers) and revenue from from loyal existing customers (obtained by cultivating and supporting, or "farming," current accounts). Successful Hunters usually have different strategies than successful Farmers. Many salespeople are expected to both hunt and farm within their territories.

**Hunter**   See *Hunter/Farmer model.*

**Ice-breaker statement**   The first sentence or two you say to a new acquaintance during a face-to-face meeting. It's usually issued in an effort to build rapport and ease any tension you or the prospect (most likely you) happen to be feeling.

**Individual zone**   The next zone beyond the confidential zone. See *confidential zone.*

**Influencer(s)**   Individual or group of individuals who are going to make a recommendation, or otherwise have significant influence over, the decision to buy your product.

**Key customers**   Customers who represent significant amounts of revenue for your organization. They're the people you should be meeting with face-to-face on a regular basis.

**Leader**   See *Authority decision maker.*

**Lockout**   Something you can offer your suspects and prospects that no one else can. Free follow-up service that your organization is willing to confirm in writing is a lockout commitment—if none of your competitors offers the same service. By highlighting that which you offer, and are willing to commit to, you "lock out" the competition.

**Maslow's hierarchy of needs**   Theory holding that human beings will always fulfill their needs from the bottom, or base, of a "needs pyramid," and move upward from there. If a lower-level need isn't satisfied, the psychologist Abraham Maslow argued, people will focus on that need before they address a higher-level one. That means that if you sell first-level physiological "essentials" (food or shelter, for instance), you'll have to contend with a different, and probably more intense, set of emotional responses and motivations than you will if you're selling alarm systems (a second-level security need). The same principle applies to memberships in country clubs or other social organizations (which correspond to third-level belonging needs), high-status purchases such as luxury automobiles (fourth-level status needs), and self-help products or demanding mountaineering trips (fifth-level self-actualization needs).

**Negotiation**   The determination of formal terms within a business agreement.

**Network of influence and authority**   System under which authority decision makers, directors, influencers, and consumers try to interact productively within your target organization. People can, on an impromptu basis, act within the level beneath them...but never the level above them. Think of the network as being similar to a bottle of Italian salad dressing. A tenth of a second after you shake the bottle, the oil and vinegar begin to separate and return to their customary (and separate!) relationships.

**Objection**   A stated reason, real or imagined, not to do something, or an expression of unwillingness, reluctance, or hesitation to buy or invest. Objections can, and often do, take the form of questions. Not doing something is often seen as being safer than doing something new, so objections are a part of everyday life for salespeople.

**Opening statement**   What you say to someone, either in person or over the telephone, to create a strong first impression and initiate the conversation. This statement has a huge effect on the environment in which your relationship with the potential customer unfolds. The only element with a greater potential impact is past experience or knowledge the contact may have about you or your organization.

**Parinello Principle**   Rule stating that 75 percent of your sales activities will yield a 125 percent quota performance...if 75 percent of your work time is managed properly, and allocated directly to supporting the sales process itself.

**Pleasantry**   Upbeat transitional phrase you use in your opening statement immediately after you've gotten your contact to say, "Yes," in response to his or her name. It's unique, it comes from your heart, and it sounds both happy and interested. ("Thanks for taking my call!")

**Preliminary suggestion**   The point of your discussion when you first make a recommendation to the buyer. (The suggestion may or may not be a request to buy.)

**Proactive selling**   Whenever you take action without being asked to, or you take action before it's absolutely necessary to do so, you are being proactive. Proactive salespeople commit to anticipating the key problems and concerns of their contacts.

**Product knowledge**   The amount of technical information and direct experience you have with the product you offer to customers and potential customers. (The term "product knowledge" is sometimes used in a general way to refer to a salesperson's level of expertise with the services his or her company provides.)

**Prospects**   These are people whom you have contacted, or who have contacted you, and who represent a realistic potential for future business.

**Quotas**   These are most useful as planning, control, and measurement tools. Your sales quota is not the same as your sales forecast. The latter is an estimate, while the former is a goal. Quotas may take many different forms dollar amounts, certain numbers of products or services sold, number of contacts made, number of calls made, etc. You should develop a strategy for earning more than your quota.

**R.O.I.**   Short for "Return on Investment." It's what the customer gets in return for investing in your organization, above and beyond the investment itself. If your product, service, or solution causes more problems than it solves, or delivers results that do not defray the costs associated in working with you, then it has not delivered any return on investment.

**References**   The answers you can give to questions like: What are other people in a similar situation doing? What kind of results have they been getting? How would they deal with this issue? A reference who is willing to back up your claims with a prospective customer can provide a powerful incentive to buy.

**Rejection**   What happens in between "yes" answers. In virtually all cases, people aren't rejecting you; they're rejecting what you have to offer.

**Retail Selling**   Everyday "across-the-counter" sales—from high-end to bargain-basement.

**Return on Investment**   See *R.O.I.*

**Sales**   The act of 1) proactively understanding the needs and problems of others, then 2) using the art of honest persuasion to highlight possible solutions to those problems, and finally 3) encouraging others to believe in what you say and to invest their money and time in what you propose.

**Sales cycle**   The average amount of time it takes to get a suspect to enter your funnel and emerge through the bottom as a customer.

**Sales forecast**   An estimate of your sales performance for a particular period in the future.

**Sales plan**   Your written document incorporating key goals and strategies that you review on a regular basis with your sales manager. Set it up! See also *Strategic plan* and *Tactical plan.*

**Sales territory**   This comprises the potential customers you want to sign up as users of your organization's product or service. A particular sales territory may or may not be defined geographically.

**75/125 Rule**   See *Parinello Principle.*

**Simple Sales Model**   One-on-one sales notable for speed in reaching an "up-or-down" decision and directness of approach.

**Sociable zone**   The next zone beyond the individual zone. See also *confidential zone.*

**Social proof**   Real-world evidence that your proposed solution works. It may take the form of a testimonial, or it may be a report or summary developed for a current customer.

**Strategic plan**   Your company's strategic plan is an overview of the approach that will be used to get the products, services, and solutions to the people who will (you hope) decide to buy.

**Suspects**   This word describes individuals or companies who are potential customers but who have not yet had any contact with you or your organization.

**Tactical plan**   Your company's tactical plan is the step-by-step process, the plan that sets out what needs to happen in each of the areas identified by the strategic plan if success is to be achieved. This is the plan that helps ensure the overachievement of revenue goals, dominance in the marketplace, compression of the production or deployment process, and containment of costs.

**Template of Ideal Prospects**   A list of characteristics shared by your company's best customers. Also known as TIP. The TIP will point you toward the most promising suspects—people whom you have not yet contacted about your product or service, but who may benefit from what you have to offer.

**TIP**   See *Template of Ideal Prospects.*

**Wholesale selling**   Selling to the distributor.

# Letters, In-Depth

The best way to make a great first impression before you meet or talk to someone by phone is to send a letter that matches the following template.

---

Headline Statement—not to exceed 30 words, this highlights benefits for leaders, advantages for directors, features for influencers, or functions for consumers. Put it in big, bold type.

Date

Contact Name

Position

Dear Mr./Ms. Lastname:

The Tie-In Paragraph is two or three short sentences that follow the lead of your headline. Get specific about the hook you've isolated in your headline. Where appropriate, provide proof in the form of statistics or endorsements that conclude the story.

➤ Then list your most compelling selling point in bullet format.
➤ Then list your next-most compelling selling point in bullet format.
➤ Then list your third-most compelling selling point in bullet format.

In the next paragraph, introduce ideas of uncertainty and doubt about reproducing your success with the target organization, and make it clear that your contact is the one who can decide what should happen next. You will probably want to mention the possibility of exploring a mutually beneficial partnership.

     Sincerely yours,

     Your Name

     Your company name

     Your phone number (Never skip the phone number!)

P.S. Say here that you will call the office at such-and-such a time on such-and-such a date. Mention the name of the person's assistant or secretary here, and suggest that he or she call you to pass along a more convenient time if this is necessary.

---

The letter must be spelled correctly from beginning to end, and must be grammatically correct.

Important: Never "ask for the order" (or anything else) in a letter designed to allow you to follow up by phone!

# The Ingredients

Here's some sample text that will help you assemble your letter—and some advice that may make it easier to write.

# The Headline

On average, people decide within about eight seconds whether or not to continue reading an unexpected piece of mail. That means you're going to need a truly compelling Headline Statement to win the readership of your prospects.

Your headline should sound the trumpet for actual events, not hypothetical situations. The headline should also ....

➤ Not extend 30 words in length.

➤ Address the prospect's interests directly.

➤ Be based on a literal quotation or on verifiable factual information, preferably from a credible source your prospect will recognize and respect.

➤ Highlight or be based on the tangible and/or intangible benefits of doing business with your company.

➤ Focus on measurable results that other real, live customers have enjoyed as a result of using your product, service, or solution.

Your headline statement may include words like guarantee, discover, benefit, advantage, value, proven results, quality, progress, growth, safe, and genuine—but if you have a compelling third-party endorsement that omits these words, there's nothing wrong with using it!

Make no mistake: You're asking 30 words to do a whole lot. I'll be honest with you; it's quite possible that it will take a good deal of time and experimentation for you to craft just the right headline. But your letter is worth it.

Here are some examples of Headline Statements that work:

We've lowered Hollis College's student registration operation costs by 25 percent in less than four months. Hollis was also in a better position to comply with the new state regulatory requirements.

We helped Metroland Hospital keep up its superior service and reduce delays in premium deliveries to donors—while reducing operating costs in Donor Services by 24 percent.

We've reduced overhead in six of the top ten law firms in Tucson—and, according to Les Reamem, of Reamem, Covertrax, and Splitt, "increased billable hours by 35 percent this quarter."

# Your Tie-In Paragraph

Your Tie-In Paragraph is the next element of your sales letter. You'll recall that its purpose is simply to carry the theme of your headline forward into the body of your letter.

Here are some examples of the kinds of tie-in paragraphs you should be using:

XYZ Company has enjoyed a 6 percent increase in annual revenue over the past year, thanks in part to their partnership approach with critical vendors. We worked together with XYZ to develop a unique inventory management system based on bar-coding technology.

Another national trading firm, with branch offices in Florida, has decreased its operating costs by $4,000,000 over the past two years. They achieved this result by using innovative solutions and ideas recommended by our company.

We helped XYZ recapture $400,000 over the past three years that helped them improve their competitive position in the video post-production industry. Our consultatitve approach helps companies to identify unique solutions to many business problems.

# The Bullets

These occupy the center of your letter and must address the most important things that your product, service, or solution does for your customers. They're short, to the point, and easy to read.

Here are some examples of bullet points that work:

➤ Streamline your operations and manage your network better.

➤ Enjoy significant reductions in your operating costs by tracking expenses 34 percent more accurately than typical off-the-shelf software systems.

➤ Manage your internal communications more effectively—and save time as a result—with the latest Gizmo 3000 server technology.

## Your Closing Paragraph

The point here is to introduce the ideas of uncertainty and doubt about whether or not you could reproduce your success with this organization. You want your reader to start thinking, "Why not? Why couldn't you make the same thing happen at my company?"

Here are some effective closing paragraphs to compare to your own:

> Could your organization benefit from the approach we used at ABC? Frankly, I'm not sure. But I would welcome the opportunity to learn more about your unique business needs, so we can take the first steps to find out.

> Whether ZYCORP can achieve these kinds of results is difficult to tell. But one thing is certain—you are the one person who can take action to find out. Together, we can quickly learn exactly what the possibilities are.

> Where does this fit in your business plan? You may be asking yourself, "Can these people actually deliver a technology based solution to my business communications problems, and save me hard dollars?" Results are not always duplicated—but we can show you, in only 20 minutes, how an outstanding partnership could result in tangible benefits for you.

## The P.S.

Don't mess around with this one. It's one of the two most important parts of your letter. People *always* skip to the bottom of the page and check out the postscript.

Use your postscript to establish credibility, persistence, and equal business stature. The postscript you see below—complete with the *correctly spelled* first name of your contact's assistant—is a time-tested winner for accomplishing all three of these goals.

> P.S.: I will call your office on Thursday, May 14, at 8:00 a.m. If this is an inconvenient time, please have Pat let me know when a better time to call would be.

*Sales letter layout.*

```
┌─────────────────────────────────────┐
│           ┌──────────────┐           │
│           │   Headline   │           │
│           └──────────────┘           │
│                                      │
│                                      │
│        ┌──────────────────┐          │
│        │ Tie-In Paragraph │          │
│        └──────────────────┘          │
│          ┌──────────────┐            │
│          │   Benefit    │            │
│          │   Bullets    │            │
│          └──────────────┘            │
│        ┌──────────────────┐          │
│        │ Ending Paragraph │          │
│        └──────────────────┘          │
│                                      │
│                                      │
│                                      │
│                                      │
│         ┌──────────────────┐         │
│         │    P.S. Action   │         │
│         └──────────────────┘         │
│                                      │
└─────────────────────────────────────┘
```

# A Letter You Can Use for Job Openings

Here's a specially targeted, and slightly expanded, letter you can use as a model for that most important of sales campaigns—your professional job search. Customize this letter to your own situation…make sure it honestly reflects your achievements…and then send it to the President of the company, executive vice president of sales, or the director of sales of your target company. The point is not to ape this letter, but to use the basic structure to put your own achievements in the best possible light. (Note that the strong results cited in the headline and the paragraph "Larger Entry Orders" below could just as easily be a summary of praise from a past supervisor about the number of customers you retained on a non-sales-related customer service job.)

---

"I shortened my sales cycle, lowered the cost of each sale, achieved 143 percent of quota, and got a promotion in the process!"

Ms. Importanto

President

Dear Ms. Importanto:

The research I've completed on your company's goals, plans, and objectives enables me to conclude the following about the prospect of me selling your innovative line of industrial solvents.

*continues*

---

*continued*

## A SHORTER SALES CYCLE

I will identify new suspects by first understanding your existing customers and your marketing initiatives. I will then apply my talents—letter-writing, telephone prospecting, and in-person cold calling—to gain an audience with the decision makers and influencers in each prospective account. In my current position I have used similar tactics to shorten the sales process by more than 25 percent.

## LARGER ENTRY ORDERS

My determination to cover every aspect of expanding initial business relationships has resulted in larger-than-average entry point orders. How much larger? My average sale is $120,000 in an industry where $80,000 orders are the norm. I accomplish this by making sure that every upper-management decision maker is aware of the results that are possible.

## DAY AFTER DAY

Imagine a dedicated team player who will bring the following values, aptitudes, and goals to your organization day after day.

➤ Honesty, integrity, and reliability. Your organization is known for its straightforward dealings with prospects and customers.

➤ Good humor, consideration, understanding of others. One of your employees, speaking of your firm, told me, "This is a people company."

➤ Street smarts, hard work, and creativity. My plan will be to overachieve any goal you set for me.

## OUR NEXT STEP

Do you believe that your sales team can use an individual with all the capabilities and traits you see here? If, so, please accept my call this week!

Lead with passion!

Will Prosper

619/555-1212

P.S.: I will call on Thursday, May 21 at 9:00 am. If this is not a convenient time, please have Robin call me and let me know of an alternate time.

# Some Thoughts on Electronic Selling

By "electronic selling," I mean selling that allows you to make initial contact with the suspect or prospect via some means other than a conversation that's conducted in person or over the phone. I don't want to get sidetracked here with an in-depth discussion of the latest telecommunications equipment—by the time you read this, whatever's out on the market now will probably be outdated anyway. But I do want to give you some ideas and strategies for using three media that are likely to help you establish contact with people when you're looking for an option that complements the phone and letter strategies you read about earlier in the book.

Of course, there's no contact method that guarantees a 100 percent connect rate with your suspects and prospects. But the ideas below may help you to establish contact with some of the vitally important players within an industry or business area you're targeting.

## Your Fax Machine to the Rescue!

You say you can't get through to a key decision maker—even though you composed a dynamic letter, made a great follow-up call, and did your very best to get on the right side of the person's secretary or administrative assistant? Not to worry. Your handy-dandy fax machine offers you three great options for leaving a positive, high-impact message that's likely to win you a return call.

## Option One: Fax That Letter

Earlier in this book, and in Appendix B, you saw how to assemble a dramatic one-page letter that serves as a prelude to a phone call with your contact. In the event that letter wasn't successful in getting your contact—or his or her assistant—to the phone at the preappointed time you specified in your letter, you should take action the following business day.

Print out another copy of your letter. Then draw a line through the P.S. and write, by hand, the new date and time when you plan to call. Follow through faithfully. If THAT doesn't work…

## Option Two: Fax an Oversized Note

You won't be faxing just any old note, mind you, but one of those "While You Were Out" messages, enlarged on your photocopier so that it takes up most of the space on a standard 8 1/2" x 11" sheet of paper. Once the form looks like it's been shot up with growth hormones, fill in the appropriate information. Who you are, what company you represent, what your telephone number is, and when you'll be calling again. If THAT doesn't bring your contact to the phone when you call (and it probably will), you should…

## Option Three: Fax a Handwritten Request

Handwritten fax messages carry a real sense of urgency. If you don't have good handwriting, find someone who does—and make sure the message is written in bold, dark ink, so it will be legible once it lands on your contact's desk. The message you fax will focus in on the "hook" statement you've developed for this person, and might look something like this message, which is directed to a leader/authority decision maker:

---

July 1

Mr. Bigshot:

John Smith over at U.S. Widget was able to reduce his operating costs by $12,000 this quarter—and INCREASE his monthly widget production at the same time. Do you think the system John used is one you and I ought to discuss? Can you call me at your convenience at 617/555-1212?

Wil Prosper

ABC Corporation

---

That's your appeal in a nutshell. If this method of fax-alert doesn't do the trick for you, it may be time to move on to the second electric selling weapon at your disposal.

# Victory by Voice Mail

There are a number of different ways you can use voice mail to your advantage. Some salespeople are most comfortable with a "minimal information" approach. This approach is pretty simple. Early in the morning, you simply punch your way through the organization's automated call system (many will allow you to access particular voice mailboxes by last name), leave your name, your phone number, and a time when you can be reached. Then hang up. A good percentage of the time, you'll get a call back—people will be pretty curious about who called. When your contact calls back, treat the call exactly as you would any other first-time phone contact with a buyer.

Perhaps you prefer a more dramatic approach. Here's a three-tiered system that has worked well for me and the people I've trained over the years. What follows is what I call a "maximum information" approach. Leave an *incredibly detailed, incredibly enthusiastic* message on the voice mail system. It might sound something like this:

> Mr. Bigshot, Wil Prosper at Widget Co. We are SO EXCITED HERE about what U.S. Widget was able to accomplish this quarter. Would you believe that Mel Atkinson at U.S. Widget was able to reduce his operating costs by $12,000 AND increase his monthly widget production during the same period? That's a staggering number, I agree—the figures even took us by surprise—but those are the kinds of results he's getting by using our system. Those kinds of numbers might be hard to match or exceed, but you know what? We have proven that they're repeatable! I'll be sitting at my desk between 3 and 5 p.m. on Thursday afternoon—give me a call if you would like to discuss this further, or have Robin call me if I've picked an inconvenient time. Thanks for listening to this long message—I truly look forward to talking with you. My number is 508/555-1212.

(Note: Robin is Mr. Bigshot's assistant.)

Wait three full days. If you don't get a call back, then launch another voice-mail. This is what message number two might sound like:

> "Mr. Bigshot, Wil Prosper at Widget Corp once again. Since the last voice-mail message you listened to, U.S. Widget announced that their overall product reliability has increased by 8.7 percent. This completes the story. What does this have to do with your operations? Everything and nothing. Everything—if you think there's room for improvement in your cost reduction efforts—and nothing—if you're totally satisfied with what's happening now in this area. Mr. Bigshot, the desire to improve may be obvious, but what may not be so obvious is how our company can play an important part in the overachievement of your strategic initiatives. I'll be in my office all day tomorrow—and again on Friday between 3:00 and 5:00, ready to take your call and answer any questions you may have. Thanks for listening to my voice-mail message. Oh, my number is 508/555-1212."

Wait another three days. If you don't get a call back, then try message number three:

> "Mr. Bigshot, this is Will Prosper at Widget Corp. You probably recognize my voice by now. I see the fact that you haven't yet returned my call as a good sign—because if you were not interested in what you've been hearing, you'd have someone call me not to call again. You haven't done that, so I'll continue to add value to your day. Besides U.S. Widget, we have 17 other customers in the widget industry—that's why we know that their results are repeatable. What we don't know yet is whether you can get similar or even greater results at your manufacturing facility. To get that

answer as soon as possible, I'll plan on coming over to meet with you for 10 minutes at 3:00 p.m. tomorrow afternoon. Mr. Bigshot, if you can't meet with me personally tomorrow, please call me at 508/555-1212 by 5:00 today. I am really looking forward to meeting you tomorrow afternoon. Thanks for listening to my voice-mail message."

That's the three-tiered system And if THAT doesn't work—if you get a call back from a secretary politely requesting that you scrap your plans for a visit, or if your drop-in effort is unsuccessful—you can always try leaving the following message on the person's voice-mail machine. It's only for use with contacts who haven't gotten back to you. I have yet to use it and not receive a return phone call.

"Mr. Bigshot—every night, before I go to bed, I talk to the man upstairs. Why can't I talk to you?"

# E-Mail Alert

Did you know that Web sites such as Yahoo!, Infoseek, and WhoWhere can point you toward the individual e-mail addresses of hundreds of thousands of Internet users?

Suppose you were to receive an e-mail message like the one below from a pleasantly persistent salesperson. How would you react?

---

```
To: Mr. Bill Bigshot

Fr: Wil Prosper

Subject: U.S. Widget

Mr. Bigshot—I was web surfing recently and decided, on a lark, to
check the Infoseek page to see if you might be listed on it. Guess
what! You are!

Here's the reason for this message: Mel Atkinson over at U.S. Widget
was able to reduce his operating costs by $12,000 this quarter—and
INCREASE his monthly widget production at the same time. Those kinds
of results might be hard to match or repeat...but do you think
they're worth talking about?

Would you like for us to get together by phone or in person to
determine whether our solutions would be of interest to you?

Best,

John Smith

508/555-1212
```

---

The beautiful thing about an e-mail message, of course, is that you have to do something to it. Your suspect or prospect has to decide how (or whether) to respond to your message. (What you put in the "subject" box will have a big influence on that decision!)

Remember: Tailor functions to consumers, features to influencers, advantages to directors, and benefits to leaders. Stay away from terms and figures that may mean little to this suspect or prospect.

As long as you're courteous, concise, and up-front about how you found out the person's e-mail address, a surprisingly high percentage of contacts you reach in this way will reply with a time for you to call!

Just make sure you check your e-mail daily if you decide to use this approach!

# More on Dealing with Gatekeepers

If you're planning on doing any amount of prospecting using a telephone, you'll be faced with the challenge of handling gatekeepers. I strongly suggest that, before you try to apply any of the advice that follows, you take a good look at their job on a personal, one-on-one level, so that you can see exactly what these people are faced with on a daily basis. By understanding their world, you'll be better prepared to win their respect and cooperation. In fact, if you work for an organization that has a receptionist, you should probably spend a day or two sitting alongside of that person, getting a good look at exactly what th ey have to put up with. Receptionist gatekeepers (and, for that matter, executive assistant gatekeepers) have a tough job—and you should never forget that!

## Don't Increase the Pressure

Don't make the job any tougher than it already is. Always try to adhere to the rules that the gatekeeper's company has set forth. Don't be overbearing. Don't cop an attitude. Let your words show that you understand that the person you're talking to has a job to do, and that you know that part of that job is to be courteous, polite, and a good ambassador for the company. (Come to think of it, those are key parts of *your* job, too!)

## Avoid Dumb Questions

Never, ever ask a receptionist for assistance in trivial matters. Track down the information you need to know—decision makers, what the company does, the current address, etc.—and then call and ask for confirmation. Do your own digging by using an online information service or an up-to-date directory. By doing this, you'll sound like an intelligent, sincere professional—rather than a lazy salesperson!

## Tell the Truth

Never lie to a gatekeeper. Too many salespeople bend (or break) the truth by saying things like, "She's expecting my call…," "He'll recognize my name…," or "I'm returning her call…." If any of these statements aren't true, don't use them! If the gatekeeper says "What's the call regarding?" answer honestly! Give an abbreviated version of your hook statement. Answer all queries directly and truthfully. If you're dealing with an executive assistant or other highly placed gatekeeper, simply pretend that person IS your prospect!

## Say "Please" and "Thank You"

Remember that gatekeepers don't work for you. They work for someone else. Treat them with the same respect you'd treat your prospect.

## Don't Go Ballistic on Hang-ups

If you're selling in the same world as the rest of us, you'll encounter your fair share of telephone hang-ups from gatekeepers. There are two ways to deal with this problem.

The first is simply to dial the number again immediately and say to the gatekeeper, "We just got disconnected—would you please connect me with Ms. Roberts? Thanks." Note that you're not picking a fight with anyone—just asking to be put through. This approach often works quite well.

The second strategy is simply to make careful note of the exact day, date, and time the person hung up on you. Later on that week, when you're out in your territory, make a point of stopping in for an in-person visit. Walk into the lobby and make eye contact with the receptionist. Say, "Hi, my name is [your name]. Were you on the switchboard on [day and date you were hung up on]?"

If the gatekeeper says "Yes, I was on then," just say, "We were disconnected somehow. Could you please let Ms. Roberts know that I'm here for an unscheduled appointment?" (Believe it or not, most of the time, you'll get in!)

If the gatekeeper says "No, I wasn't on then," say, "Your other receptionist and I were disconnected somehow. Could you please let Ms. Roberts know that I'm here for an unscheduled appointment? (Ditto!)

# Index

# S

## U - V

## W

## Y - Z

# When You're Smart Enough to Know That You Don't Know It All

For all the ups and downs you're sure to encounter in life, The Complete Idiot's Guides give you down-to-earth answers and practical solutions.

## Personal Business

**The Complete Idiot's Guide to Terrific Business Writing**
ISBN: 0-02-861097-0 ▪ $16.95

**The Complete Idiot's Guide to Winning Through Negotiation**
ISBN: 0-02-861037-7 ▪ $16.95

**The Complete Idiot's Guide to Managing People**
ISBN: 0-02-861036-9 ▪ $18.95

**The Complete Idiot's Guide to a Great Retirement**
ISBN: 1-56761-601-1 ▪ $16.95

**The Complete Idiot's Guide to Protecting Yourself From Everyday Legal Hassles**
ISBN: 1-56761-602-X ▪ $16.99

**The Complete Idiot's Guide to Surviving Divorce**
ISBN: 0-02-861101-2 ▪ $16.95

**The Complete Idiot's Guide to Getting the Job You Want**
ISBN: 1-56761-608-9 ▪ $24.95

**The Complete Idiot's Guide to Managing Your Time**
ISBN: 0-02-861039-3 ▪ $14.95

**The Complete Idiot's Guide to Speaking in Public with Confidence**
ISBN: 0-02-861038-5 ▪ $16.95

**The Complete Idiot's Guide to Starting Your Own Business, 2E**
ISBN: 0-02-861979-X ▪ $17.95
Available February 1998!

You can handle it!

## The Complete Idiot's Guide to Learning French on Your Own
ISBN: 0-02-861043-1 ▪ $16.95

## The Complete Idiot's Guide to Dating
ISBN: 0-02-861052-0 ▪ $14.95

## The Complete Idiot's Guide to Hiking and Camping
ISBN: 0-02-861100-4 ▪ $16.95

## The Complete Idiot's Guide to Cooking Basics, 2E
ISBN: 0-02-861974-9 ▪ $16.95
Available November 1997!

## The Complete Idiot's Guide to Learning Spanish on Your Own
ISBN: 0-02-861040-7 ▪ $16.95

## The Complete Idiot's Guide to Gambling Like a Pro
ISBN: 0-02-861102-0 ▪ $16.95

## The Complete Idiot's Guide to Choosing, Training, and Raising a Dog
ISBN: 0-02-861098-9 ▪ $16.95

You can handle it!

**The Complete Idiot's Guide to Trouble-Free Car Care**
ISBN: 0-02-861041-5 ▪ $16.95

**The Complete Idiot's Guide to the Perfect Wedding, 2E**
ISBN: 0-02-861963-3 ▪ $17.99

**The Complete Idiot's Guide to Trouble-Free Home Repair**
ISBN: 0-02-861042-3 ▪ $16.95

**The Complete Idiot's Guide to Getting into College**
ISBN: 1-56761-508-2 ▪ $14.95

**The Complete Idiot's Guide to First Aid Basics**
ISBN: 0-02-861099-7 ▪ $16.95

**The Complete Idiot's Guide to the Perfect Vacation**
ISBN: 1-56761-531-7 ▪ $14.99

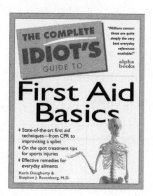

# The Purchase of This Book Offers You Access to the Author's Tele-Mentoring Program!

Anthony Parinello, a success coach for over one million professionals, is eager to guide you on the journey to maximum success. As a purchaser of this book, you can take advantage of his tele-mentoring program!

Each month you'll join Parinello's teleconference calls, where you can ask critical questions to help you make any sales. You'll also be listening to others as they meet their own challenges on the way to total sales success!

Here's what people have to say about Tony's mentoring:

"My coach is the nation's leading expert—that's why I am at 184 percent of quota!"

—David Wilson, Charleston, NC

"Tony is for real! Real experience, real ideas, and real commitment to his students' success."

—Vinnie Deschamps, San Jose, CA

"In the last seven months, my team has generated $18 million in new sales. We couldn't have done it without Tony's tele-mentoring!"

—Mike Adami, vice president, Moore Business Solutions

Register for your mentoring session today! Send the sales receipt for this book along with your name, address, and telephone number to:

Parinello Inc.
P. O. Box 875
Julian, California 92036

Upon receipt, a registration card will be sent to you outlining the details of the program.

To register for your mentoring session, call 1-888-275-8486. Do it today!